Why Does My Bird Do That?

A Guide to Parrot Behavior

Second Edition

JULIE RACH MANCINI

BICENTENNIAL
1807
WILEY
2007
BICENTENNIAL

Wiley Publishing, Inc.

Library of Congress Cataloging-in-Publication Data is available from the publisher upon request.

ISBN-10 0-470-03971-X
ISBN-13 978-0-470-03971-7

Printed in the United States of America

10   9   8   7   6   5   4   3   2   1

Second Edition

Book production by Wiley Publishing, Inc. Composition Services

CONTENTS

For my husband, Ron, who is every
bit the animal lover I am.

ACKNOWLEDGMENTS

Thank you to some special people who helped make the second edition of this book possible:

First, my stepdaughter, Rhonda Mancini, who has demonstrated to me her talents as a bird trainer and photographer countless times.

Next, to my friends Pamela Higdon and Mary Selby for their insights on owning species of birds I haven't had the opportunity to know well.

Also, to an outstanding avian veterinarian, Gary Gallerstein, and the staff of his clinic, Acacia Animal Hospital, for their wonderful care of my bird over the years.

And finally, to the many bird owners I've spoken to or corresponded with over the years. Without your stories and questions, this book would not be possible.

INTRODUCTION

Welcome to the second edition of this book! I hope you will find it useful in understanding your bird's normal behaviors and in helping you resolve any behavior problems your bird may have.

Parrot behavior is a subject that has fascinated researchers and frustrated bird owners for years. Researchers have long been intrigued by the natural intelligence of these clever creatures. That same native intelligence and cleverness initially charms an owner and then causes that same owner to throw up his or her hands in frustration when the birds consistently "misbehave." Many of these birds end up rehomed, retired, or released into the wild.

Rehoming an adult parrot presents its own set of challenges, but with patient care and gentle nurturing, an adult parrot can become a welcome member of the family. Retirement facilities can provide lifetime care for parrots who cannot be placed in suitable new homes. Owners pay monthly maintenance fees to have their birds cared for, and the birds live out their days surrounded by bird-loving caretakers.

Releasing a bird into the wild is not an option. It is, in fact, cruel beyond belief. What does a domestically raised bird know of life in the wild? How would he find food when he has had food presented to him during his life in captivity? If an owner does not release a problem parrot into the wild, he might choose to euthanize the bird because he became too much of a problem to handle.

Ten years of living with a wild-caught, feather-picked African grey confirmed for me that coping with an adult parrot's behaviors can try an owner's patience, sometimes severely. Over the years, I've watched friends cope with bites and bruises to their fingers and their egos as their birds matured and demonstrated behavioral changes, and I learned a few things along the way about biting, screaming, sexually motivated behaviors, and other potential perils of parrot ownership.

In the ten years I had my parrot, I had to deal with her biting me and screaming at me out of fear, developing her confidence, improving her health, and distracting her from picking her feathers, which was a long-established habit in her previous home. I also had to find ways to encourage her to eat a wider variety of healthful foods and to play with toys. At times, it would seem that we made tremendous progress, but at other times I seriously doubted I would ever make headway with all her problems.

After a few years of feeling disappointed with her progress, I realized that many of these so-called problems were far bigger issues for me than for her. I dreamed of a talking, whistling, singing, fully feathered, outwardly perfect parrot when an almost fully feathered, content bird in reasonably good health was a more realistic expectation. When I examined my own hopes, then considered the many changes that she had undergone, I readjusted my expectations and we're both much happier—I accepted her for what she was, not what I thought she should be.

THE LIFE SPAN OF PET BIRDS

Ideally, bird ownership should be a lifelong commitment between you and your pet, but many people get into owning birds without considering how long some parrot species can live. Many pet owners are accustomed to the relatively short life spans of other companion animals, such as pocket pets, cats, and dogs, and they are unaware of how long-lived some birds can be.

The following list gives you some idea of expected life spans for many common parrot species:

- African grey parrots   up to 50 years

- Amazon parrots   up to 80 years

- Cockatiels   up to 30 years

- Cockatoos   up to 40 years

- Conures   up to 40 years

- Lovebirds   up to 15 years

- Macaws   up to 50 years

- Parakeets   up to 20 years

The bird world has several stories of particularly long-lived pet birds. While I worked there, *Bird Talk* magazine reported on a 106-year-old Amazon who lived in Alaska. When I lived in California, I regularly visited the San Diego Zoo, which erected a statue to its longtime greeter, King Tut, a Moluccan cockatoo, near its main entrance. King Tut was a zoo resident for more than 60 years, and many of those were spent meeting people as they entered the zoo grounds.

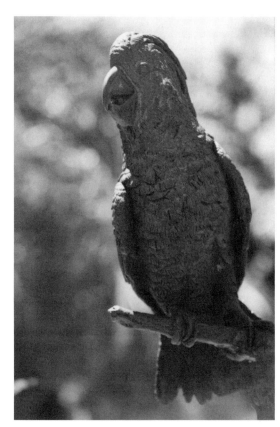

The San Diego Zoo honored its longtime greeter, a Moluccan cockatoo named King Tut, with a statue near its main entrance. King Tut retired in 1989 after many years as the zoo's greeter. (PHOTO BY JULIE RACH MANCINI)

Because questions concerning parrot behavior were frequently raised in many letters and phone calls I received when I was an editor at *Bird Talk* magazine, I can attest that understanding behavior is a common concern of pet bird owners. The other editors and I thought behavior was such an important topic, in fact, that we tried to include an article about behavior in each issue of the magazine, as well as providing a monthly question-and-answer column on avian behavior.

Since I've left the magazine, I've seen frequent stories in the news and documentaries on public television about research into parrot behavior, and parrot behavior conferences that bring bird owners and behavioral experts together are more popular now than they've ever been.

*Keeping canaries became
popular among wealthy
Europeans during the
Renaissance.* (PHOTO BY
ERIC ILASENKO)

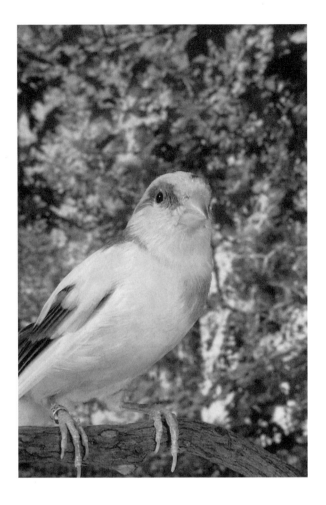

Bird owners today have more resources to consult if their birds develop behavior problems than ever before. Bird breeders and pet store staff members can be valuable sources of information because they have spent quite a bit of time working with different captive-bred species of pet birds. Parrot behaviorists are important parts of many avian veterinary practices now, and students with an interest in parrot behavior can pursue courses of study in animal behavior that will allow them to become animal trainers or behaviorists when they graduate from college.

A Long History

Birds have been on the earth for about 140 million years. They first appeared in the late Jurassic period, and the first bird was *Archaeopteryx lithographica,* which was about the size of a crow and lived in the cycad forests.

Because bird bones are so fragile, few representatives of early birds left behind remains in the fossil record. Nevertheless, fossil remains have been found that indicate that birds were on the scene during the Cretaceous period, which occurred about 110 million years ago.

The earliest fossil parrot may be *Archaeopsittacus verreauxi* from the lower Miocene period of about 30 million years ago. It was described from a bone found in France. Some experts believe that this particular specimen is not a parrot, however, and that the first fossil parrot was *Conuropsis fratercula,* fossils of which were found in Nebraska. *Conuropsis fratercula* lived about 20 million years ago. Representatives of the *Pionus* and *Aratinga* genera were in existence less than one million years ago.

Now that we have established the beginnings of parrots, let's look back at the beginnings of the association between people and parrots. The ancient Egyptians are credited as being the first people to keep birds, particularly pigeons. Queen Hatsheput (1504–1482 B.C.E.) is said to be the first monarch to create a royal zoo, which included exotic birds. The ancient Persians also knew about talking birds as early as the fifth century B.C.E., when a court physician and naturalist wrote about talking birds who were described to him by Indian merchants.

From Egypt, bird keeping spread to Greece and Rome. Alexander the Great receives credit from some historians for discovering the Alexandrine parakeet, and the Greeks are credited with popularizing parrot keeping outside of the birds' native lands of Africa and Asia.

Well-to-do Romans built extensive garden aviaries and employed mockingbirds in the entryways of their homes as feathered doorbells that would announce visitors. The Romans are also thought to be the first bird dealers, bringing different types of birds to Great Britain and the European continent.

Until the Renaissance, bird keeping was considered a hobby that only the wealthy could pursue. After canaries were introduced to Europe by Portuguese sailors, bird keeping began to flourish, although it was still confined largely to upper-class fanciers. Spanish monks began to propagate canaries for the royal families of Europe and other wealthy bird fanciers. The monks tried to keep tight control over their birds, allowing only the males to be exported, but somehow female canaries made it to other parts of Europe. By the 1600s, the Dutch were producing show canaries. Some of these birds were exported to Britain, and bird keeping began to be more accessible to the masses.

At about the same time, in the British penal colony of Australia, a forger named Thomas Watling first described the ability of the budgerigar (better known in the United States as a parakeet) to mimic human speech. This bird was able to greet Watling's employer by saying, "How do you do, Dr. White?"

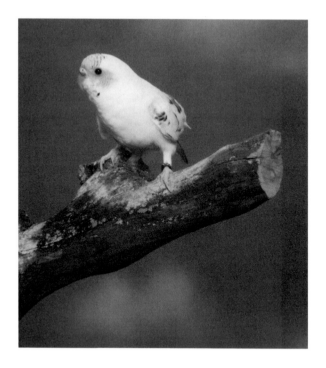

The parakeet has been the most popular pet bird in the United States for more than 50 years. (PHOTO BY RHONDA MANCINI)

Bird keeping as we know it today can trace its beginnings to Victorian Great Britain, when bird sellers in the British Isles would offer goldfinches and larks to ship captains en route to the West Indies. These common European birds would then be traded in the islands for species commonly found there.

In the United States, bird keeping began to boom after World War II. The parakeet rose to its position as most popular pet bird in the 1950s, and the bird care industry began to grow steadily and significantly in the 1980s.

What began as a few companies packaging birdseed and selling cages soon grew to a multifaceted industry that provides a variety of foods, cages, treats, toys, grooming utensils, talking tapes and compact discs, books and videotapes on bird care, veterinary specialization, and behavioral counseling for both pets and owners.

A Wild Harvest

At the start, parrot keeping depended heavily upon trapping parrots in the wild to turn them into pets. Until the late 1970s, this procedure was accepted as the normal way of procuring a bird. At this point in time, some forward-thinking parrot keepers began to set up pairs of commonly imported species to produce parrots specifically for the pet trade.

A LINK TO DINOSAURS?

In 2001, scientists announced that a 130-million-year-old feathered dinosaur fossil had been discovered in China. The first dinosaur found with its body covering intact, it was identified as a Dromaeosaur, a small, fast-running dinosaur closely related to Velociraptor, with a sickle claw on the middle toe and stiffening rods in the tail. According to the American Museum of Natural History, Dromaeosaurs are advanced theropods, which is a group of two-legged predators that includes Tyrannosaurus rex. Dromoaesaurs had sharp teeth and bones that are very similar to those of modern-day birds.

The fossil was found in Liaoning Province in northeastern China. It was described as looking like a large duck with a long tail. The animal's head and tail were covered with downy fibers, and it had other featherlike structures on the back of its arms and on other parts of its body.

The first feathered dinosaur was found in China in 1995. This discovery, Sinosauropteryx, was also a theropod dinosaur, and it was also found in Liaoning Province. Sinosauropteryx dates from between 121 and 135 million years ago, and it falls in between Archaeopteryx, the earliest known bird, which lived about 150 million years ago, and Protarchaeopteryx robusta, which lived at about the same time as Sinosauropteryx but probably could not fly, despite the presence of feathers on its body.

Fossils of birdlike dinosaurs and dinosaurlike birds have been found in Madagascar, Mongolia, and Patagonia, as well as in China. The Eoalulavis, found in Spain, was one of the earliest birds who could maneuver well during flight, thanks to a feather tuft on its thumb called an alula. This feature is found on birds today, and it helps them with takeoffs and landings. Some scientists theorize that birds evolved from dinosaurs, while others are still seeking an earlier reptile ancestor for birds. In June 2006, scientists in China announced the discovery of *Gansus yumenensis*, a web-footed, feathered bird that lived 110 million years ago.

By the 1980s, some species, such as sun and jenday conures, were bred with regularity in captivity. These domestically bred birds had all the exotic appeal of their wild-caught cousins without some of the common behavior problems, such as fear biting, screaming, or hiding in the corner of the cage. The pet-owning public began to respond to these domestically bred birds, and breeders turned their attention to other species. Wild-caught parrots still dominated the market, however.

When parrots were caught in the wild and imported into the United States and Europe in great numbers, trappers used nets, snares, and other methods to catch the birds, who were usually enticed to the capture site with a lure bird tied or glued to the spot by the trappers. In some cases, nesting trees were cut down and parent birds killed while trappers robbed the nest of chicks. Birds were taken from the jungle to holding stations, from which they were exported.

Along the way, these captured birds were fed whatever food happened to be available with little concern shown for proper nutrition. The food that the birds received in captivity may or may not have been what they were used to in the jungle, and some of the birds died from the different diet or from the stress of being captured.

If birds were injured in the capture process, little to no veterinary care was available to them. Many died from their injuries, while others were crippled for life. Once in the country of export, birds were held at import stations to ensure that they did not carry any communicable diseases, such as Newcastle disease, and then they were distributed to pet stores.

The birds who survived all this were stressed, to say the least. As wild animals snatched from the jungle, they hadn't the foggiest notion of how to be pets or what humans expected of them. Humans had, after all, taken them from their familiar surroundings and hurt many of them along the way, so why should these intelligent, sensitive creatures want to associate with the humans who would buy them as pets?

As a result, these wild-caught birds often made less-than-desirable pets. They screamed, they bit, they pulled their feathers, or they cowered in the corners of their cages. My own parrot did all these things when I first adopted her, and it took six years of constant care on my part and the efforts of several avian veterinarians and behaviorists to restore her health and to curtail her feather-picking and biting habits.

Early taming procedures for wild-caught birds were fairly brutal. Trainers often encouraged owners to break their birds' spirits by handling the birds with heavy gloves, throwing the birds on the ground, striking the birds' cages, or, even worse, striking the birds themselves. Not surprisingly, many of these untamed birds became even more impossible to handle. Some particularly incorrigible specimens were labeled broncos, with the implication that they, like the wild horses they were named for, would never be tamed.

Some breeders took these unhandleable birds and set them up in breeding programs, where some of the birds proved to be suitable parents. Breeders pulled some of the chicks and hand-raised them to improve the chicks' pet qualities, and, in time, domestic-bred birds largely replaced wild-caught birds in the pet market.

A Better Option

In the early 1990s, the importation of parrots was outlawed in the United States, so domestic-bred birds were the primary option available to most people seeking a parrot, although some wild-caught adults were still offered for sale by owners who were unable to turn these birds into the loving pets they desired. Because the domestic-bred birds bonded with humans almost from the instant they hatched, they made much better pets than their wild-caught counterparts. And because breeders wanted to ensure their livelihood for the future, the domestic-bred birds were healthier than their wild-caught brethren, too, which also helped make them more suitable pets.

Today's domestic-bred birds still need behavior modification from time to time, but fortunately, parrot behavior consultants now tout kinder, gentler methods of reprimanding birds who occasionally get out of hand. These include "time-outs" similar to those given to unruly children, stern tones of voice, and praising good behavior instead of punishing misbehavior. When owners take the time to see things from the birds' point of view, this helps them better understand some behaviors that had been considered problems (by people) but are perfectly normal for the birds.

I hope this book will help clarify some of the mysteries of bird behavior as they relate to the kinds of birds most commonly kept as pets. To help you better understand your bird and his behavioral patterns, read on!

chapter 1

FLOCK BEHAVIOR IN THE WILD AND HOW IT APPLIES IN THE HOME

To understand parrot behavior in the home, one must first start in the jungle. Parrots can be found in the wild on the continents of North America, South America, Australia, Africa, Asia, and on some islands in the Caribbean and the South Pacific.

Most of the species are confined to relatively small areas of the world. Brazil, for example, is home to seventy parrot species, while Australia is home to another fifty-two. Colombia and Venezuela are home to forty-nine and forty-eight species, respectively, and New Guinea is home to an additional forty-six species.

Parrot lovers who want to witness behaviors in a natural setting can visit the Tambopata Research Center in southeastern Peru. The center, which has been in operation since 1990, is located near Manu National Park, where Charles Munn of the Wildlife Conservation Society began studying the habits of wild macaws, particularly as they apply to a clay lick in the park.

Birds visit the lick to obtain sodium that is missing from their diets, and they also may consume the clay to help neutralize toxins that they consume in some fruits and vegetables. Researchers led by Donald Brightsmith, Ph.D., of Duke University now know that visits to the clay lick are somewhat determined by the area's weather. Macaws are less likely to visit the lick on rainy or foggy days than they are on sunny days. They usually do not visit the lick if the morning is rainy, even if the rest of the day becomes sunny and clear. Nine of the fourteen parrot species seen at the lick visit it before 7:30 A.M., while the other species use it at almost any time of day. The birds are most likely to visit the licks between August and December, and they are least likely to visit the lick in May. Researchers believe the changes in visits to the lick throughout the year may tie into the migrations of some birds away from the area at different times of the year and changes in the food supply during the year.

Visitors to Tambopata can see macaws and other parrots at the clay lick and in the surrounding jungle. Some of these birds are macaws that the research center staff hand-fed, then released back into the wild. These birds, affectionately known as chicos, are still tame enough to willingly approach staff members and visitors for special treats. The chicos have formed a semi-wild flock, and they forage with the resident birds during the day and return to the center for attention from people in the evening. Some of the birds have paired up with wild macaws and successfully raised chicks.

In addition to providing an ecotourism opportunity for bird lovers, the research center is devoted to improving the reproductive rates of macaws in the area. It has done this by providing additional artificial nest sites using nest boxes made of PVC or wood. The center has also provided natural nesting sites in aguaje palm trees by cutting the palms in such a way as to allow the center to rot and create a suitable nesting chamber for the macaws. In addition to hand-feeding some chicks as noted earlier, staff members have also provided supplemental feedings to some second- and third-hatched chicks in the nest, which has improved the survival rates for some of the second chicks, but not for the third chicks. They hope someday to be able to apply the lessons learned about macaw reproduction to other parrot species in the area.

Initially, researchers were concerned that the ecotourists themselves might interfere with the daily activities of birds and other animals around the clay lick, but this has not proven to be the case. Preliminary reports indicate that the birds do not seem to be affected by the presence of observers, as long as the observers remain quiet and stay about 500 feet away from the lick. Further research on the birds' behavior as it relates to tour groups is underway.

Bird Watching

If you don't want to travel to Peru and you live in a temperate climate, you may be able to see feral parrots in your area. Bird-watchers in the Los Angeles area may have the chance to observe psittacine behavior in the wilds of canyons, parks, and residential streets because feral flocks of conures (cherry heads, mitreds, and nandays are the most frequently seen species), Amazons, and other psittacine species have been reported in the area.

Bird lovers from the Pacific Palisades to Pasadena have been delighted by the antics of these feral birds, which regularly perform gymnastic routines on power lines or raid nut trees. The birds stay in an area for a few days, then move over a few city blocks to start the routine over again.

One flock of feral parrots has become quite well known. They are a group of conures that live on Telegraph Hill in San Francisco. Mark Bittner began caring for the birds in the 1990s when he was a caretaker for one of the neighborhood's cottages, and he studied their activities closely. His observations led to articles about the flock in local and national magazines and newspapers, a book, *The Wild Parrots of Telegraph Hill: A Love Story . . . with Wings,* and a documentary film, *The Wild Parrots of Telegraph Hill,* both of which were released in 2005. (See appendix B, "Resources," for further information on ordering copies of the book and film.) Bittner continued to keep the birds in the news in California after the movie was released. In early 2006, an agreement was reached between Bittner and a property owner on Telegraph Hill to maintain a stand of Monterey cypress trees the birds used as nesting sites. The property owner had originally planned to cut down the trees, but the cutting was stopped after Bittner threw himself in front of a tree-cutting crew. The new plan calls for additional trees to be planted to support and replace the original trees, which were in danger of falling and damaging nearby property.

Flocks of feral parrots may also exist in San Diego County in southern California, and in Texas, Florida, and other temperate climate zones. Feral flocks of Quaker parrots have been reported in less-temperate climates, such as Seattle and the New England region. In early 2006, animal lovers in Connecticut took legal action to stop a utility company in the state from destroying Quaker parakeet nests that were built on utility poles. The utility company maintains that the nests are a hazard, causing transformer fires and blackouts. The legal action asks that the utility undertake a maintenance plan that prevents the birds from nesting on the poles, rather than the current plan of destroying the nests and the birds after the nests are built.

How any of these parrots got loose is anyone's guess; some attribute the birds to a pet store fire, while others say that a smuggler who was about to be captured freed his supply of birds. Still others with a more realistic attitude attribute their presence to a great many lost (or intentionally freed) pets who were lucky enough to escape predators and band together.

Wherever they live in the world, parrots are naturally social creatures and live together in flocks ranging from a few individuals to several hundred birds. Lowland tropical rainforest is the most typical habitat for parrots, but they can also be found in semiarid climates, mountain areas, or savannahs. Some species are even seen in parks and other urban environments in South America and Australia.

Certain species are found in specialized wild habitats, such as Australia's ground parrot, found in a very restricted mountain heath area in southern Australia. Others, such as thickbilled parrots or glossy cockatoos, seem to live in habitats that contain a particular foodstuff that the parrots enjoy. In the case of thickbills, it's pine nuts, while glossy cockatoos prefer the seed of the casuarina tree.

Some species adapt in different ways to different environments. For example, parakeets living in central Australia have adapted to the harshness of the environment by reproducing at young ages and having many chicks in the hope that some will survive the rigors of life in this part of the country. Parakeets living on the coast and in the central southern areas, where the climate is less extreme, do not demonstrate this ability to breed early and often.

In the wild, another Australian species, the cockatiel, is active during the early morning and the late afternoon. These are the times when the birds usually head toward a water source to drink, being sure to land, drink, and leave quickly rather than become a meal for a passing bird of prey. They spend a good bit of their days on the ground, searching for food, but they are likely to spend midday blending into their surroundings by sitting lengthwise along tree branches, usually dead limbs that are free of foliage.

Most parrots eat seeds and different types of fruits that they find in the treetops or on the ground. Many medium-sized and large parrot species use one foot (usually the left) to pick up and hold food while they eat.

To open a seed, a bird uses his tongue to steady the seed against the underside of his upper beak (a parrot's upper beak has ridges in it that help hold food steady) and peels away the seed husk with his sharp lower beak.

Some parrots, such as lories and lorikeets, are specialized feeders. These brush-tongued parrots live strictly in trees, where they feed on nectar, pollen, and soft fruits.

Some species actually change their diets significantly in the wild when the opportunity is right. For example, the kea parrot of New Zealand changed its diet from fruits and seeds to lamb after settlers in the area began raising sheep. The importance of lamb in the kea's diet has been overemphasized by some, so much so that a bounty was paid on keas in the past. According to Joseph Forshaw's *Parrots of the World*, these large, stocky parrots only feed on sheep trapped in snow, sick or injured animals, or animals the birds perceive as dead. Keas are now under limited protection of the New Zealand government. (See appendix B for more information on the Forshaw book.)

A Daily Routine

In the wild, the flocks greet the dawn by vocalizing. They do so to alert members of the flock that they will be moving soon, and they also let other flocks in the area know where they are. After the flock is awake, they move from their roosting trees to find food.

Bird language in the wild includes calls to signal the flock that food has been found, calls that indicate a mate has been won, calls that indicate danger is near, calls that bring the flock together at the end of a day, songs to establish territories and to attract mates, and chattering that some researchers believe resembles human conversation.

The birds forage and eat throughout the day, alerting other members of the flock to their location and to potential dangers through a series of calls and other vocalizations.

When they aren't foraging or eating, parrots in the wild spend a good part of their day playing. Young birds learn about their environment through play, and older birds use the opportunity to play to exercise and to reaffirm their position in the flock.

As the day ends, the birds call to each other to gather flock members together, and the flock goes back to roost, starting the cycle again in the morning.

Parrots become sexually mature at around 2 years of age for smaller species and at around 3 years of age for larger species. Because males and females frequently look the same, it is often difficult for humans to differentiate between the sexes. An exception to this rule is the eclectus, in which males are green and females are purple and red. The extreme difference in the coloring of the sexes, called sexual dimorphism, led early scientists to believe that they had actually discovered two different species of parrots!

Sexual dimorphism, or the outward differences between male and female birds of the same species, is not usually as pronounced as it is in this pair of gang-gang cockatoos at the San Diego Zoo. The male has a bright-red head and a fluffy crest, while the female is less conspicuously colored. (PHOTOS BY JULIE RACH MANCINI)

Most psittacine species are monogamous, and many mate for long periods, perhaps for life. Pairs demonstrate pair-bonding behavior, such as mutual preening or sitting very close to one another, throughout the year. Experts believe that a strong pair bond helps parent birds be more successful at laying fertile eggs and raising chicks.

A variety of conditions, including rainfall, an increase in the food supply, and gradually longer days, stimulate parrots to breed in their natural environments. In breeding facilities and pet homes, owners will notice that their birds begin to go into breeding mode in the late winter, spring, or summer. Few parrots are year-round breeders.

In the wild, parrots nest in tree cavities, termite mounds, niches carved in faces of sandstone cliffs, and other natural crevices. Few parrots excavate a nest from scratch, according to parrot expert Joseph Forshaw, but they will enlarge or expand an existing nest site that has been abandoned by other species of birds.

Parrot chicks are altricial when they hatch, meaning that they are blind, featherless, and helpless. However, by the time they are about 3 weeks old, like these cockatiel chicks, their eyes have opened and they have started to develop feathers. (PHOTO BY GARY A. GALLERSTEIN, DVM)

The nests are predominantly enclosed and parrot eggs are most typically white, so a parent bird can easily see them in the darkness of the nesting chamber. Clutch size ranges from two to five eggs for larger species, and can be as large as eight for smaller species. Eggs are laid on an approximately every-other-day schedule. The incubation period ranges from fourteen to more than thirty days.

Newly hatched young are altricial. This means they are blind, naked, and completely dependent upon their parents. A chick's eyes open about two weeks after hatching, and chicks stay in the nest for three weeks to three months, with smaller species leaving the nest sooner than their larger cousins.

As a rule, parrots do not build what we think of as nests. An exception to this rule is the Quaker, or monk, parrot, which can build quite elaborate nests out of sticks.

From Treetop to Cagetop

What does all this mean to a parrot owner? Whether they are in the jungle or in your living room, parrots demonstrate some similar behaviors. They eat and play, they call to mates and other flock members, and they vocalize at sunrise and sunset. These are all normal behaviors that are unlikely to be modified significantly, although you can usually work with your parrot to modulate his noise level.

Whether in the wild or in your home, parrots communicate by whistling and vocalizing. Often, vocalizing crosses the line into screaming or loudly speaking the phrases you have so lovingly taught your bird, if you are fortunate enough to have a talking parrot. While these sounds may be music to your ears, your neighbors (especially if you're in an apartment or condominium) may not find your pet's antics so charming.

If noise is a concern, do not select a cockatoo or a macaw for your pet because these two species are among the noisiest of parrots. Cockatoos often greet the dawn by screaming, and some feel compelled to acknowledge sunset in the same way. Certain species, such as Moluccans, may hoot and stamp their feet as part of their natural display. Macaws' screams are higher-pitched than cockatoos, which may make them even more grating on your ears or those of your neighbors.

Cockatoos in general like to be the life of the party and the center of their owners' universe. They are emotionally needy birds that require a great deal of time and attention from their owners. If they do not receive it, cockatoos can become destructive feather pickers; some even turn to self-mutilation.

For those considering a medium-sized parrot, keep in mind that Amazons, although lively clowns, may whistle and scream frequently throughout the day. The good news is that their noise level should not bother neighbors. How you feel about sharing space with a noisy green parrot is another matter. For close quarters where noise may be a factor, choose a smaller bird, such as a parakeet, lory, or African grey.

If your bird spends time on the floor in your home, you must be careful that you don't step on him or that he doesn't injure himself by chewing something that he shouldn't.
(PHOTO BY JULIE RACH MANCINI)

For those of you concerned about chewing, realize that all parrots chew to some extent. However, some species, such as conures, are more voracious than others. By providing your parrot with access to appropriate chewables, such as food, nuts, or toys, you fulfill his need to chew while reducing the possibility of your bird chewing on some of your possessions.

Another behavior that concerns new parrot owners is biting. If you start with a young bird and handle him properly, you should not be bitten too often, but you must realize that being bitten is part of parrot ownership and, as a longtime bird-owning friend of mine once put it, "Nobody ever died from a bird bite."

Some parrots are more prone to biting during certain times of the year, such as breeding season, or they are incited to bite by their owners roughhousing with them. By being careful in the way you handle your bird, you will significantly reduce your chances of being bitten.

If space is a concern, I would recommend eliminating the large parrots, such as macaws and cockatoos, from consideration. Kept in appropriate-sized cages, these birds can occupy as much space as a full-sized refrigerator! If these large parrots are not allowed the opportunity to exercise outside their cages, they may develop some behavior problems, such as screaming or biting.

Remember that your bird needs the largest cage you can afford in order to benefit from daily exercise. The cage you select should be large enough so your bird can fully extend his wings without having the wings touch the sides of the cage. The bird should also have ample clearance for his head from the cage ceiling and his tail from the cage floor when sitting on his perch. In addition to your bird, the cage must hold a few perches, some toys, a food bowl, a water bowl, and possibly a bathtub.

When choosing your bird's cage, keep in mind that pet birds are like little airplanes, flying across an area, rather than little helicopters that hover up and down. For this reason, long rectangular cages that offer horizontal space for short flights are preferred to tall cages that don't provide much flying room. All cage birds—finches, canaries, softbills, and parrots—need to fly across their cages, so make a long, rectangular cage a priority regardless of the species you keep.

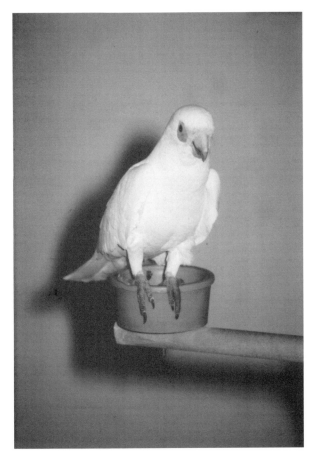

Parrots, such as this bare-eyed cockatoo, will sometimes eliminate in their food or water dishes. Be careful when placing bowls in your bird's cage or when placing your bird on a T-stand. (PHOTO BY GARY A. GALLERSTEIN, DVM)

When setting up a cage for a young parrot, you may want to keep the perches fairly low. Some young birds, particularly African greys, are notoriously clumsy when they're first getting the hang of perching and climbing. Once you see that your bird is navigating around the cage with ease, you can raise the perch heights.

When placing perches in your bird's cage, try to vary the heights slightly so your bird has different "levels" in his cage. Vary the diameters slightly, too, so your bird can exercise his feet by sitting on a perch of recommended size part of the time and on one that's slightly larger than the recommended diameter the rest of the time.

Recommended perch diameters are as follows:

- ³/₈ inch for finches and canaries

- ¹/₂ inch for parakeets

- ⁵/₈ inch for cockatiels

- ³/₄ inch for conures

- 1 inch for Amazons and other medium-sized parrots

- 2 inches for cockatoos and macaws

Perches are available in a variety of different materials, including wood, rope, and concrete. Providing more than one type of material can give your bird some variety in his perching surfaces, which can help exercise his foot muscles. (PHOTO BY JULIE RACH MANCINI)

Don't place perches over food or water dishes because birds can and will contaminate food or water by eliminating in it. Finally, place one perch higher than the rest for a nighttime sleeping roost. Parrots like to sleep on the highest point they can find to perch, so please provide this security to your pet.

Domed or round cages may cause some birds to develop behavioral problems, such as screaming, feather chewing, or self-mutilation because they feel uneasy without a corner to settle into. This information helped me to better understand my parrot's situation in her previous home. She had lived in a large, round, domed cage, and she chewed her feathers. She now lives in a smaller, rectangular cage and doesn't pick her feathers. I believe she didn't feel completely comfortable in her old cage because it was difficult for her to get around in, given her crippled legs and reduced mobility. In her present cage, she can maneuver quite well and, I would surmise, feels more at ease.

As you select a cage, you'll need to keep in mind one other dimension: bar spacing. This is the distance between the cage bars, and it's important because birds can get themselves stuck between the bars or even escape from a cage if the bar spacing isn't right for them.

Here are the bar spacing recommendations for commonly kept pet birds:

- $3/8$ inch for parakeets, canaries, finches, and lovebirds
- $1/2$ inch to $3/4$ inch for cockatiels and small conures
- $3/4$ inch to 1 inch for Amazons, African greys, and other medium-sized parrots
- $3/4$ inch to $1^1/2$ inches for macaws and cockatoos

Reject any cages that have sharp interior wires that could poke your bird. Also be aware that birds may injure themselves on the ornate scrollwork that decorates some cages.

Examine the finish of the cage you select carefully before making your final selection. Make sure the finish is not chipped, bubbling, or peeling, because a curious pet bird may find that spot and continue removing the finish. This can cause a cage to look old and worn before its time, and some cages may start to rust without their protective finish. And if your pet ingests any of the finish, he could become ill.

If you are choosing a cage for a parrot, make sure the cage you choose has some horizontal bars in it so your bird will be able to climb the cage walls if he wants to exercise. Climbing is good exercise that helps a parrot burn off energy he might otherwise use to scream or bite or pull his feathers, so be sure to encourage your pet to exercise inside his cage and out of it. Finches, canaries, and softbills are more apt to hop and flit across the cage than they are to climb the cage walls, so horizontal bars are not as great a requirement for them as they are for hookbilled birds.

Parrots like to climb. Be sure to provide your pet with climbing opportunities in your home. (PHOTO BY JULIE RACH MANCINI)

If you find wooden or bamboo cages in your shopping excursions for a parrot cage, reject them immediately unless the wood is lined with wire or wire mesh. Although they may be suitable for finches and songbirds, a busy hookbill beak will soon make short work of a wooden or bamboo cage, and you'll be left with the problem of finding a new home for your pet!

Acrylic or Wire?

Birdcages are traditionally made of metal wire, but you may see acrylic cages in magazine advertisements or at your local pet store. These cages are better at containing seed hulls, loose feathers, and other debris your bird creates, which may make bird keeping easier and more enjoyable for you. Although it sounds like a sales pitch, I can attest that acrylic cages clean up easily—simply wipe inside and out with a damp towel and regularly change the tray that slides under the cage itself.

Before they moved to Texas with their owners, I regularly bird-sat a pair of Pacific parrotlets who had a tendency to fling food around with the greatest of ease. When they were kept in a traditional wire cage, my dining room table and walls bore lasting reminders of each visit, no matter how diligently I scrubbed them. When the birds returned later in an acrylic cage, nothing remained to mark their passing after their owners took them home.

I also bird-sit a canary who lives in an acrylic cage. He is the easiest bird I have ever cleaned up after, because the feathers, seed hulls, and treat scraps remain within the cage. All I have to do for this bird is change the cage paper daily and clean and refill his food and water bowls twice a day. My own bird's wire cage, on the other hand, requires frequent vacuuming and diligent care.

If you choose an acrylic cage for your pet, make sure it has numerous ventilation holes drilled in its walls to allow for adequate air circulation. Be particularly careful about not leaving your bird in direct sunlight if you house him in an acrylic cage, because these cages can get warm rather quickly and your bird could become overheated. (Pet birds in wire cages shouldn't be left in direct sunlight either, as they can overheat, too.)

If you select an acrylic cage for your pet, make sure to include a couple of ladders between the perches to give your pet climbing opportunities he won't be able to take advantage of on the smooth sides of an acrylic cage.

Making Your Bird Feel at Home

Some birds have special caging requirements. My parrot, for example, lived for many years in a rectangular rabbit cage because it had smaller mesh that she could hook her beak into easily. With her physical limitations, this helped her get around more quickly. However, the galvanized finish made her ill over time, so she was moved into a cockatiel cage with a bright brass finish. The bar spacing was not as convenient for her, but the health benefits were greater.

A parakeet I know named Calvin was handicapped as a chick. (I think his mother sat on him too tightly in the nest and squashed his developing skeleton a bit.) As a result of injuries he suffered early in life, Calvin didn't perch too well and had trouble getting around in and living in a conventional wire birdcage. His owner searched through pet stores to find the best cage for her physically challenged pet, and her solution was a wire hamster cage with climbing ramps and resting platforms, rather than traditional perches. Because the platforms and ramps were wide and had both horizontal and vertical bars on them, Calvin could maneuver around his cage pretty well.

You'll probably notice that your bird spends a lot of time moving around his cage. This mimics the movements of flocks in the wild. During these movements, he often uses his beak as much as his feet. Parrots are very good at using their beaks to climb, reach, hold, bite, hang, eat, preen, or play, depending on what their current activities call for.

In your home, your parrot probably won't spend much time foraging for his food. To provide an outlet for those foraging tendencies, consider offering food in different forms from time to time. Offer whole green beans or peas in the pod to encourage your bird to work for his food a little bit. You can also give your bird nuts in the shell to challenge his mind as well as nourish his body. (You may want to crack the nuts slightly the first time you offer them, especially if your bird is young, so he knows what's inside the nutshell.)

To further help your bird expend the energy he would use to forage and feed in the wild, give him ample opportunities to play. Busy, occupied birds are less likely to misbehave, and they become well-adjusted, content companions. Birds who might otherwise scream, pull their feathers, or become aggressive can channel their energies into play if provided with the chance.

Parrots need suitable toys to play with. If you try one type of toy—for example, a chain with a bell on it—and your bird doesn't like it, don't give up! You may have to try several different types of toys before you find one that your bird likes.

When selecting toys for your bird, be sure they are of an appropriate size for your pet. Small birds, such as parakeets or cockatiels, can become frightened if they are presented with toys that are too large for them, and toys that are too large can even injure them. By the same token, large parrots such as macaws or cockatoos, with their powerful beaks, can easily splinter toys made for smaller birds and the splinters can injure them. Most bird toys are sold with bird-size recommendations printed on their price tag, or you can ask the staff of your bird supply store for recommendations.

In addition to selecting correctly sized toys, make sure the toys you choose for your bird are safe. Avoid toys that attach to cages with split-ring fasteners because some birds can open these rings enough to catch their beaks, tongues or toes in them. Choose toys that attach with C-clips instead.

Select toys that are made from vegetable-tanned leather and that use food-safe dyes. These are important ingredients in a bird-safe toy because your pet will spend a lot of time chewing on his toys, and you don't want him to become ill from chemically treated leather or dyes that are not food-safe.

Some birds do not react well to brightly colored toys, while others love them. A friend who has a flock of three birds reports that her pets seem to favor toys that have colors similar to those of the birds' plumage. Perhaps these birds perceive items of a similar color as less threatening than those that are brightly colored and foreign to them.

In addition to playing with toys, your parrot needs a chance to flap his wings, climb, hang off of a perch or play gym, or chase a ball. All these activities will help your pet burn off energy. Again, each parrot will have activities that he prefers, so you will have to see which type of exercise appeals to your parrot.

Remember to take time to play with your bird, too. Parrots are flock animals, so your bird would naturally expect to have some company while he's playing. You can roll your bird over and pet his "tickle spots," you can play tug-of-war with him, you can introduce him to a new toy, or you can hold him on your hand or arm while he flaps.

Toys can be colorful or plain, complicated or simple. You will have to determine which type is right for your bird. (PHOTO BY JULIE RACH MANCINI)

Select toys that are appropriate to the size of your bird. These toys are suitable for a parakeet or other small parrot. (PHOTO BY JULIE RACH MANCINI)

These toys are suitable for a larger parrot, such as an Amazon or African grey.
(PHOTO BY JULIE RACH MANCINI)

You can encourage your bird to play by challenging him to a game of tug-of-war.
(PHOTO BY JULIE RACH MANCINI)

chapter 2

PARROT BEHAVIOR EXAMINED

Parrot behavior has been studied in a laboratory setting for more than fifty years. Today, however, it's difficult to discuss parrot behavior without mentioning an amazing African grey parrot who's been the subject of study by an evolutionary biologist for almost thirty years.

Alex the Grey

In 1977, Irene Pepperberg, Ph.D., purchased an African grey parrot selected at random from the birds at a Chicago pet store as part of a research project to examine animal intelligence and communication skills.

That bird is Alex, and he has proved to be an exceptional research subject in the ensuing years. Dr. Pepperberg has learned that Alex not only uses human language to communicate, but he uses language appropriately. Alex is able to note differences and similarities in objects that are shown to him and to tell researchers the colors of the objects and the materials from which they are made. He can identify seven colors and can count up to six.

One of Alex's most remarkable moments came in 2005 when he told researchers "none" after being asked to identify a group of five objects on a tray in front of him. Subsequent testing showed Alex was able to say "none" correctly when the tray in front of him did not have the correct number of objects. None of the researchers who work with Alex taught him to say "none" when he was not presented with an appropriate number of objects, but he did learn to use the word when presented with two like-sized objects and asked to say which was the larger. He apparently made the leap to a zero-like concept on his own.

While this may not seem significant, researchers say that children do not grasp this zero-like concept until they are between 3 and 4 years of age.

In addition, Alex asks for toys or treats in the course of his day at the lab or to be carried from one part of the lab to another, and he tells researchers "No!" forcefully if they bring him the wrong treat or toy or if they try to set him down in a part of the lab he didn't ask to visit.

Alex also apologizes to people in the laboratory if he bites them (although he is likely to bite them again). When Dr. Pepperberg left Alex at a veterinary hospital for surgery, he said to her, "Come here. I love you. I'm sorry. I want to go back." Apparently, Alex thought he was being punished by being left at the hospital.

Alex spends about eight hours a day in a lab room with researchers and is confined to a roomy cage when he is alone. His diet consists of Harrison's Bird Diet, organic fruits and vegetables, and water.

When he responds to a question about an object correctly, Alex often receives the object to play with as a reward for giving the right answer. If he does not answer correctly, he is told to try again or to give a better response. If he asks for a treat by name, he is given that treat immediately after he answers the trainer's question correctly.

In the early 1990s, two African grey chicks joined Alex in the laboratory. These birds, Griffin and Wart, began by identifying objects, such as paper or cork. Then they learned to distinguish items, including the number of a particular item, its relative size, the material it is made from, and its color. Finally, the birds learn phonemes (distinctive sounds) and how to combine them.

Alex and the other birds in Dr. Pepperberg's lab are not the first African greys studied in this manner. Researchers in Europe developed a method of communicating with African greys in the 1940s and 1950s, and a German researcher popularized the use of the model/rival technique to teach and study African grey parrots.

In the model/rival method, the teacher shows one of two students (either avian or human) an object and asks what it is. If the student identifies it correctly, the teacher gives the object to the student to examine and play with. If the student gives an incorrect answer, the teacher and the other student "model" the correct response, then the teacher asks the first student the question again. Tests conducted on Alex indicate that he can correctly answer 80 percent of the questions asked him.

Dr. Pepperberg became interested in studying animal intelligence in 1973 while completing her doctorate in chemical physics at Harvard. After seeing the success others had in teaching chimps to use sign language, she began studying animal intelligence with a special emphasis on vocal communication. She spent about forty hours each week researching animal intelligence while devoting another forty hours a week to completing her doctorate.

In the course of her research, Dr. Pepperberg read reports in which psychologists had studied parrots' abilities to solve problems and to communicate. She believed that earlier investigations had failed to achieve meaningful communication with their study subjects because of inappropriate training practices and set out to test her theory with Alex, a borrowed laboratory, some volunteer assistants, and some used equipment.

Within two years of beginning her study, Dr. Pepperberg could show that Alex used language with meaning to identify objects. He could identify more than thirty items by name, shape, and color and had averaged 80 percent accuracy on tests administered to chart his progress.

Alex now knows the names of almost one hundred items, he can count to six, and he can name about seven colors and about seven different types of materials. He has also made up his own names for some items, such as "yummy bread" for carrot cake, "banana cracker" to describe a banana chip, "cork nut" to ask for an almond in its shell, and "rock corn" to distinguish dried corn from fresh. Depending on his level of interest on a given day, Alex's attention span ranges from a few minutes to more than two hours.

From the beginning of the study, Alex has been allowed regular interaction and cuddling with Dr. Pepperberg and her student assistants. They believe this interaction mimics the attention Alex would receive from his flockmates. They also think this attention is vital to Alex's success and to getting him to cooperate in the research project. Alex has a method of testing new students in the program: He rattles off a list of items that he desires, sending the student scrambling to fetch what may end up being dozens of foods and toys. To some, it seems as though Alex wants to know if the new person speaks the same language as he does.

At the beginning of the study, Alex was approximately 1 year old and had received no prior speech instruction. He was domestically bred, but he was not a hand-raised parrot. The chicks that joined the study in 1992 were domestically bred and hand-raised.

The Parrot's Brain

Although the term *birdbrain* is not usually a compliment, Alex has demonstrated that a bird's brain is really capable of quite amazing feats. Parrots have one of the largest brains in the class Aves. They are thought to have large brains because they need to forage for food in the wild. Their large brains also help them function in flock situations, allowing them to learn from other parrots, which helps them have a better chance of survival.

Parrot brains differ from mammal brains in several ways, according to Bonnie Munro Doane. The major differences are found in the sizes of the cerebral cortex and the striatum. In mammals, the cortex is large and the striatum is small. In parrots, the reverse is true. The striatum is the center of birds' intelligence. Although parrots use a different part of their brains than we do to think, it is apparent that they do indeed have the capability to process information and use it intelligently.

Alex is apparently not alone in his mental abilities. In 2006, stories began to surface about a parakeet named Victor who was able to speak in a conversational manner. Victor's owner, Ryan Reynolds, established a Web site about the bird and other parakeets who could converse with their owners. Reynolds also created the Budgie Research Group to allow owners of birds with outstanding verbal abilities to network and share stories about their special pets.

Pet Bird Behavior Compared

Certain personality characteristics are shared by particular species of commonly kept cage birds. The chart on pages 32–35 can be used to determine the characteristics that are important to you, which may in turn help you to select a pet bird that you will enjoy.

Know from the start that all parrots will occasionally scream, bite, chew, or otherwise misbehave from a human point of view. The goal of a good parrot-owner relationship is to minimize the number of episodes of misbehavior that a bird is involved in each day.

More information about the different types of pet birds is available in appendix A, "Pet Bird Personalities."

How to Select a Parrot

Parrots can be purchased through several sources, including bird breeders, private owners, bird shows and marts, and pet stores. Each source provides advantages and disadvantages.

Bird Breeders

Bird breeders advertise in newspapers, online, or in bird specialty magazines when they have young birds for sale. Some breeders may also offer older birds for sale. These are most likely breeder birds who are too old to produce chicks but are still good candidates for pet situations.

If you buy your bird from a private breeder, you will probably be shown only the birds that the breeder has for sale. Do not be offended or upset if you cannot see all the birds that the breeder keeps; some birds are sensitive about the presence of strangers during breeding season, and sensitive birds may destroy eggs or kill chicks when they're upset. If, however, a breeder is willing to show you around his or her facility, consider it a special treat and an honor that few people have bestowed on them.

Bird breeders can be excellent resources for first-time bird owners because they frequently offer follow-up care and advice after they've sold a bird.

Private Owners

Private owners often place classified advertisements in newspapers or online when they want to place their pet birds in new homes. A previously owned bird can be a wonderful investment, or it can be an extremely frustrating experience. Proceed cautiously if you have never owned birds before because private owners often do not offer follow-up care after they've sold a bird.

Bird Shows and Bird Marts

Bird shows and marts offer bird breeders and bird buyers an opportunity to get together to share a love for birds. Bird shows can provide prospective bird owners with the chance to see many different types of birds in one place (usually far more than many pet shops would keep at a time), which can help you narrow your choices if you're undecided about which species to keep.

A bird mart is a little different from a bird show. At a bird mart, various species of birds and a wide variety of bird-keeping supplies are offered for sale, so you can go and shop to your heart's content. However, little follow-up care or advice is usually available, so it may be better to look at different species at a bird mart, but to do your actual purchasing from a different source that offers follow-up care.

Pet Stores

Pet stores may or may not be the ideal place to purchase a parrot. You'll have to check with stores in your area to determine if they even sell pets because many stores discontinued selling livestock in the early 1990s. These stores will be listed as "pet supply stores" in your phone book and may be the places you'll want to go to get the cage, food, dishes, perches, toys, and other accessories you'll need before your bird comes home.

If a store in your area sells live pets, you'll need to visit the store and make sure it's clean and well kept. Walk around the store a bit. Are the floors clean? Do the cages look and smell as though they're cleaned regularly? Do the animals in the cages appear alert, well fed, and healthy? Do the cages appear crowded, or do the animals inside have some room to move around?

Did someone greet you when you walked into the store? Is the store staff friendly? Do they seem to care that you came in to shop? Remember that you will be visiting a pet store every week or two to purchase food, toys, and other items for your pet, so you will want to select a store with friendly and knowledgeable people behind the counter.

After you've determined whether the store is clean and the employees are pleasant, find out if the staff tries to keep their birds in good health. Do they ask you to wash your hands with a mild disinfectant before handling their birds or between handling birds? If they do, don't balk at the request. This request is for the health of the birds, and it indicates that the store is concerned about keeping its livestock healthy. Buying a healthy bird is much easier and more enjoyable than purchasing a pet with health problems, so don't be afraid to follow the rules in a caring store.

Pet Bird Behavior

Species	Activity level	Noise level	Playfulness	Destructiveness
African Greys	Moderate	Moderate	Moderate	Moderate
Amazons	High	Moderate to high	High	Moderate to high
Brotogeris	Moderate	Moderate to high	Moderate to high	Low
Budgerigars/ parakeets	High	Low	High	Low
Caiques	High	Low to moderate	High	Low to moderate
Canaries	Low to moderate	Low	Low	Low
Cockatiels	Moderate to high	Low to moderate	Moderate	Low
Cockatoos	High	High to extremely high	High	Moderate to high
Conures	High	Moderate to high	Moderate to high	Moderate to high
Diamond Doves	Low	Low	Low	Low
Eclectus	Low to moderate	Moderate	Low	Moderate
Finches	High	Low	Low	Low
Grass Parakeets	High	Low	Low	Low
Hawkheaded Parrots	Moderate	Moderate to high	High	Moderate

Cuddly?	Require regular interaction with owners?	Shoulder bird?	Talking potential	Biting potential
Possibly	Yes	Possibly	High	Moderate
Low to moderate	Yes	Possibly	Moderate to high	High to extremely high
Moderate to high	Yes	Possibly	Moderate	Moderate
Moderate	If kept as single pet, yes.	Yes	High	Low
Possibly	Yes	Yes	Low	Low
No	No	Possibly	Low	Low
Possibly	If kept as single pet, yes.	Yes	Low	Moderate
Yes	Yes	No	Low	High
Possibly	Yes	Possibly	Low	Moderate
No	No	No	Low	Low
No	Yes	No	Low to moderate	Moderate
No	No	No	Low	Low
No	No	No	Low	Low
Possibly	Yes	Possibly	Low to moderate	Moderate

continues

Pet Bird Behavior *continued*

Species	Activity level	Noise level	Playfulness	Destructiveness
Kakarikis	High	Moderate	High	Moderate
Lories	Moderate to high	Moderate	High	Low to moderate
Lovebirds	High	Low	Moderate to high	Low
Macaws	Moderate to high	High	High	High
Mynahs	Moderate	High	Moderate	Low
Parrotlets	High	Moderate	Moderate	Low to moderate
Pekin Robins	High	Low	Low	Low
Pionus	Low	Moderate	Moderate	Low to moderate
Quaker Parrots	Moderate to high	Moderate to high	Moderate to high	Moderate
Ringnecks	Moderate to high	Moderate to high	Moderate	Moderate
Rosellas	Moderate	Low	Moderate	Low
Senegals	High	Moderate	Moderate to high	Low to moderate
Tanygnathus	Low	Moderate	Low	Moderate to high
Toucans	High	Moderate to high	Low	Low
Touracos	Moderate	High	Low	Low

Cuddly?	Require regular interaction with owners?	Shoulder bird?	Talking potential	Biting potential
No	No	No	Low	Low to moderate
No	Yes	Possibly	Moderate	Moderate
No	If kept as single pet, yes.	Possibly	Low	Moderate
Possibly	Yes	No	Low to moderate	High
No	Yes	Yes	High	Low
Possibly	If kept as single pet, yes.	Yes	Low	Moderate
No	No	No	Low	Low
Possibly	Yes	Yes	Low	Low
Possibly	Yes	Yes	Moderate to high	Low to moderate
Possibly	Yes	Possibly	Moderate to high	Moderate
No	Yes	No	Moderate	Low
Possibly	Yes	Possibly	Low	Low
Possibly	No	No	Low	Low
No	No	No	Low	Low
No	No	No	Low	Low

If something about the store, staff, and livestock doesn't feel quite right, choose another establishment with which to do business. If the store and its livestock meet with your approval (as they often will), then it's time to get down to the all-important task of selecting your pet bird.

Look at the birds that are available for sale. If possible, sit down and watch them for a while. Don't rush this important step. Do some of them seem bolder than others? Consider those first because you want a curious, active, robust pet rather than a shy animal that hides in a corner. Are other birds sitting off by themselves, seeming to sleep while their cagemates play? Reject any birds that seem too quiet or too sleepy because these attributes can indicate illness.

Here are some of the indicators of a healthy parrot. Keep them in mind when selecting your pet.

- Bright eyes
- Clean cere (the area above the bird's beak that covers her nares, or nostrils)
- Upright posture
- Full-chested appearance
- Actively moving around the cage
- Clean legs and vent
- Smooth feathers
- Good appetite

Remember that healthy birds spend their time engaged in three main activities: eating, playing, and sleeping. If you notice that a bird seems to want only to sleep, for example, reject that bird in favor of another whose routine seems more balanced.

You may think that saving a small, picked-upon parrot from her cagemates seems like the right thing to do, but please resist this urge. Do not buy a bird because you feel sorry for it. You want a strong, healthy, spirited bird rather than the "runt of the litter." Although it sounds hard-hearted, automatically reject any birds that are being bullied, are timid, or hide in a corner or shy away from you. It will save you heartache in the end.

When you approached the parrots under consideration, did they hold their ground, or did they retreat into a safe corner of the cage? Did they take an interest in you, or did they shy away? Birds who hold their ground and take an interest in store visitors have better pet potential than those who flee or hide in a corner.

BIRD RESCUE GROUPS

Another resource to consider when looking for a bird is a bird rescue group. Bird rescue groups have become more popular as bird ownership has grown and as some people realize that parrot ownership just isn't for them.

Bird rescue groups often have a wide variety of birds available for adoption. Each group has its own requirements for new bird owners. Some groups have potential owners take parrot ownership classes, for example, while others may require reference letters from avian veterinarians or other parrot owners before they let you adopt a bird.

Bird rescue groups often provide follow-up care for the birds they place. They can also make referrals to avian veterinarians and offer other valuable information to first-time owners.

Look in the Yellow Pages or online for bird rescue groups in your area.

You can further test the pet potential of a parrot you're considering by putting your hand slowly up to the bird's cage or perch. If the bird stays where she is on the perch or cage or acts curious about your hand, she has better pet potential than if she scoots away from you or flies to the back of the cage.

If possible, let your new pet choose you. Many pet stores display their birds in colony situations on play gyms, or a breeder may bring out a clutch of babies for you to look at. If one bird waddles right up to you and wants to play, or if one comes over to check you out and just seems to want to come home with you, that's the bird you want!

One Bird or Two?

First-time bird owners who are considering smaller birds, such as parakeets, cockatiels, and lovebirds, often ask, "Should I get one bird or two?" Single-pet birds generally make more affectionate pets because you and your family become the bird's substitute flock. But a pair of birds can be quite entertaining as they chase each other around the cage and generally encourage each other into all sorts of avian mischief.

One small drawback of owning two pet parakeets or cockatiels, especially young ones, is that they may have a tendency to playfully tug on one another's tail feathers. Sometimes these feathers come out, leaving you with two considerably shorter birds until the next set of tail feathers grows in. If you have a pair of birds who suddenly become tailless, check the cage bottom for feathers and watch your birds to see if they chase and pester each other. If not, you have nothing to worry about. If so, please alert your avian veterinarian to the problem and ask for further guidance. Two birds are also less likely to learn to talk because they can chatter to each other in their own language rather than learning the language of their substitute "flock."

Let the size of your home, the size of the cage you have chosen, and the amount of time you have to devote to your birds decide how many you will take home with you. Remember, two birds means more work than one, but they can also double your amusement and enjoyment of birds.

If you initially decide on a single pet bird and later add another, plan to house the birds in separate cages, at least at first. Introducing a new bird to another bird's cage opens up the possibility of territorial behavior on the part of the original bird. This behavior can include bullying the newcomer and keeping her away from food and water dishes to the point that the new bird cannot eat or drink.

To avoid this problem, house the birds in separate cages until you can supervise their interactions. Let the birds out together on a neutral play gym and watch how they act with each other. If they seem to get along, you can move their cages closer together. Some birds will adjust to having other birds share their cages, while others prefer to remain alone in their cages with other birds close by.

Don't try to house a significantly larger or smaller bird with your existing pet because one or both of the birds could become injured during play or in a dispute over perches or food bowls. Moreover, certain small birds do not make good cagemates for other small birds of a different species. For example, parakeets may tend to bully finches and canaries, keeping them away from food and water bowls, while cockatiels and lovebirds may exhibit the same behavior toward parakeets.

To keep peace in your avian family, make sure that every bird has her own cage, food, and water bowls. Some birds will get along with other birds during supervised playtime on a play gym, while others do not work or play well with others and enjoy being the only pets out on the gym.

The Pre-Owned Parrot

Many pet bird owners start with young, hand-fed birds, but some people adopt an adult parrot. You may be wondering which option is the right one, but there is no one right answer. If you have the time to devote to a hand-fed parrot's needs, then you should explore that option. If you don't want to start with a young bird, then by all means look into adopting an adult parrot.

Keep in mind that adopting a young parrot may be less demanding because the bird hasn't had a chance to develop many bad habits. In some cases, bringing home an adult bird could be a great mistake if the bird has a number of behavioral problems. On the other hand, it could be the best investment you'll ever make.

People put adult birds up for sale for many reasons. Perhaps the bird detects stress in the home and begins to pull her feathers, and the owners have neither the time nor the patience to solve the problem. The owners may now have a child and suddenly no longer have time for the parrot, or they may be moving and cannot take their pet with them. Some people simply lose interest in their birds and sell them after a few years.

My experience with a previously owned adult parrot has been completely satisfying, but it required a considerable investment of time, patience, and money to restore my African grey's health and allow her charming personality to come through. I can't guarantee that you'll find a diamond in the rough like I did when I adopted my adult bird, but I would certainly encourage you to consider an adult bird when you're looking for a pet.

If you do consider an adult bird, get as much background information as possible from the bird's current owner. Has the bird been moved from home to home, or is the current owner the bird's first owner? Why is the bird being put up for adoption? Has the bird been seen by a veterinarian recently?

Examine the bird closely. Does the bird seem to have all her feathers? Does she scream the entire time you're visiting the current owner? Does she cower in the corner of the cage? Does she seem to want to make your acquaintance, or does she seem uninterested in her surroundings?

Listen to what your heart and your head tell you when you see this bird. Don't adopt her because you feel sorry for her—you are bound to regret your decision later. If you and the bird seem to have a bond, consider adopting her. If, however, the bird shows all her problem behaviors in a single visit, look elsewhere for your chosen pet.

Adopting a previously owned parrot can provide a bird owner with a great deal of enjoyment, or it can cause a lot of heartache. Think carefully about bringing home an adult bird. (PHOTO BY JULIE RACH MANCINI)

chapter 3

NORMAL PARROT BEHAVIORS

Parrots display a wide range of personalities. Some parrots are naturally outgoing and enjoy showing off. They sing or do tricks for complete strangers. Others will talk for family members, while still others talk only for their favorite person in the home. Some parrots are real cuddlebugs, requiring regular sessions of cuddling and scratching, while others prefer to be admired from a distance. Some are playful, while others are reserved.

Regardless of the personality of the parrot you select as a pet, keep in mind that all parrots like routine. They seem to appreciate knowing that they will be fed about the same time every day, and that at other times of the day someone will take them out and pay attention to them, perhaps putting them on a play gym or maybe just cuddling them while watching television. Parrots also like to know that bedtime will occur at about the same time every night. As a result, you may find yourself with a little feathered alarm clock on your hands.

Parrots do not know the difference between workdays and weekends. Don't be surprised if your parrot wakes you at 7:30 on weekend mornings if that's the time he's accustomed to getting his morning round of attention and his breakfast.

Some parrots can be subtle about the way they wake you up. They may rustle lightly under their cage covers or bump into their toys quietly. Others take a more direct approach, talking or whistling or even yelling for attention until someone comes to uncover them.

Although they are creatures of habit, parrots can accept changes in their routines and schedules. You can vary your pet's routine a little bit, but you should be prepared to meet your pet's needs on a regular basis. Don't serve him breakfast at 6:30 on the weekdays and expect him to wait until 11:00 to eat on the weekends. After your bird has had some attention and you've served him breakfast, he will

Some parrots enjoy cuddling, while others like to be admired from afar. (Photo by Pamela L. Higdon)

usually let you crawl back in bed for those last few precious minutes of weekend catch-up sleep.

To illustrate how much time a parrot requires, let me outline my morning schedule. I come downstairs and let my parrot, Sindbad, out of her cage. I remove her evening food and water bowls and hold her over the trash can so that she can eliminate.

While I'm waiting for her to take care of business, I pet her head, scratch her back, and rub under her wings. Not only does she get attention this way, but it's also the perfect opportunity for me to check her over for lumps, bumps, scrapes, ingrown feathers, food that's stuck to her face and beak, and anything else that seems out of the ordinary. On a good day, this routine takes about twenty minutes. If she is feeling neglected or in need of more attention than usual, it can take thirty minutes or more.

After Sindbad has relieved herself, I put her on top of her cage and make her breakfast. I chop her fruits and vegetables, add them to the Nutriberries and almonds I've already placed in her bowl, and serve the meal to Sindbad. While I make my own breakfast and get ready for the day, she's left atop her cage to play for another thirty minutes or so.

In addition to her morning attention, Sindbad has come to expect attention during the day and in the evening, too. When I worked outside the home, I usu-

Sindbad falls over to attract attention when she believes that she is being ignored. (PHOTO BY JULIE RACH MANCINI)

ally came home for lunch to give her some time out of her cage at midday, and then she expected more time out of her cage before dinner and as much attention as I would give her in the evenings. This could have been as simple as having her sit next to me while I read or watched television or as involved as an extensive cuddling session in which I helped her preen hard-to-reach feathers.

Now I work at home, and she's come to expect short bits of attention throughout the day, either by a visit from me or by a trip to my home office to "help" me write. (She does this mostly by sitting on my desk, clicking her beak at pictures of African greys in my office, and looking at me.) If she doesn't receive the expected attention, she falls over in her cage and taps lightly on the side of the cage to have me come rescue her. Since she does this only when I am in the same room with her but am not paying attention to her, I believe this is a learned behavior that resulted from earlier experiences in my home. When she first came to me, Sindbad would fall over because of a variety of physical ailments. She would tap on the side of the cage with her beak to alert me that there was a problem, and I would pick her up and fuss over her. I believe she enjoyed the attention greatly and knows how to receive more of it.

All in all, Sindbad gets a minimum of two hours of attention from me each day—and that's about as little as a parrot can stand.

Safe and Sound

Your parrot needs to feel secure. You can help him feel secure by providing him with a safe home in a large cage that is set up in a part of your house that is fairly active. In this way, your parrot feels that he is part of your family or flock. By giving him a cage, you also give your pet a place where he can relax and just be a bird. Be sure this cage has at least one solid wall behind it. Being housed in the middle of a room may unduly stress your parrot because he may be on the lookout for surprise attacks from all sides of the cage.

Your bird may benefit from having a window near his cage, but make sure that your pet is not exposed to long periods of direct sunlight. (Photo by Julie Rach Mancini)

You can add variety to your bird's environment by putting his cage near a window. Be sure, however, not to place the cage completely in the window because your bird may overheat in the direct daylight. Parrots cannot sweat as mammals can, so owners have to be sure to protect their pets from temperature extremes.

The Empathetic Parrot

A parrot can read his owner's moods very well. If you're in a hurry and rushing around, don't be surprised if your bird's behavior takes a turn for the worse. If I try to rush my bird, she reacts by throwing miniature tantrums, becoming fussy and unhandleable.

When she first arrived in my home, my bird would show her displeasure with being rushed by biting me, and I still have the scars on my hands to show for my lack of judgment. Fortunately for my fingers, she has chosen to vocalize at me more than bite for the last five years, and I have learned to heed those vocalizations and slow down rather than get both of us excited over some minor stress. Interestingly, Sindbad has learned to express herself with increased moderation: the screams followed the biting period for about a year, and the screams have now been replaced with a series of squeaks, trills, and other noises that are delivered with a variety of intonations.

When I worked at *Bird Talk* magazine, we received a few letters from readers whose birds were especially tuned into their owners' needs. One woman had seizures, and her bird would act differently when she sensed the woman was about to have a seizure. This different behavior allowed the woman time to lie down before she had the seizure, which lessened her chances of injury.

The Animal Planet television network featured a parakeet with a similar ability on its show *Animal Miracles*. Sammy the parakeet flies around in a very animated fashion when he senses an impending seizure in his owner so she, too, has a chance to lie down before she has the seizure. Since she brought Sammy home, the woman reported that her seizures have decreased in frequency, which helps support the widely held theory that having a pet is good for your health!

Common Conduct

The following common avian behaviors are listed, in alphabetical order, to help you better understand your new feathered friend.

Aggression

While it may seem like we're starting off on a negative note, aggressive behavior is within the realm of normal parrot behavior. In the wild, birds often show aggressive behavior toward one another when competing for favorite foods or the best mates.

In captivity, parrots show aggression in many ways. They may click their beaks in a short series of clicks, raise one foot, or raise their wings above their backs like little eagles ready to swoop down and attack. Sometimes these behaviors are bluffs, designed to scare off more passive birds, but you need to pay attention to any sort of aggressive behavior from your pet, especially during breeding season. Mature birds are often ruled by their hormones during such times, and their normal behavior may seem quite abnormal to you, particularly if you are bitten (and yes, being bitten is a normal outcome if you do not heed your bird's warning signs).

Aggressive birds may also signal their intentions by fanning their tails, pinning their eyes, or wiping an already clean beak on a perch.

Other aggressive gestures include raising the nape and back feathers while keeping the head feathers low and crouching like a tightly coiled spring. The mouth is open, and the bird is ready to strike if you are foolish enough to put your hand near. Some birds drum their wings to indicate that you are invading their space and an attack may be in the offing, while still others lean away from their cagetop or perch with beaks open to defend their space.

Attention-Getting Behaviors

As your parrot becomes more settled in your home, don't be surprised if you hear subtle little fluffs coming from under the cage cover in the morning. It's as if your bird is saying, "I hear that you're up. I'm up, too. Don't forget to uncover me and play with me!" Other attention-getting behaviors include gently shaking toys, sneezing, or soft vocalizations. In addition to the early-morning attention-getting behavior, some parrots will try to distract their owners when they are on the phone or have their attention otherwise diverted from the bird. My parrot acts up by vocalizing loudly while I'm on the phone, yet when I'm out of the room working or watching television in the same room as she is, she's a perfectly well-behaved bird.

Amazons and cockatoos may display for attention. They will throw their heads back, open their wings, and fan their tails, almost as if they're demanding that everyone in the room look at them.

Some birds will beg to be petted by crouching low on their perches and holding their wings slightly away from their body. A begging bird will also stare at the neglectful offender. Extreme examples of attention-getting behavior include screaming and biting.

Bathing

In their natural habitats, birds bathe according to the opportunities presented to them. Some parrots, such as those that live in the canopy of the rainforest, bathe in rainfall. In captivity, these birds like showers or misting because it is similar to the rainfall to which their ancestors were accustomed.

Others bathe in puddles of water or by rolling around in wet grass. These birds will likely bathe in a shallow dish of water or by rolling in damp greens, including those in their food bowls.

Many birds seem to enjoy taking baths. You will have to experiment with your pet bird to see which type of bath he prefers. If you want to mist your pet, remember to use a spray bottle filled with only warm, clean water. Rather than spraying the water directly into the parrot's face, spray the water over the bird's head so that the mist falls on him like rain. Be sure the bottle itself hasn't held any chemicals, because these could be harmful to your bird's health. Mark the bottle as a bird sprayer to ensure that other family members won't use it to fertilize plants or clean the windows.

Beak Clicking

If your bird clicks a single click of his beak at you and pins his eyes but otherwise looks unthreatening, he is merely greeting you. If your bird clicks a series of short clicks with his beak and raises his foot at you, he is guarding his cage against attack, and the click is a warning for you to back off or the bird will attack you.

Beak Grinding

If you hear your bird making odd little grinding noises as he drifts off to sleep, don't be alarmed. Beak grinding is a sign of a contented pet bird, and it's com-

Beak grinding is an activity that shows that a parrot is content. Owners often hear their pets grinding their beaks as the birds drift off to sleep at night. (PHOTO BY JULIE RACH MANCINI)

monly heard as a bird settles in for the night. Some experts believe that this action helps a bird keep his lower beak in top condition for eating, and the bird grinds his beak at bedtime to be ready to eat again first thing in the morning.

Beak Wiping

After a meal, it's common for a parrot to wipe his beak against a perch or on the cage floor to clean it. Your pet will also wipe his beak on your arm or shirt if they are within reach when his beak is dirty.

If another bird is in the area, the bird who is wiping his beak is marking his territory. You will also see the territory-defending bird move toward the intruding parrot's feet with his beak. In some cases, the defender will chase the intruder off, while in others the defender will decide to back off.

Burrowing

Some species, especially *Brotogeris,* macaws, conures, and caiques, think it's great fun to burrow under their owners' clothing to play hide-and-seek. Conures will also hide under their cage papers or cage covers if allowed to do so. If your bird likes to burrow, be careful that he doesn't get sat upon or squashed while playing. You may also want to wear a certain special "birdie outfit" for these play sessions because some birds like to chew on their owners' clothing!

Chewing

Birds love to chew, and they do it quite well. The reasons behind chewing range from keeping a bird's beak in condition to burning off nervous energy. Whatever the cause, your bird will need a variety of chew toys to destroy in order to keep him happy and healthy. If a bird doesn't have chew toys, he may gnaw on his

Brotogeris, *such as this grey-cheeked parakeet, are happy to burrow under an owner's clothing.* (PHOTO BY GARY A. GALLERSTEIN, DVM)

perches, the paper in his cage tray, or other items that are not good for him to chew on, such as houseplants, doorjambs, antique furniture, or electrical cords.

If your bird is a chewer, be sure to check the finish on his cage to ensure that the finish is not chipped, bubbled, or peeling because your pet may find the spot and continue removing the finish, which, if ingested, can cause your bird to become ill. If you are considering a galvanized cage, be aware that some birds can become ill from ingesting pieces of the galvanized wire. You can prevent this "new-cage syndrome" by washing down the cage wires thoroughly with a solution of vinegar and water and then scrubbing the cage with a wire brush to loosen any stray bits of galvanized wire. Rinse the cage thoroughly with water and allow it to dry before putting your bird into his new home.

Supervise your bird when he's out of his cage: A well-watched bird can't destroy the television remote. He can't chew through phone cords or electrical wires, and he can't nibble on houseplants, baseboards, or furniture. Think of your

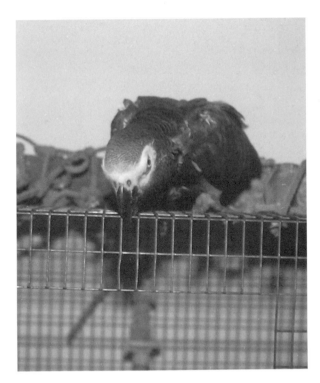

If your bird likes to chew on his cage, make sure that he can't injure himself by ingesting pieces of the cage finish. (PHOTO BY JULIE RACH MANCINI)

bird as his own worst enemy in many cases because his natural curiosity can lead him into all sorts of temptation. As a conscientious bird owner, you want to protect your pet from all dangers, including itself and his curious nature.

Climbing

Parrots are agile creatures who often use their beaks as a third foot to help them get where they want to go. In his quest to move from point A to point B, your parrot is liable to climb chains, cage legs, lamp cords, and curtain ropes.

Drinking

You will notice that your bird drinks water by scooping the water up in his lower beak and then tipping his head back to let the water run down his throat.

You will need to provide your parrot with fresh, clean drinking water to maintain good health. Change the water at least twice a day, and more often if your bird has a tendency to drop food in his bowl or if he eliminates in the bowl.

You can offer water to your bird in a shallow dish that clips onto the side of the cage, or you may find that a water bottle does the trick. If you are considering a water bottle, be aware that some clever parrots have been known to stuff a

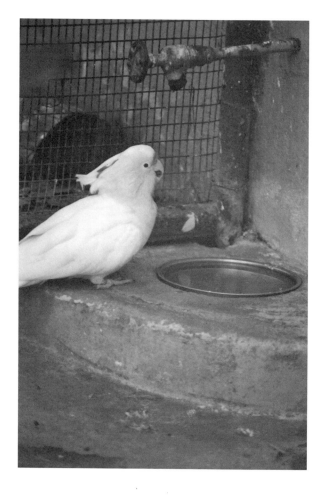

Birds drink by scooping up water in their lower beaks and then tipping their heads back to let the water run down their throats. (Photo by Julie Rach Mancini)

seed into the drinking tube, which allows all the water to drain out of the bottle. This creates a thirsty bird and a soggy cage, neither of which are ideal situations.

Note: If you would like to convert your bird from using a water dish to a water bottle, make sure he knows that the bottle contains water and how to use it before you stop offering the bird water in a bowl.

If you want to share a beverage with your bird, make sure that he has his own drinking vessel. Don't share caffeinated drinks, such as coffee or soda, and don't offer your pet alcohol. Neither caffeine's stimulant effects nor alcohol's sedating nature are good for your pet bird. Better choices for your pet are clean, fresh water or unsweetened fruit juice.

Eating

For your bird, eating does more than just fill his nutritional needs. An interesting array of fresh foods can help stimulate your bird's brain and make his daily routine a little more interesting. Offering your pet a balanced diet may also help him avoid behavioral problems, such as biting, screaming, or chewing, and it may help increase the bird's playfulness and activity levels.

Some birds shred their food, which is a normal play behavior and shouldn't be a cause for concern. Others root through their food bowls rather abruptly, raking across the top of the food to find choice morsels. The food that gets tossed aside in the hunt for the extra-special goodies may be completely ignored, or your bird may give it a second look later in the day.

At the start of each meal, my parrot goes through her dish looking for almonds, which are currently her favorite food. Other favored foods in the past have included cheddar cheese, walnuts, apple slices, and pomegranates. After she finds her favored food, she eats it, and then she goes back to select something else from the bowl. She tends to ignore any food that is thrown out of the bowl and ends up on the floor of her cage, but she will sort through the contents of the dish several times during the day to ensure that she hasn't missed anything. Sometimes I encourage her to go back for seconds or thirds by adding things to her dish throughout the day.

Birds generally eat only during daylight hours, although you may hear your pet rustling around under his cage cover to get a last bite or two of supper before he goes to sleep at night. Birds eat small quantities of food throughout the day to replenish their metabolisms, which is why many bird keepers provide a constant supply of food (seeds or pellets) to their pets at all times. Others prefer to feed their birds once in the morning and once in the evening. Whichever method suits you and your bird is fine.

I choose to have food available to my parrot at all times, day or night, and she has become accustomed to this. She has seeds and nuts available to her in the evening, and I offer more seeds, nuts, and fresh foods during the day.

Parrots are social eaters, which means that they may dive into their food bowls when they see you sit down to a meal. Your pet may also take an interest in

Some foods can double as chew toys. Challenge your pet's mental faculties by offering him a variety of foods, some of which require a little work to enjoy.
(PHOTO BY JULIE RACH MANCINI)

whatever you are eating. Some parrots seem to think that the crackling sound your hand makes as it works down into a salt-free pretzel bag or the opening of a fresh bag of just-popped microwave popcorn is an open invitation for you to share whatever you're eating.

Sharing healthy people food with your parrot is completely acceptable, but sharing something that you've already taken a bite of is not. Human saliva contains bacteria that are perfectly normal for people but are potentially toxic to birds. For your bird's health and your peace of mind, always give your bird his own portion or plate. (And speaking of healthy food, see chapter 12, "Behaviors Every Bird Owner Should Know," for what foods your parrot should *never* eat.)

Eye Pinning

When your bird sees something that excites, frightens, or interests him greatly, his pupils will dilate, then contract, and then dilate again. This behavior is known as eye pinning. Birds pin their eyes when they see a favorite food, a favored person, another bird, or a special toy. They also pin their eyes when they are sexually excited, upset, or aggressive. Some experts describe eye pinning as "flashing" or "blazing."

In larger parrots, eye pinning can also be a sign of confused emotions that can leave an owner vulnerable to a nasty bite. Watch your bird carefully if you see him pin his eyes. He could be greeting you warmly, or this could be an indication that the bird will bite soon!

Facial Feather Twitching

Cockatiels and cockatoos are prone to twitching their facial feathers. This gesture often occurs when the bird is startled or mildly irritated by something, although some birds do this when they are intrigued.

Eye pinning can indicate that a bird is very interested in something. Here, Sindbad pins at the prospect of a favorite treat—a slice of green apple. (PHOTO BY JULIE RACH MANCINI)

Fluffing is a common parrot behavior that often precedes preening. (PHOTO BY JULIE RACH MANCINI)

Fluffing

Fluffing is often a prelude to preening or a tension releaser. However, fluffed feathers can also be an indicator of illness, so if your bird fluffs up, stays fluffed, and resembles a little feathered pinecone, contact your avian veterinarian for an appointment.

Flying in Place

Parrots with clipped wings sometimes exercise their wing and chest muscles by flying in place. These birds tightly grip their perch or the top of their cage and flap furiously for a few moments. The "flying" parrot will also hold onto a cage wall with his beak while flying in place.

Flying in place may indicate that a bird wants your attention. It can also mean that the bird is happy or is trying to tell you something important.

Foot Tapping

Cockatoos are most likely to demonstrate this behavior, although other species may do so. A bird who feels threatened in his space may tap his foot to establish his dominance over the area. It is often used as a bluff, but a bird may follow it up with other aggressive behaviors, so be cautious.

Hanging Upside Down

Some birds enjoy hanging upside down from the curtains or drapery rods or inside their cages. My bird used to do this quite often to demonstrate that she was content and at peace with her surroundings, but it caused the veterinarian's office staff a great deal of concern the first time they saw her do it. Hanging upside down is perfectly normal behavior for some birds, but it can be a bit unsettling if you aren't ready for it.

Head Shaking

Some cockatiels shake their heads when they hear particular noises or pitches. Experts disagree as to the meaning of this behavior; some believe that the bird is reacting negatively to the sound by shaking his head, while others argue that head shaking indicates that the bird is enjoying the sound.

Interacting with Their Owners

One of the simplest ways that parrots interact with their owners is to seek out some scratching. A bird with an itchy head will nudge his head under your hand until your fingers fall on the itchy spot, or he will approach you with his head down in a gesture of solicitation. If your parrot is molting when he comes to you seeking a scratch, pet him very gently because incoming feathers are often sensitive to the touch.

Parrots also like to interact with their owners during mealtime (pull a portable perch up to the table and let your bird join your family) or while the owner is watching television or reading (your bird can perch on the arm of your chair while you take part in these activities). Remember that parrots are social creatures who need interaction with other members of their flock, and in the home, you and your family are your bird's substitute flock.

Jealousy

Some birds become very possessive of their owners, and when they feel that they are not being given enough attention, they demonstrate their displeasure in a number of ways. These demonstrations can include tearing up their cages, nibbling on or biting their owners' hands, and screaming or making other noises when their owners are on the phone.

To prevent your bird from becoming a problem pet, be sure to provide him the opportunity to entertain himself in his cage from time to time. Don't reward his screaming for attention (you'll soon learn which screams are just for the joy of making noise and which ones indicate a pet in danger or pain), and don't bribe your pet into silence with treats while you are out of the room or on the phone. If you do, your bird will soon have you wrapped around his wing feathers and will take full advantage of the situation.

Mobility

Most psittacine birds walk pigeon-toed and appear to waddle when they walk, while passerines and softbills hop from perch to perch. Birds kept in captivity should have their wings clipped to prevent them from flying into windows, mirrors, and walls or escaping through an open door or window. Obviously, owners can carry their pet birds from place to place. Take care to keep the bird at chest level or slightly below to maintain control of your pet.

Some birds display affection for their owners by preening their hair. (PHOTO BY PAMELA L. HIGDON)

Mutual Preening

This part of the preening behavior, described later in this section, can take place among birds or between birds and their owners. Mutual preening can also be a way for birds to "kiss and make up" after a disagreement. Mutual preening is a gesture of affection reserved for best friends or mates, so consider it an honor if your bird wants to preen your eyebrows, hair, mustache or beard, or arms and hands.

If your bird wants to be preened, he will approach you with his head down and will gently nudge his head under your hand as if to tell you exactly where he wants to be scratched and petted, usually in an area that the bird cannot reach, such as the top of his head or under his chin.

Napping

Don't be surprised if you catch your parrot taking a little catnap during the day. As long as you see no other indications of illness, such as a loss of appetite or a fluffed-up appearance, there is no need to worry if your pet sleeps during the day.

Parrots need about twelve hours of sleep daily. They occasionally take short naps in the middle of the day. (PHOTO BY JULIE RACH MANCINI)

Pair Bonding

Pair bonding is usually discussed in the context of breeding; however, not only mated pairs bond. Best bird buddies of the same sex will demonstrate some pair bonding behavior, including sitting close to each other, preening each other, and mimicking the other's actions, such as stretching or scratching.

As you watch a bonded pair, you will see that one bird is generally dominant and the other is submissive. The submissive bird will usually let his partner eat first and have the best spot on the perch.

Perching

During the day, your parrot will alternate the feet on which he perches. He will draw one foot or the other up into his belly feathers to rest it. If you see your bird resting on one foot with his beak tucked into his back feathers, it's a happy bird who's about to take a nap.

If your bird perches on both feet all the time, he may be showing signs of illness, or he may be uncomfortable in his environment. If he sits low on the perch with his feathers fanned out over his feet, he's a happy bird who's keeping his feet warm. However, if your bird perches low on the perch and shows any signs of illness, such as labored breathing or watery eyes, contact your avian veterinarian immediately for an evaluation.

Picking His Feet

Healthy parrots groom their feet as part of their regular routine. Occasionally bits of food become stuck to a bird's feet, or small flakes of dead skin will need to be removed.

In certain cases, a bird can overgroom his feet, picking the skin until the foot bleeds. A small injury may be the cause of this behavior, but not all parrots who overgroom their feet have injured feet before the picking begins. If you see that your parrot has become overly interested in grooming his feet, contact your avian veterinarian for an evaluation.

Playing

Playing is a vital part of a bird's life. Play gives parrots something to do physically and mentally with the energy they would expend in the wild while foraging for food. Playing helps fill the time when a bird's owners are unable to entertain him. It also helps a bird reduce frustration. Finally, playing simply lets birds have fun!

To help your bird play more productively, you will need to provide him with some toys. If your bird doesn't have any toys, he will make some by using his own feathers, dishes, food, or other items within his cage.

Good choices for store-bought toys include sturdy wooden toys (either undyed or painted with bird-safe vegetable dye or food coloring) strung on closed-link chains or vegetable-tanned leather thongs, colorful toys that are made of parrot cookies, soft wooden blocks to encourage chewing, and rope toys. If you purchase rope toys for your parrot, make sure to trim his nails regularly to prevent them from snagging in the rope, and discard the toy when it becomes frayed to prevent your bird from becoming tangled in the toy and accidentally injured.

Unsafe toys include brittle plastic toys that can be shattered easily by a parrot's strong beak, lead-weighted toys that curious birds can crack open to expose the dangerous lead, loose-link chains that can catch toenails or beaks, and jingle-type bells that can trap toes, tongues, or beaks.

Some entertaining toys can be made at home. Give your bird an empty paper towel roll or toilet paper tube (from unscented paper only, please), string some uncooked pasta on a piece of vegetable-tanned leather, or offer your bird a dish of raw pasta pieces to destroy.

Some fun toys can be made at home. Offer your pet some uncooked pasta, large nuts and bolts, or an empty paper towel roll as a change of pace from his other toys. Make sure that nuts, bolts, and other small items are clean and of a size that your pet can't swallow them. (PHOTO BY JULIE RACH MANCINI)

Introduce new toys to your bird by setting them next to your pet's cage for a few days before putting them inside. (PHOTO BY JULIE RACH MANCINI)

You might want to leave the toy next to the cage for a few days before actually putting it inside. Some birds accept new items in their cages almost immediately, but others need a few days to size up a new toy, dish, or perch before sharing cage space with it.

Possessiveness

Some parrots can become overly attached to one person in the household, especially if that same person is the one who is primarily responsible for their care. Indications of a possessive parrot can include hissing and other threatening gestures made toward other family members, and pair bonding behavior with the chosen family member.

You can keep your bird from becoming possessive by having all members of the family spend time with your bird from the moment you bring him home. Encourage different members of the family to feed the bird and clean his cage, and make sure that all family members play with the bird and socialize with him while he's out of his cage.

Preening

Preening is part of a parrot's normal routine. You will see your bird ruffling and straightening his feathers each day. He will also take oil from the uropygial or preen gland at the base of his tail and put the oil on the rest of his feathers, so don't be concerned if you see your pet seeming to peck or bite at his tail. If, during molting, your bird seems to remove whole feathers, don't panic! Old, worn feathers are pushed out by incoming new ones, which makes the old feathers loose and easy to remove.

Birds with crests, such as cockatoos and cockatiels, appreciate a little help from their owners when it comes to preening the crest feathers. (PHOTO BY PAMELA L. HIGDON)

Regurgitating

If you see your bird pinning his eyes, bobbing his head, and pumping his neck and crop muscles, he is about to regurgitate some food for you. Birds regurgitate to their mates during breeding season and to their young while raising chicks. It is a mark of great affection to have your bird regurgitate his dinner for you, so try not to be too disgusted if this occurs.

Scratching

Parakeets and cockatiels have remarkably flexible leg joints and are able to bring their legs up and behind their wings to scratch their heads. Larger parrots bring their heads and feet together in front of their bodies to execute a scratch.

Larger parrots may entice their owners to come over and pet them by slowly scratching their own heads, chins, or necks while fluffing their head feathers.

Preening is another common parrot behavior. Pet birds spend a lot of time grooming their feathers during the course of the day. (PHOTO BY JULIE RACH MANCINI)

Sensory Overload

If your bird suddenly pins his eyes, puffs up his feathers, and seems to be a bundle of frenzied energy, look out! He has just gone into sensory overload, and he may bite you if you try to approach him under these conditions. If your bird acts like this, leave him alone until he calms down enough to be handled safely. Amazons seem quite prone to this behavior, but parakeets and African greys are also subject to overstimulation.

Shyness Around Strangers

Some birds are reluctant to talk or perform around people who are unfamiliar to them. This is normal behavior, and if an owner has properly exposed the bird to new people and places the bird will warm up to a new person rather quickly.

Sidestepping

Sidestepping is a common movement frequently seen in parakeets working their way across their cage on a perch. The bird scoots sideways along the perch and reaches his chosen destination rather quickly.

Sneezing

In pet birds, sneezes are classified as either nonproductive or productive. Nonproductive sneezes clear dust or a stray feather from a bird's nares (what we think of as nostrils) and are nothing to worry about. Some birds even stick a claw into their nares to induce a sneeze from time to time, much as a snuff dipper would take a pinch to produce the same effect. Productive sneezes, on the other hand, produce a discharge and are a cause for concern. If your bird sneezes frequently and you see a discharge from his nares or notice that the area around his nares is wet, contact your avian veterinarian immediately to make an appointment.

Stress

Stress can show itself in many ways in your bird's behavior, including shaking, diarrhea, rapid breathing, wing and tail fanning, holding feathers tightly against the body, screaming, feather picking, poor sleeping habits, and loss of appetite. The bird may also sit up tall on his perch and try to make himself appear as thin as possible. (We'll examine a bird's feather-picking behavior more closely in chapter 4, "Behaviors That Indicate Illness," and we'll look at stress in more detail in chapter 5, "Behaviors That Indicate Stress.")

Over a period of time, stress can harm your pet's health. To prevent your bird from becoming stressed, try to provide him with as regular a routine as possible.

For the most part, parrots are creatures of habit, and they don't always adapt well to sudden changes in their environment or schedule. If you do have to change something, talk to your parrot about it first. I know it seems crazy, but telling your bird what you're going to do before you do it may actually help reduce his stress.

Avian behaviorist Christine Davis advises owners to explain upcoming events to their birds. For example, I explain what I'm doing every time I rearrange the living room or when I have to leave my bird at the veterinarian's office for boarding during business trips. If you're going to be away on vacation, tell your bird how long you'll be gone, and count the days out on your fingers in front of the bird or show him a calendar.

Stretching

All parrots seem to engage in occasional bouts of stretching. An otherwise calm bird will suddenly grab the cage bars and stretch the wing and leg muscles on one side of his body, or he will raise both wings in imitation of an eagle. Again, this is normal behavior.

Tail Bobbing

If your bird's tail pumps or bobs when he's breathing, this is an indication of respiratory distress. However, it can also indicate exuberant vocalizing. If you see other signs of illness in conjunction with the tail bobbing, contact your avian veterinarian for an appointment.

Tail Flipping

Tail flipping is generally a sign that a bird is feeling happy. He seems to say, "Look at me, I am just on top of the world!" Or, as a parrot-owning friend of mine says, when a bird flips his tail, "You can just imagine a little thought bubble over their heads with the word 'Yahoo!' in it."

Tail Wagging

Birds who wag their tails may be expressing happiness at seeing their owners, showing their interest in something, or merely straightening their tail feathers. Tail wagging is often seen as part of an overall feather-fluffing greeting.

Tasting/Testing Things with the Beak

Birds use their beaks and mouths to explore their world in much the same way that people use their hands. For example, don't be surprised if your bird reaches out to tentatively taste or bite your hand before stepping onto it the first time. Your bird isn't biting you to be mean; he's merely investigating his world and testing the strength of a new perch using the tools he has available.

Thrashing

African greys, some cockatoos, and lutino cockatiels seem prone to a condition that is described as "night frights," "cockatiel thrashing syndrome," or "earthquake syndrome." Birds who experience thrashing episodes will be startled from sleep by loud noises or vibrations that cause them to awaken suddenly and try to take flight. In the case of caged pet birds, the thrasher may injure his wing tips, feet, chest, or abdomen on toys or cage bars when he tries to flee from the perceived danger.

To help protect their pets from harm, bird owners can install a small night-light near the bird's cage to help the bird see where he is during a thrashing episode, or place an air cleaner in the bird's room to provide "white noise" that will drown out some potentially frightening background noises, or place the bird in a small sleeping cage that is free of toys and other items that could harm him if he became frightened.

Threats

If your bird wants to threaten a cagemate, another pet in the home, or one of his human companions, he will stand as tall as he can and open his mouth. He will also try to bite the object of his threats.

Tongue Wiggling

When they see something they like very much, cockatiels and cockatoos open their beaks slightly and wiggle their tongues, then lick their beaks as if they've just eaten something tasty.

Vocalization

Many parrots vocalize around sunrise and sunset, which I believe hearkens back to flock behavior in the wild when parrots call to each other to start and end their days.

You may notice that your pet calls to you when you are out of the room. This may mean that he feels lonely or needs some reassurance from you. Tell him that he's fine and that he's being a good bird, and the bird should settle down and begin playing or eating. If he continues to call to you, however, you may want to check on him to ensure that everything is all right in his world.

If you hear your bird softly muttering to himself as he goes to sleep at night, chances are he is practicing talking. Listen to him carefully and see if you can deduce what he is trying to say. Many parrots practice their speech lessons quietly to themselves before trying their talking abilities on a larger audience.

Weak Legs

Some birds suddenly develop "weak legs" when they are put in their cages for time-out or at bedtime. A cockatoo I used to bird-sit was a master of this behavior, and it usually occurred when I was trying to put him up for the evening before he wanted to go to bed.

No matter how hard I tried to put him on his sleeping perch, his legs were too "weak" to support him, and he had to stay on my hand until he felt up to the challenge of perching for the night. This routine usually lasted between five and ten minutes, and when he felt that he had had adequate attention, he remembered how to perch in time to go to bed.

Wing Flipping

When birds are happy, they sometimes flip their wings to get their feathers just right. If they are preening, they may also flip their wings to get the feathers fluffed up so that they can be preened back in place. Note, however, that wing flipping can be tricky to interpret. It can also mean that a bird is settling down to sleep, is angry, or is in pain.

Wing Lifting

Birds often lift their wings to stretch them. They also lift their wings when they are warm in order to equalize their body temperatures. Birds have no sweat glands, so they must pant and lift their wings to remove excess heat from their bodies.

Yawning

You may notice your pet yawning from time to time or seeming to want to pop his ears by opening his mouth wide and closing it. Some bird experts would say your bird needs more oxygen in his environment and would recommend airing out your bird room (be sure all your window and door screens are secure before opening a window or sliding glass door to let in fresh air). Other experts would tell you that your pet is merely yawning or stretching his muscles. If you see no other signs of illness, such as forceful regurgitation or vomiting, yawning is no cause for concern.

This Is *My* Space!

When visiting bird stores and the pet birds of friends, be aware that birds are territorial; this is a normal bird behavior. Don't poke your fingers into a cage that holds a bird you do not know well. The bird will take this gesture as a threat and will probably bite you for invading his space.

Be wary of strange birds, particularly larger parrots such as Amazons, cockatoos, and macaws. Birds who do not know you may perceive you as a threat and may bite. At best, these bites pinch a finger and hurt a lot; at worst, you can end up like a customer at a pet store in Orange County, California, who required plastic surgery on her ear after being bitten by the store's scarlet macaw.

Species-Specific Behaviors

In addition to the common parrot behaviors described above, some behaviors are specific to certain species.

African Greys

Like many parrots, African greys can see detail and discern colors. Unlike many parrots, greys can be highly sensitive to changes in their food dishes and other cage accessories and may refuse to eat. Be aware of this when selecting cage accessories for your pet. Some seem excited by a different-colored bowl, while others act fearful of the new item. My African grey recognizes her black food trays and her red, blue, brown, and ivory water bowls, but if I offer her food or water in a different-color tray or bowl, she hesitates to eat or drink right away. She must become accustomed to the new food vessel before she will use it, a process that can take as little as a few minutes or as long as half a day.

Some wild-caught greys have refused to eat from a bowl if it was a different color than the bowls to which they were accustomed, while others would eat only if the person feeding them wore the same clothes each day at feeding time.

African greys are clumsy, particularly when they are chicks. Make your grey feel more comfortable when you hold him or carry him by allowing him to rest his beak on your chest as he perches on your hand. Many birds feel more secure when they are held or carried in this manner.

Amazons

Amazons may beak-fence with one another, which is a prelude to mating. In this gesture, two birds face off and try to grab the other's beak. If one bird manages to grab hold of the other's beak, the caught bird needs only to cry out a little, and then the grabbing bird lets go. The birds then preen each other, followed by more fencing.

Amazons may also demonstrate their excitement by blowing and snorting air through their nares. An excited Amazon may crouch low on his perch, pin his eyes, hold his wings away from his body, and snort. Owners of Amazons may notice that their birds' eyes rapidly dilate and contract when the bird is excited, frightened, or pleased. The birds will also fan their tail feathers and fluff their neck feathers under these circumstances in order to look larger and more intimidating. To prevent yourself from being nipped severely, keep your hands away from any parrot who is pinning his eyes and fluffing his feathers. The bird could feel he needs to defend himself from a perceived threat (you, whether you're threatening or not) and will respond by biting or striking at you.

At around 3 or 4 years of age, yellow-naped Amazons have a tendency to become extremely possessive of their owners during breeding season. I saw two different yellow nape owners get bitten severely by the other person's bird during breeding season one year. In each case, the bird perceived the other person as a threat to his owner, and the bird chased off the intruder. Usually, yellow napes are really just interested in their owners and will bite them as punishment for daring to have interests unrelated to the bird itself.

Budgies/Parakeets

Be sure to offer only uncovered dishes to your parakeet, because many parakeets would rather starve to death than eat out of a hooded or covered feeder.

When you're feeding your bird, check the dish daily to ensure that he has enough food. Because they are such neat eaters and drop the used hulls right back in their dishes, parakeets can often fool you into thinking that they haven't finished their meals. Don't just look in the dish, but actually remove it from the cage and blow lightly into the dish to remove seed hulls. (You might want to do this over the kitchen sink or the trashcan.)

Cockatiels and Cockatoos

Cockatiels and cockatoos can say a lot with their crests, and observant owners can quickly learn how to read their pets' moods. Here's what to look for:

- Content birds keep their crests lowered. Only the tips of the feathers point upward.

- Playful, alert birds raise their crests vertically. This position indicates that the bird is ready for action.

- Agitated birds raise their crests straight up with the feather tips leaning forward slightly.

- Frightened birds whip their crests back and hiss in a threatening manner. They also stand tall, ready to fight or flee as the situation dictates.

- Male cockatiels declare their love for their mates (or their owners) by raising their wings sideways after the wings are fully extended. The male cockatiel also bows his head and may dip his whole body forward as part of this courtship ritual.

Conures

Conures have several interesting behaviors, one of which is snuggling under something when they sleep. Don't be surprised to find your bird under a corner of his cage paper if the cage he lives in doesn't have a grille to keep the bird out of the cage tray. You can provide your conure with a washcloth, a fuzzy toy, or something else cuddly to snuggle with.

Conures also fall asleep in their food bowls, often on their backs with their feet in the air. Bird owners might consider this an awkward or uncomfortable position, and upon first encountering this behavior some owners panic, fearing that their pet has died. Despite its alarming first impression, there's nothing wrong with your conure if he naps on his back. Some parent birds even feed their chicks when the chicks are lying on their backs, and this is a perfectly comfortable position for a conure.

Conures are also great bathers, and they'll try to bathe in their water bowls if nothing else is available. Conures really prefer to be dunked under the water faucet or to stand under a light shower in the kitchen sink. Be sure the water is lukewarm before letting your conure take a quick dip, and allow plenty of time for your bird's feathers to dry before he goes to bed (a blow-dryer set on low can accelerate the drying process).

Austral and slender-billed conures like to forage on cage bottoms for roots, tubers, leaf buds, seeds, nuts, and fruits. Although bird owners are generally cautioned to be concerned if their birds seem to always be on the cage bottom, for these two conure species, it's perfectly natural behavior.

Eclectus

Female eclectus are conditioned to protect the food supply at all costs to ensure the survival of the species. When Rosebud, a female eclectus I have known since she was hatched in southern California about fifteen years ago, gets defensive of her food bowls, she hovers in a "zone" near the bowls. Her owners cannot get her out of the zone and someone will get bitten if they remain in the area. Rosebud's owner has stopped handling any of her dishes when the bird is near.

Rosebud is so defensive that she recently "attacked" when her owner was washing another parrot's dishes, which look completely different from Rosebud's. Rosebud's eyes turned a pale yellow, and she clamped down on her owner's finger and would not let go. The owner had to press on the skin that connects the upper and lower mandibles. Because her owner knows that this is an instinctive behavior on the part of her pet bird, she simply has to leave Rosebud in her cage whenever she's preparing food—or suffer the consequences. Trying to punish the bird or alter this behavior is a lost cause.

Female eclectus are notorious for attacking bare toes. If you have a female eclectus and allow her to roam free on the floor in your home, make sure that you wear shoes or prepare to be bitten. (PHOTO BY PAMELA L. HIGDON)

The Young Parrot

Parrot chicks spend most of their time eating and sleeping. As they grow and mature, they go through developmental stages: their feathers grow, they develop motor and flight skills, and they become increasingly self-sufficient. Young parrots will also stretch their wings and scratch themselves in an effort to be more comfortable.

Owners of hand-raised chicks may notice that their birds will go through an "independent" phase in which the chicks move from being cute and dependent upon their owners to exploring their world. The birds will need a combination of nurturing to encourage them to explore and discipline to protect them from their curious natures.

It's up to you, the owner, to nurture and discipline your young parrot and to continue to do so throughout his lifetime. It is important to discipline your parrot, but discipline should be clearly distinguished from punishment. Parrots don't understand and therefore do not respond fruitfully to most forms of punishment used by pet owners. Traditional forms of punishment often frighten, harm, or anger parrots rather than achieve your desired result of getting them to behave better. "Time-outs" and other discipline methods used with children who are just starting school are very effective with most parrots. Withholding attention briefly or otherwise denying them a pleasure, such as a cuddle or a head scratch, will do more to encourage your parrot to behave than traditional forms of punishment.

The Mature Bird

When birds are between 2 and 5 years old, they reach sexual maturity. This stage of development brings with it another set of behaviors, many of which coincide with breeding season. These can include biting, screaming, or striking at an owner who puts his or her hand into a bird's cage to change food or water bowls. Note

Young birds need guidance from their owners to ensure that they will be good pets.
(Photo by Gary A. Gallerstein, DVM)

that these actions are normal parrot behaviors. Once your parrot reaches sexual maturity, his hormonal drives during breeding season will largely determine his conduct. Unfortunately, you are not a parrot, so you may not see these behaviors as normal. They are, and they will pass. You may need to alter your behavior somewhat during breeding season to ensure that you get through it with flying colors.

Just as dogs or cats can be altered, so can pet birds. However, this surgery is not routinely recommended. It's a far riskier procedure for birds than for other pets, and it's not necessary in most cases. (See the sidebar on page 135 in chapter 7, "Breeding Behaviors.") A veterinarian *might* recommend that you spay your female bird if she is a chronic egg layer and if other methods of treating the problem, such as hormone shots, have failed.

Senior Parrots

As your parrot grows older, you may notice some changes in his behavior and some subtle changes in his appearance and habits. He may molt more erratically, and his feathers may grow in more sparsely as he ages, or he may seem to preen himself less often. You will need to pay more attention to your older bird's behavior and his routine because changes in his behavior may indicate illness.

Although little is known about the nutritional requirements of older pet birds, avian veterinarians Branson W. Ritchie and Greg J. Harrison suggest in their book *Avian Medicine: Principles and Applications* (coauthored with Linda R. Harrison) that older pet birds should eat a highly digestible diet, allowing them to maintain their weight while receiving lower levels of proteins, phosphorus, and sodium. They also suggest that this diet contain slightly higher levels of vitamins A, B12, and E, as well as thiamin, pyridoxine, zinc, linoleic acid, and lysine to help birds cope with the metabolic and digestive changes that come with old age. (See appendix B, "Resources," for more information about this book and other avian veterinary titles.)

Older pet birds are prone to a number of health problems, including tumors, vision problems, thyroid gland insufficiencies, chlamydiosis, and upper respiratory infections.

If you notice that your pet's breastbone sticks out a little more than it used to or that your bird has difficulty perching, schedule an evaluation with your avian veterinarian. Both of these signs indicate possible tumor development. Tumors develop in pet birds most frequently in the nerves off the bird's spine. A tumor in this spot can impair kidney and gonad function, which can put pressure on the nerve that runs into the bird's leg.

Vision problems can show themselves in several ways. Your pet may no longer be able to judge distances well, or his eyes may appear clouded over. Just as in older people, cataracts can appear in older birds, especially parakeets and macaws.

Thyroid problems occur frequently in older parrots and are usually a result of either a deficiency in the bird's hormonal system or a need for supplemental iodine in the diet. If your bird suddenly gains weight and develops fat deposits that resemble tumors, contact your avian veterinarian to have your pet examined.

Although they may not seem to be connected, a thyroid problem may show itself in a longer-than-average molt. If you notice that your bird's molting period seems unusually long as he ages, talk to your avian veterinarian. A hormonal supplement may be in order to help keep your bird healthy.

You may need to pay more attention to the temperature of your bird's room as he grows older. Add supplemental heat by using an incandescent bulb covered with a reflector on one end of your bird's cage. This allows a bird to move closer to the heat source if it is cold and away from it if the bird becomes too warm. Make sure that the bulb is sufficiently far from the cage so that your pet cannot burn himself on the reflector or the bulb.

How to Help Your Bird Act Normally

Helping your bird maintain normal behavior is much easier than trying to solve behavior problems, and it's not that difficult to do. By having realistic expectations that your bird is, after all, a bird and he will behave as a bird normally does, you will save yourself a great deal of frustration.

In addition to having reasonable expectations of your bird's behavior, you can help him act normally by following a few simple tips:

- **Offer variety.** You enjoy a varied schedule in your day, so why wouldn't your bird? Help your bird be a bird by giving him different toys from time to time and by letting him spend time with you in bird-safe places in your home outside his cage, such as a perch near the table at mealtime or on a play gym in the family room as you watch television in the evenings. If he begins to act up while he's away from his cage, quietly return him to his cage for a little "time-out" of about 20 minutes. Don't yell at him or threaten him for his bad behavior because your actions and tone of voice will actually *encourage* bad behavior in your bird (he loves the drama!). When he returns to his cage, your bird can rest, eat, have a drink of water, or eliminate. After he has had an opportunity to regroup, he can be rejoin you on his perch or play gym.

- **Prevent behavior problems from occurring.** I know this sounds like a tall order, but you can do it fairly easily if you're paying attention to your bird and his normal behaviors. Make a point of playing with your bird or at least talking to him regularly so he knows he has your attention before he begins to misbehave. Greet your pet every time you walk into the room his cage is in, and remember to tell him good-bye when you leave. If your bird feels he has your attention and you know he's there, he won't be as likely to act up to attract your attention.

- **Don't reward misbehavior.** Although it's very tempting to speak loudly to your bird or even yell at him when he's acting up, resist. Ignore his bad behavior because any action on your part to shout him down or otherwise react to his antics will actually reward him and encourage him to behave badly in the future. It's very difficult to do, but it can be done.

When your bird acts up, don't pick him up or look at him. Don't talk to him, and, above all, don't yell at him. As I mentioned earlier, parrots have a flair for the dramatic, and they like all the commotion provided by being yelled at for misbehaving. In his mind, arm waving and yelling and stomping around the bird's room are all good things, and none of them are particularly healthy for you. If you react to your bird's misbehavior in any of these ways, the bird will feel rewarded and will misbehave again just to see you go through the motions of getting excited. Very soon, you will be well trained, and you will think that you have an impossible parrot on your hands.

- **Remember that your bird is an intelligent creature and treat him with respect.** If you respect your bird's intelligence and treat him accordingly, he will be better behaved than if you treat him as "a dumb animal."

- **Make sure your bird is socialized.** Expose your bird to new places and people regularly throughout his life, and begin this process shortly after he becomes part of your family. Play games with him regularly and be sure to give him consistent attention from day one. This doesn't mean that you should hover over his cage twenty-four hours a day, but rather that you should set up a workable schedule that lets your bird know there will be time each day that will be spent with you, as well as time during the day that he has to entertain himself. To help him entertain himself, make sure he has access to interesting toys, and rotate them regularly to keep them interesting. Allow him to become comfortable in several places in your house (his cage, his perch and his play gym, for instance) and introduce him to other family members so that he does not become overly dependent on one person in the family.

- **Recognize your pet's fears and help him overcome them.** If something new in your home scares your bird, make time to help him overcome the fear. You may notice that your bird reacts differently if you change the color or style of your hair or if you suddenly start wearing glasses. In time he will become accustomed to the new you, but you may have to reassure him regularly during the first few days or week he sees the "new you."

NO SHOULDER SITTERS!

One of the best ways to keep your bird well behaved is to keep him off your shoulder. This prevents your bird from considering you as an equal, which he would do if he could see eye to eye with you. Birds who are allowed to sit on their owners' shoulders often try to dominate their owners, which can result in the birds biting their owners regularly, as well as being difficult to handle.

In addition to these potential problems, parrots on shoulders may entertain themselves by nibbling on their owners' jewelry, pulling their hair, or investigating their moles. None of these are desirable activities, and many can lead to injury for either the bird or the owner.

To help keep your bird under control, hold and carry him at chest level. Keep your bird close to your body so he can feel secure, and the sound of your heartbeat may calm him even further.

Some readers may already have shoulder-sitting birds, and they may be wondering what to do to retrain their pets. Here's how to proceed:

Begin training him to perch on your knee when you're watching television or to sit on the arm of your chair. If your bird tries to climb up to your shoulder, place your hand in front of your bird and tell him to step up, then place the bird back where you want him to sit. Eventually, your bird will get the idea that your shoulder is off-limits.

If you remember to keep your arm bent at the elbow and tucked in close to your ribcage, your bird will not have a ready-made ramp (your arm) to run up from your hand to your shoulder. This will also help discourage a former shoulder sitter from regaining his position of power.

If the bird isn't sure about a new toy, for example, leave the toy out where the bird can see it for a few days and become adjusted to it before you put it in your bird's cage. You may even have to play with the toy yourself where your bird can see you to show your pet that there's nothing to fear from a new toy. In some cases, you may even have to put the toy away for a while and reintroduce it later, but your patience will pay off.

- **Talk to your bird.** Look your bird in the eye and speak to him in a pleasant, animated voice. This is the way birds talk to each other in the wild, and you may notice that your bird talks back, either in human words or in little chirrups or feather fluffs.

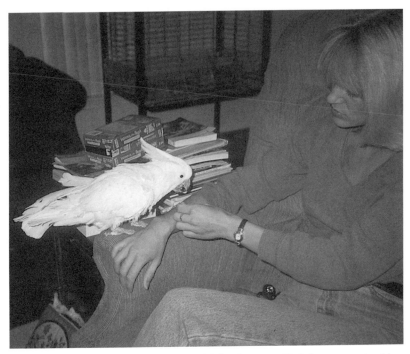

To avoid possible problems associated with having your bird sit on your shoulder, encourage him instead to sit on the arm of your chair as you watch television or read. (PHOTO BY PAMELA L. HIGDON)

Use Your Surroundings

Certain environmental factors can be used to help control your bird's behavior. These include height, territory, location, and light.

Let's look at the first factor, height. Parrots generally behave well with people they have to look up to, but they tend to bully those they look down upon. To keep your pet handleable, make sure he stays between the level of your chest and your waist whenever you hold or carry him.

Territory is another important consideration, and territorial behavior is often seen in birds who do not come out of their cages regularly. They tend to defend their cages against intruders, including their owners' hands, which results in bitten fingers and hurt feelings on the part of the person trying to pick up the parrot. To help prevent territorial behavior in your bird, make sure he has several places around your home in which he feels comfortable. These can include a portable perch that rolls from room to room, a T-stand that's permanently set up in another part of your home, or a play gym the bird can use while he joins the family for an evening of watching television or playing games in the family room.

Location can become either a positive or a negative in bird behavior, depending on where the bird spends most of his time. If he is left alone in an otherwise unused room, he will likely become like a prisoner in solitary confinement and will not behave well on the rare occasions he is allowed to join in on family activities. If, on the other hand, the bird is made to feel part of the family on a consistent basis, he will likely behave better toward all members of the family, especially if they all take part in his daily care. Instead of only one family member handling the feeding and cage-cleaning chores, divide the duties among all family members. This way, your bird becomes a family pet that everyone can enjoy and interact with daily.

Birds need regular exposure to light to maintain their good health, but too much or too little light can cause health and behavior problems. Discuss your bird's light requirements with your avian veterinarian, and see that your bird receives adequate amounts of light each day.

By taking time to understand what your bird needs from you in order to behave well, you will help him be a more enjoyable pet, and you will also save yourself endless frustration for years to come.

chapter 4

BEHAVIORS THAT INDICATE ILLNESS

Despite their reputations as delicate pets, many parrots are really quite hardy if given proper daily care and attention. From time to time, however, your parrot may fall ill, and it's up to you to see that she gets proper veterinary care in order to make a full recovery. Here are some clinical signs of illness to be on the lookout for:

- **Activity:** Is your bird suddenly less active than she was a few weeks ago? Is she less interested in her toys that were previously her favorites? Does she want to sleep all the time and sits fluffed up on a perch in her cage? Is she talking less? Any change in activity level may be an indicator of illness.

- **Appearance:** Does your bird sit with her feathers ruffled all the time? Does she sit on the cage bottom frequently and seem unable to perch? Are her feathers rough and ragged? Does her abdomen appear full or distended? Changes in appearance can also indicate illness in a pet bird.

- **Appetite:** Has your bird lost interest in food? Or is she eating everything in sight and needing additional servings? Is she drinking less water than normal? Is she drinking more water than normal? Is she losing weight? Appetite or weight changes can be indicators of illness.

- **Breathing:** Is your bird gasping or choking instead of breathing normally? Does she make clicking or popping noises when she breathes? Does she seem to pant after only a little movement? Does her tail bob as she inhales and exhales? Do you notice discharge from her eyes or nares (nostrils)? Has she lost her voice? Breathing problems can present in a number of ways, and they all can indicate illness.

- **Digestion:** Is your bird regurgitating food? Are her droppings loose? Does she seem to strain to relieve herself? Do her droppings contain blood, mucus, or whole seeds? All of these digestive problems can be indicators of illness.

- **Droppings:** Has the number of droppings increased or decreased? Have they changed color? Are they looser or more compact than usual? Like digestive problems, changes in the color, consistency, or frequency of a bird's droppings can indicate illness.

- **Eye problems:** Does your bird have swollen eyelids? Are they pasted shut? Do her eyes appear cloudy? Is she squinting frequently? Is she blinking more than normal or rubbing her face against her wing or the side of the cage? Untreated eye problems may lead to blindness, so it's important to have any issues with your bird's eyes examined immediately.

- **Feather problems:** Has your bird gone through a prolonged molt? Is she chewing her feathers or picking them out of her body? Are her latest feathers broken, crushed, deformed, or otherwise damaged? Feather problems can indicate a number of illnesses.

- **Skeletal problems:** Is your bird unable to walk normally? Is one of her wings suddenly droopy? Does she sit differently on her perch? Changes in a bird's muscles and skeletal system often show up as a change in posture or mobility, and such changes can be indicators of illness.

- **Skin problems:** Does your bird suddenly have unexplained lumps or bumps? Is her skin flaky? Has her beak started to peel noticeably? Are her nails overgrown? Any of these signs can indicate illness in your pet.

If your bird shows any of these signs, please contact your veterinarian's office immediately for further instructions. Your bird should be seen as soon as possible to rule out any illnesses.

Be aware that your bird may be quite discreet in showing signs of illness. Her routine may change subtly: She may just sleep a little more in the afternoon, or she may eat a little less. You may not really see a drastic change in her routine, but something may feel different. Experience has taught me to listen to those feelings. It's up to you as the bird's owner to be alert to any changes in your bird's routine and to bring these changes to the attention of your avian veterinarian.

Common Avian Health Conditions

In the wild, birds are masters of hiding illness or weakness, because to demonstrate ill health makes the bird an easy target for predators. As a result, by the time many parrots show obvious signs of illness, they are really quite ill and they may

If you suddenly notice that your bird is favoring one leg, it could indicate illness or injury. (PHOTO BY JULIE RACH MANCINI)

not be able to be nursed back to health. Here's a closer look at the most common health problems.

Aspergillosis

Aspergillosis is caused by a fungus, *Aspergillus*. It can settle in a bird's respiratory tract and cause breathing difficulties. This disease was once considered untreatable, but the use of antifungal medications from medicine designed for humans has brought some hope for a remedy.

Bumblefoot

Bumblefoot is an infection of the sole of a bird's foot. It can cause redness and inflammation, swelling, and lameness. Antibiotics, bandages, and surgery may be needed to treat the condition, which can be prevented by keeping a bird's cage clean and feeding her a well-balanced diet.

Candida

Candida is a disease caused by the yeast *Candida albicans*. Young birds seem to be particularly susceptible to candida infestations, which occur when a bird's diet is low in vitamin A. Signs of candida include white cheesy growths in the bird's mouth and throat, a loss of appetite, regurgitation or vomiting, and a crop that is slow to empty.

Many adult birds show no signs of this condition, and therefore diagnosis is problematic. A breeder may not even know that he or she has infected birds until the parent birds pass the yeast to the chicks during feeding. Even hand-fed chicks are not immune to the condition because it can affect them if feeding tubes damage their throats. Veterinary assistance in the form of antifungal drugs and a diet high in vitamin A may be your best weapons against candida.

Giardia

Giardia is caused by a protozoan called *Giardia psittaci*. Signs of a *Giardia* infection include loose droppings, weight loss, feather picking (especially under the wings), loss of appetite, and depression. Because the *Giardia* organism is difficult to detect in a bird's feces, arriving at a proper diagnosis may be very time-consuming. The disease can be spread through contaminated food or water, and birds do not develop an immunity to it. Your veterinarian can recommend an appropriate medication to treat *Giardia*.

Goiter

Goiter is an enlargement of the thyroid gland in a bird's throat. It is caused by an iodine deficiency and is most often seen in parakeets who eat seed-only diets. Symptoms include difficulty breathing and swallowing and regurgitation. Your veterinarian can determine whether your parakeet has a goiter through X-rays and blood tests. Iodine supplements are used to treat the condition.

Gout

Gout may be associated with kidney problems. Specifically, gouty birds have kidneys that are unable to remove excess nitrogen from the bird's bloodstream. This causes uric acid and urates to build up in the bird's body or joints.

The exact cause of gout is unclear at this time, but high levels of dietary sodium or calcium and inadequate fluid intake may contribute to gout. Two forms of gout occur:

- Articular gout, which affects a bird's lower leg joints as shiny, cream-colored swellings. Articular gout is a painful condition that causes an affected bird to go lame.

- Visceral gout, which affects a bird's internal organs and is difficult to diagnose.

Presently, no cure exists for gout, but treatment includes lowering protein levels and increasing the amount of fruits and vegetables in the bird's diet, along with treating any underlying infections that may have an impact on kidney function. Veterinarians may be able to lower a bird's uric acid levels with medication, and they can also prescribe drugs to ease the bird's pain. Padded perches also seem to offer comfort to afflicted birds.

Obesity

Obesity may be caused by a malfunctioning thyroid gland, but it is most often caused by a bird eating far more calories than she burns in a day. An overweight bird has increased stress on her bones, joints, and internal organ systems. She may also be more prone to developing diseases such as diabetes, pancreatic and liver disease, thyroid problems, atherosclerosis, and heart disease.

To prevent this from happening to your pet bird (particularly your parakeet, Amazon, or cockatoo), make sure that she eats a well-balanced diet that is low in oil seeds and nuts (sunflower seeds, millet, peanuts, walnuts) and that she receives ample opportunity to exercise both inside her cage and outside of it during supervised "out times" on a play gym.

If your bird is overweight, you may notice that she has developed a fatty growth, or lipoma, that may impair her ability to fly. Some experts think that lipomas are linked to a lack of exercise in pet birds. The good news is that most lipomas can be removed safely by your veterinarian.

Papillomas

Papillomas are benign tumors that can appear almost anywhere on a bird's skin, including her foot, leg, eyelid, or preen gland. If a bird has a papilloma on her cloaca, the bird may appear to have a "wet raspberry" coming out of her vent.

This parakeet is obese. It's a good idea for owners to weigh their birds regularly and to chart their weights. Always use a gram scale to weigh your bird, since it is considerably more accurate for our feathered friends than a traditional scale. (PHOTO BY GARY A. GALLERSTEIN, DVM)

To encourage your parrot to exercise, you can place her food atop her cage so that the bird has to climb up to dine. (PHOTO BY JULIE RACH MANCINI)

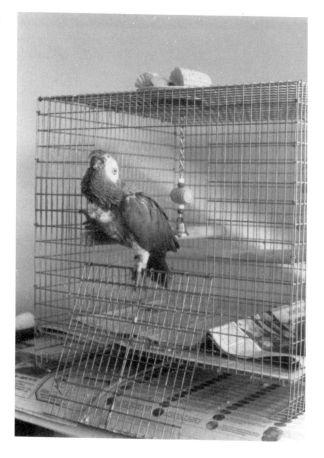

These tumors, which are caused by a virus, can appear as small, crusty lesions, or they may be raised growths that have a bumpy texture or small projections.

Many papillomas can be left untreated without harm to the bird, but if a bird picks at the growth and causes it to bleed, removal will be necessary.

Polyomavirus

Polyomavirus, which is sometimes called French moult, causes flight and tail feathers to develop improperly or not to develop at all. Polyomavirus can be spread through contact with new birds, as well as from feather and fecal dust. Adult birds can carry polyomavirus but not show any signs of the disease. These seemingly healthy birds can pass the virus to young birds who have never been exposed, and these young birds can die from polyomavirus rather quickly.

Sick birds can become weak, lose their appetites, bleed beneath the skin, have enlarged abdomens, become paralyzed, regurgitate, and have diarrhea. Some birds

HELP YOUR BIRD STAY FIT AND TRIM

Obesity is becoming a more common health problem with pet birds. Some avian veterinarians consider it the number one health problem facing pet birds today.

To help your bird maintain her proper weight, you will need the assistance of your avian veterinarian. Discuss your bird's ideal weight with your avian veterinarian, and monitor your pet's weight at home weekly with a kitchen scale that measures weight in grams. This will match the weight measurement used at your veterinarian's office and will help you monitor your pet's weight most effectively.

Schedule daily exercise periods for your bird, and make sure she climbs on a play gym or flaps her wings while she perches on your hand or takes part in some active exercise for a few minutes each day to help her maintain good muscle tone and burn off extra calories. You'll soon see that a well-exercised bird looks better and behaves better, too, because she has an exercise outlet for any pent-up energy.

with polyomavirus suddenly die. Have your bird vaccinated against this disease to protect her from falling ill.

Proventricular Dilatation Syndrome

Proventricular dilatation syndrome, formerly known as macaw wasting disease, is a serious disease of a bird's digestive system. Affected birds are unable to digest their food properly. Signs of proventricular dilatation syndrome include regurgitation, undigested food in the bird's droppings, diarrhea, and severe weight loss. This disease is fatal, and no cure exists at present.

Psittacine Circovirus 1

Psittacine circovirus 1, originally known as psittacine beak and feather disease syndrome or PBFDS, is caused by a virus first detected in cockatoos. It was originally thought to be a cockatoo-specific problem but it has since been determined that more than forty species of parrots can contract this disease, which causes a bird's feathers to become pinched or clubbed in appearance. Other symptoms include beak fractures and mouth ulcers. This highly contagious, fatal disease is most common in birds less than 3 years of age, and there is no cure.

THE IMPORTANCE OF QUARANTINE

You can protect your pets against polyomavirus and other diseases. Quarantine new stock, and shower and change your clothes before handling your pet when you've gone to other bird owners' homes, to bird marts that have large numbers of birds from different vendors on display, or to bird specialty stores with unhealthy stock.

Psittacosis

Psittacosis (also known as chlamydiosis or parrot fever) is a disease that some birds carry all their lives, although symptoms may not surface for many years. Signs of the disease include nasal discharge, diarrhea, lime-green droppings, loss of appetite, weight loss, and depression. Some afflicted birds simply suffer a sudden death. Birds with psittacosis can be treated with tetracycline-laced pellets. Parrots can transmit this disease to people, and individuals with suppressed immune systems are particularly susceptible. However, transmission to humans is quite rare. Affected people display flulike symptoms and should seek antibiotic treatment from their physicians.

Roundworms

Roundworms, or ascarids, can infest birds that have access to dirt, which is where roundworm eggs are found. The worms themselves are 2 to 5 inches long and resemble pieces of white spaghetti. Minor infestations of roundworms can cause weight loss, appetite loss, growth abnormalities, and diarrhea, while heavy infestations can result in bowel blockage and death. To diagnose roundworms, your veterinarian will analyze a sample of your bird's droppings. He or she can then prescribe an appropriate course of treatment to alleviate the problem.

Sarcocystis

Sarcocystis, another parasite, can be a problem in North American areas with large opossum populations. Sarcocystis infections seem to be more prevalent in the winter months, and male birds seem more susceptible to this parasite than females. Birds affected by sarcocystis often appear healthy one day and are dead the next. Those birds that do show signs of illness before dying become lethargic, cannot breathe easily, and pass yellowish droppings. Preventing opossums from gaining access to your aviaries can eliminate the threat of this disease. However, cockroaches can also pass along this parasite by consuming opossum feces and then being eaten by an aviary bird.

Scaly Face

Scaly face is a condition caused by the *Knemidokoptes* mite, which burrows into the top layers of a bird's skin around its cere, eyelids, vent, or legs. This burrowing leaves white crusts on the bird's cere or the corners of the mouth.

If allowed to progress, scaly face can cause lesions to develop on a bird's beak, eyelids, throat, vent, legs, and feet. Advanced cases can also cause beak deformation and horny appendages on a bird's face and legs. The appendages can interfere with a bird's ability to move its legs and toes. If your avian veterinarian suspects your pet has scaly face, he or she will diagnose the condition by examining skin scrapings under a microscope.

Although scaly face has the potential to be a serious condition, the good news is that it can be easily treated by a veterinarian using Ivermectin, which will remove the mites and restore the skin to its normal appearance. Although some over-the-counter remedies are sold to treat scaly face, a veterinarian-supervised course of treatment using Ivermectin will alleviate the problem more quickly and more easily.

Stress

The appearance of white lines or small holes on the large feathers of a bird's wings and tail indicate that the bird was experiencing stress as its feathers were developing. Not surprisingly, these lines or holes are referred to as "stress bars" or "stress lines." If you notice stress bars on your parrot's feathers, discuss them with your avian veterinarian. Be prepared to tell the doctor of anything new in your bird's routine because parrots are creatures of habit who sometimes react badly to changes in their surroundings, diet, or daily activities.

I find stress bars on my bird's feathers each time she completes a course of antibiotic treatments, and I also find stress bars on her tail feathers regularly. I attribute the stress bars on her tail to the fact that she is a rather clumsy parrot and often catches or bends her developing tail feathers in the cage bars and floor grate.

Upper Respiratory Infections

Upper respiratory infections are commonly seen in pet birds that eat seed-only diets without vitamin or fresh food supplements. Signs of an upper respiratory infection include nasal discharge, tail bobbing, watery eyes, and fluffed feathers. Antibiotics prescribed by an avian veterinarian are in order to treat this condition in your pet bird. (Please don't use over-the-counter antibiotics to treat your bird

Stress bars on your bird's
feathers are an indication
that something is not quite
right in your parrot's environment. (PHOTO BY JULIE
RACH MANCINI)

for any illness, because antibiotics work only on bacterial infections. To be effective, an antibiotic dosage must take into account the weight of the animal being
treated, which is why you should use only medications prescribed by your bird's
veterinarian.)

Vitamin A Deficiency

Vitamin A deficiency, or hypovitaminosis A, is a common health problem seen in
pet birds that eat seed-only diets. Signs of vitamin A deficiency include respiratory problems, vision problems, mouth sores, and frequent yeast infections.
Treatment includes supplemental vitamin A injections and antibiotics to combat
any additional infections the bird has.

Vitamin A deficiency can be easily prevented by feeding a bird a varied diet
that includes dark orange and dark green vegetables, such as sweet potatoes, broccoli, carrots, and red peppers, and fruits such as papaya, apricots, and cantaloupe.

Poor Behavior or Poor Health?

If your bird suddenly begins misbehaving, make an appointment with your avian
veterinarian for an evaluation. Some behavior problems indicate illness, and you
want to rule out this possibility before beginning to resolve your bird's behavior
problems.

You should also evaluate changes in your bird's environment—did you move
her cage, change her feeding schedule, or stop taking her out for playtime?

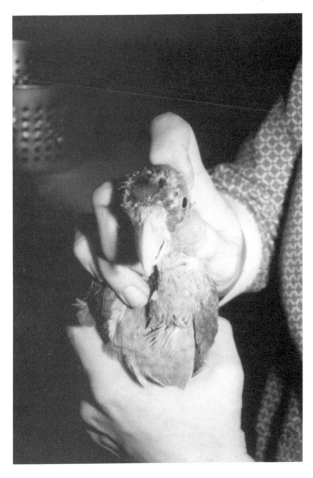

This Amazon is recovering from an upper respiratory infection that caused her to rub her head excessively against the cage bars. Notice the dried debris around the cere and the clumpy feathers on the top of the bird's head. (PHOTO BY GARY A. GALLERSTEIN, DVM)

Remember that birds often do not respond well to sudden changes in their routines, and they may react by misbehaving. If the behavioral problem persists after your avian veterinarian gives your pet a clean bill of health, you may need to consult an avian behaviorist for further assistance.

Avian behaviorists, also called parrot behavior consultants, help parrots and their owners better understand one another. They do this through lectures at conventions, through articles in magazines and on the Internet, and through personal consultations on the telephone or in person. In a perfect world, the behaviorist would meet with new parrot owners while their parrot is still a chick in order to prevent the development of problem behaviors. However, many pet owners seek the advice of behaviorists only after problems have begun.

Avian behaviorists have learned how to address parrot behavior problems by studying bird behavior, dog and cat training techniques, and human psychology. Some of them have worked in veterinary hospitals or raised birds as well.

TAKE CARE WITH KISSES

To avoid possible exposure to human saliva, please don't kiss your bird on the beak. Kiss her on top of her little head instead. Do not allow your parrot to put her head into your mouth, nibble on your lips, or preen your teeth. Although you may see birds doing this on television or in a magazine and think that it's a cute trick, it's unsafe for your bird's health and well-being. It could also leave you open to a nip on the lip, cheek, or nose from your pet because your bird may not be in the mood to play this game with you.

Parrot owners can find avian behaviorists online, through referrals from an avian veterinarian, or through classified advertisements in bird specialty magazines and pet care newsletters and newspapers.

How to Help Your Bird Maintain Good Health

Your bird relies upon you for her daily care, and it's up to you to ensure she receives fresh, healthy foods and clean fresh water each day. Change the food and water regularly to ensure your pet is not exposed to any spoiled or tainted food or water. Change the cage paper daily, too, to help protect your pet from the debris that falls into the cage tray. A curious parrot may climb to the cage floor and attempt to play with or eat food that has been fouled by droppings or may be spoiled because it has been in the cage all day. The simple act of changing the cage paper will help keep your pet's home looking better and will also help her maintain good health.

Make sure she has daily opportunities to exercise, too, because not only will exercise help maintain her weight and health, but it will also help her be a well-behaved bird because she won't need to expend her excess energy by misbehaving.

If you notice any signs of illness in your pet bird, contact your avian veterinarian's office immediately for an appointment. Remember that birds are very good at hiding signs of illness until they are extremely ill, so it's important to take your bird in for an evaluation as soon as you see any indications of illness to give her the best chance at recovery.

In addition to consulting with your avian veterinarian regularly, you may want to discuss your bird's health and behavior with her breeder. Bird breeders have a wealth of knowledge and experience gained from working with different species of birds over the course of many years. Your breeder is a good person to consult with when you have questions about bird care, nutrition, or behavior. He or she will have provided you with contact information at the time you purchased your bird, so be sure to stay in touch with him or her.

Feather Picking

Feather picking—an extreme form of grooming in which a parrot not only preens her feathers but also picks at or pulls them—is one of the most common avian behaviors. It can indicate illness, stress (see chapter 5, "Behaviors That Indicate Stress"), or boredom (see chapter 6, "Behaviors That Indicate Boredom").

Feather picking may have physical causes, such as a dietary imbalance, a hormonal change, a thyroid problem, or an infection of the skin or feathers. It can also result from a bird breaking a feather while she is a clumsy youngster. The feather hurts, so the bird picks at it to remove the source of the pain. If the bird has difficulty removing the feather, she may come to believe that picking helps alleviate pain. Be sure to check your bird's feathers regularly and remove any broken feathers promptly. Ask your avian veterinarian for information on how to remove a broken feather.

Feather picking can also be caused by an emotional upset, such as a change in the owner's appearance, a change in the bird's routine, another pet being added to the home, a new baby in the home, or a number of other factors.

Once feather picking begins, it may be difficult to get a bird to stop. Although it looks painful to us, some birds find the routine of pulling out their feathers emotionally soothing. Birds who suddenly begin picking their feathers, especially those under the wings, may have an intestinal parasite called *Giardia*. If you notice that your bird suddenly starts pulling out her feathers, contact your avian veterinarian for an evaluation.

Your Bird's Health Care Team

Your bird's avian veterinarian is an important ally in your efforts to keep your bird healthy. He or she can provide the latest health and nutrition information, and the office staff can also provide support by answering your grooming questions or providing up-to-date care information.

Your veterinarian's office may have an avian behaviorist on staff, and he or she can also be an important resource to help you determine which behaviors are normal for your bird and which ones indicate something may need to be corrected in your pet's diet or environment. Avian behaviorists have invested considerable time and energy in studying the behavior of pet birds, so put their knowledge to good use in helping your bird maintain good health and good behavior.

Work with the members of your avian veterinarian's staff to form a well-balanced health care team for your bird. Don't be afraid to ask questions or to

Feather picking can be caused by illness, such as a Giardia *infestation. If your bird begins picking her feathers, have her evaluated by an avian veterinarian to rule out physical causes for the picking.* (PHOTO BY JULIE RACH MANCINI)

request additional information if you don't understand a treatment procedure or if you need care instructions repeated. The staff is there to help you help your bird regain or maintain her good health, and it's important for you to understand your role in making that happen.

Visit the Veterinarian Regularly

With good care, a large pet parrot such as an Amazon can live up to eighty years. Along with a balanced diet and daily attention from you, regular visits to an avian veterinarian will go far to prolong the life of your pet.

As a caring owner, you want your bird to have the best chance at living a long, healthy life. To that end, you will need to locate a veterinarian who understands the special medical needs of birds and with whom you can establish a good working relationship. The best time to do so is when you first purchase your pet. If possible, arrange to visit your veterinarian's office on your way home from the breeder or store. This is particularly important if you have other birds at home,

DISEASES SHARED BETWEEN
BIRDS AND PEOPLE

Zoonotic diseases, or diseases that can be passed between animals and people, have gotten a great deal of attention in the first part of the twenty-first century, thanks to outbreaks of diseases such as bird flu, which came to public attention in late 2003 when outbreaks were reported in Asia. By early 2006, outbreaks had been reported in 54 countries and 230 people worldwide had contracted the disease from birds. As this book went to press, the Centers for Disease Control and Prevention had a plan in place to combat avian flu in the event an outbreak occurred in the United States, and vaccines to combat the disease are under development.

Bird flu is an infectious disease that is caused by Type A strains of the influenza virus. It infects mostly waterfowl, such as ducks, but it can spread to domestic poultry. Wild birds worldwide may be carriers of bird flu. Carrier birds often do not show signs of illness, but they shed the virus through their droppings, nasal secretions, or saliva.

Bird flu is of particular concern to poultry farmers in the United States. Since 1997, about 16 outbreaks of bird flu have been reported on U.S. poultry farms. These outbreaks were classified as low pathogenic, which means that few birds became ill or died. This is in direct contrast to the cases reported in Asia in 2003 and 2004, when thousands of birds became ill or were euthanized to stop the spread of the disease.

People can catch bird flu by coming in contact with the droppings of infected birds or with the birds themselves. This is what happened in Asia during the outbreaks in 2003 and 2004. Symptoms of bird flu in people can range from the typical flulike symptoms, such as fever, cough, sore throat, and muscle aches, to eye infection, pneumonia, and other life-threatening complications. Clinical signs in birds can vary, from birds who show no signs of illness to any of the following: lack of energy and appetite, decreased egg production, soft-shelled or misshapen eggs, nasal discharge, sneezing, lack of coordination, or loose droppings.

Let me emphasize that it is extremely unlikely that your pet parrot is a carrier of bird flu or that you could catch bird flu from your pet. Bird flu is a greater concern for poultry farmers and bird breeders than it is for the average pet bird owner, but I am including information on it because the topic has received widespread media attention.

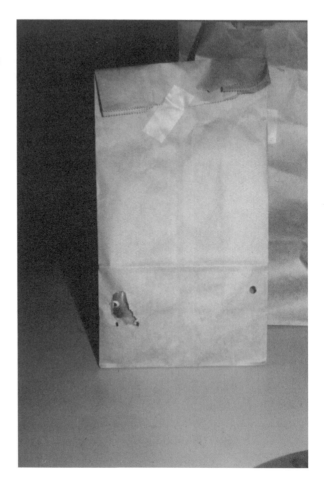

A paper bag is not an appropriate bird carrier. A parrot, such as this Fischer's lovebird, can chew through the bag and escape. Use a proper, safe carrier when taking your pet to visit the veterinarian. (PHOTO BY GARY A. GALLERSTEIN, DVM)

because you don't want to endanger the health of your existing flock or your new pet.

Finding an Avian Veterinarian

If you don't know an avian veterinarian in your area, find out where the person from whom you bought your bird takes his or her birds. Talk to other bird owners you know and find out whom they take their pets to, or call bird clubs in your area for referrals.

If you have no bird-owning friends or can't locate a bird club, you might be able to find a veterinarian in the Yellow Pages. Read the advertisements for veterinarians carefully, and try to find one who specializes in birds. To find a vet in your area, you can also go to www.aav.org. Many veterinarians who have an interest in treating birds will join the Association of Avian Veterinarians and advertise

A better carrier for trans-porting your bird to the veterinarian's office is a small pet carrier, such as those used to transport cats and dogs. (PHOTO BY JULIE RACH MANCINI)

themselves as members of this organization. Some veterinarians have passed a special examination that entitles them to call themselves avian specialists.

Once you've received your recommendations or found likely candidates in the telephone book, start calling the veterinary offices. Ask the staff how many birds the doctor sees in a week or a month, how much an office visit costs, and what payment options are available (cash, credit card, check, or time payments). You can also inquire if the doctor keeps birds as personal pets.

If you like the answers you receive, make an appointment for your bird to be evaluated. Make a list of any questions you want to ask the doctor regarding diet, how often your bird's wings and nails should be clipped, or how often you should bring the bird in for an examination, and take it with you when you go to the appointment.

Preparing for Your Visit to the Veterinarian

Bird owners should not be afraid to ask their avian veterinarians questions, but they should also be prepared to provide a good deal of information. When you take your bird in for an exam, the doctor may ask you for answers to these questions:

- Why is the bird here today?

- How would you describe the bird's normal activity level?

- How is the bird's appetite?

- What does the bird's normal diet consist of?

- Have you noticed a change in the bird's appearance lately?

Be sure to explain any changes in as much detail as you can, because changes in your bird's typical behavior can indicate illness.

During the initial examination, the veterinarian will probably take his or her first look at your pet bird while she is still in her cage or carrier. The doctor may talk to you and your bird for a few minutes to give the bird an opportunity to become accustomed to him or her, rather than simply reaching right in and grabbing your pet. While the veterinarian is talking to you, he or she will check the bird's posture and its ability to perch.

Next, the doctor should remove the bird from its carrier or cage and look it over carefully. He or she will particularly note the condition of your pet's eyes, beak, and nares (nostrils). The bird should be weighed, and the veterinarian will probably feel your pet's body and wings for any lumps, bumps, or deformities that require further investigation. Feather condition will also be assessed, as will the condition of the bird's vent, legs, and feet. Your veterinarian will also listen to your pet's lungs with a stethoscope, and may also check the bird's mouth, throat, and ears.

After your veterinarian has completed your bird's physical examination, he or she may recommend further tests. These can include:

- Blood tests, which help a doctor determine if your bird has a specific disease. From a blood test, the doctor can obtain a complete blood count, showing the number of red and white blood cells that your bird has. This information can help diagnose infections or anemia.

- Radiographs or X-rays, which allow a veterinarian to study the size and shape of a bird's internal organs, along with the formation of its bones. X-rays also help doctors find foreign bodies in a bird's system.

- Microbiological exams, which help a veterinarian determine if any unusual organisms (bacteria, fungi, or yeast) are growing inside your bird's body.

- Fecal analysis, which evaluates a small sample of your bird's droppings to determine if she has internal parasites or a bacterial or yeast infection.

Once the examination is concluded and you've had a chance to discuss any questions you have with your veterinarian, the doctor will probably recommend a follow-up examination schedule for your pet. Most healthy birds visit the veterinarian annually, but your doctor may recommend a different schedule.

To keep your pet from suffering long-term health risks, keep a close eye on her daily activities and appearance. If something suddenly changes in the way your bird looks or acts, contact your veterinarian immediately.

chapter 5

BEHAVIORS THAT INDICATE STRESS

Birds experience "positive" stress that produces excitement and enjoyment, such as a play session with a favored person or a ride in the car. However, stress frequently has negative ramifications and can cause illness and behavioral problems in your bird. A bird can be stressed by a number of things, even detecting tension in the home between partners. Stress can result from feeling insecure because his cage is in the center of the room. Birds need to feel secure in their cages, so make sure that your bird's home has at least one solid wall behind it. A solid wall "protects" your bird from being approached from behind by predators and other scary things; this it will help your bird relax.

Ideally, your bird will encounter some combination of positive stress and negative stress throughout his life. Try to minimize the negative stress and provide some positive stress. It's impossible to remove all stresses from your bird's life, just as it's impossible to remove them from your own. However, by striking a balance, you can help your bird live a more comfortable, less stressed life.

Be sure that your bird's cage is up against a solid wall to provide him with a feeling of security. (Photo by Julie Rach Mancini)

Among the common stressors for birds are:

- New people in the home
- New pets in the home
- Loud noises
- Earthquakes
- Sudden movements
- Rearrangement of the furniture in the bird's room
- Sensing stress in his owner's life
- Dirty feathers

- Attaining sexual maturity and being unable to breed
- Boredom
- Insecurity
- Malnutrition
- Lack of sleep
- Loneliness
- Lack of toys
- Owner's reinforcement of feather picking

Sometimes, a frightened bird needs to be cuddled and reassured that all is well in his world. (PHOTO BY JULIE RACH MANCINI)

How Stress Affects Birds

Stress can affect a pet bird in a number of ways. One of the most important ways stress can affect a pet bird is by diminishing his ability to fight off disease. Birds who are stressed by one or more factors in their environment are more likely to become ill than birds who feel content in their surroundings. Take steps to ensure that your bird feels comfortable in your home to help him stay healthy.

Another way stress can affect birds is through the fight-or-flight response. This instinctive reaction helps all animals survive, but in captive conditions, this response can lead to health or behavioral problems because the bird wants either to flee the situation or to put up a fight to defend himself, but he can do neither one successfully.

Stress can also lead to abnormal behaviors in birds, many of which are outlined in the following sections.

Biting

Birds under stress sometimes take out their frustration with their environment by biting their owners. These birds may have chosen to start biting their owners because their owners did something to frighten them or to hurt them, or they may have tried to force the bird into doing something he didn't want to do, such as playing or rough-housing when the bird was ready to go to bed.

Whatever the cause, a bird bite hurts physically and emotionally, and it's easy to do something to "get back at" a biting bird, such as striking it or causing it other physical harm. Do not hit or otherwise harm your bird if he bites you; instead, try to determine why he bit you and take steps to change your behavior in order to keep him from biting in the future.

Handle your bird with consistent, gentle discipline, and be aware of his moods. Don't make him play with you if he's tired, for instance, and don't be mean to him or otherwise tease him. By sending a consistent message to him, you're more likely to have a well-behaved bird who is routinely easy to handle.

Fear

Generally, frightened birds hold their feathers flat against their bodies and try to make themselves as "thin" as they can. They also stretch their necks, stare with small pupils, and may raise themselves off their perches. When the fear passes, the bird raises all his feathers and shakes them.

Birds can also show fear by puffing their feathers, screaming, growling, hiding, flying away from whatever has scared it, raising the crest (if the bird has one), or becoming aggressive.

To help calm your bird when he becomes scared, you can talk to him, cuddle him, or cover his cage. You will have to experiment to see which reaction your bird shows to things that frighten him and which kind of attention works best to allay your pet's fears.

Feather Picking

As mentioned in chapter 4, "Behaviors That Indicate Illness," stress can cause one of the most obvious behavior problems in parrots—feather picking. Some species, such as African greys, seem more prone to feather picking than others, but almost any parrot can develop this problem.

Don't confuse picking with normal preening. Once feather picking begins, it seems to be a compulsive habit. It actually calms some birds, even though it appears to us to be painful. Birds who suddenly begin picking their feathers, especially those under the wings, may have an intestinal parasite called *Giardia*. If you notice that your bird suddenly starts pulling his feathers out, contact your avian veterinarian for an evaluation.

For the first six years my African grey, Sindbad, lived with me, she picked her feathers regularly. She came to me without anything more than downy underfeathers from just below her lower beak to her vent, and her crop was picked down to pink skin. Gradual changes in a variety of factors in her life eventually taught her to leave her feathers alone, though she still has a small bare area on her

Some birds show fear by hiding in a corner of their cages. (PHOTO BY JULIE RACH MANCINI)

chest that may never be fully feathered, as it is likely that she damaged the feather follicles themselves with her picking.

The first step was to determine whether there was a physical cause for her picking. When I knew that her health was relatively stable, my next step was to consistently provide a routine in my bird's life. I have put her cage in approximately the same place in each of the apartments we have lived in, set the same pieces of furniture around it, and hung the same pieces of artwork on the walls over the cage. I have also made sure that she is served her meals at approximately the same time every day and that she receives consistent attention from me.

In addition to her routine, I offered my bird a varied and well-balanced diet that included some visually and (I hoped) mentally interesting items, such as corn on the cob, carrot sticks, zucchini wedges, pomegranate slices, green beans, and peapods. In this way, I believed I was not only feeding my bird's body, but also feeding her mind by giving her something interesting to play with in her food bowl.

One of the biggest challenges was to encourage my bird to play. Perhaps she didn't have toys that interested her in her previous home, or maybe her health wasn't good enough to allow her to play, but she didn't seem to understand what toys were all about when she came to me. By spending time around a variety of birds at my friends' homes and at her veterinarian's office and through trial-and-error introduction by me, I eventually found some toys that interest her enough so that she destroys them and doesn't chew on her feathers quite so frequently.

In addition to stress, psychological causes for feather picking can include boredom, insecurity, breeding frustrations, and nervousness. After Sindbad's veterinarian determined that her picking had a psychological cause, I began to look at the world through her eyes. What seemed strange or frightening? What was comforting and familiar? What had owners of other birds who picked found successful in helping their pets stop this habit? I soon discovered I had many more questions than answers, but I pressed on.

As much as I'd like to tell you differently, my efforts were neither overwhelmingly nor universally successful. Sindbad would leave her feathers alone for a week or so and then preen them down to the skin with a vengeance. Some weeks she would pull the feathers on her chest, while other weeks she would destroy the feathers on her back or the tips of her wings. It seemed that for every two steps of progress, she took three steps backward into more serious picking. Still I persevered. I knew that if she was still picking, something was not right in her universe, and I continued to try to find out what was making her so unsettled and insecure.

I didn't try using any of the spray-on products touted to be cures for feather picking. Birds preen their feathers to keep them clean, so if you apply something to that feather, the bird is going to work extra hard to clean the feather, even to

Feather picking can occasionally progress to self-mutilation of a bird's skin.
(PHOTO BY GARY A. GALLERSTEIN, DVM)

BEHAVIOR MODIFICATION
FOR FEATHER PICKERS

To help your bird behave better, praise him when he does the following things:

- Sits quietly on his perch.

- Plays with his toys.

- Vocalizes quietly.

Do not react whenever he begins to pick his feathers, because you are actually rewarding the behavior by your reaction.

---

the point of chewing the feather off! If you're going to spray anything on your bird, make sure it's no stronger than clean, warm water, and also be sure your bird enjoys being misted before you make this a regular part of his routine.

As her health improved, Sindbad's picking lessened. One day, I happened to notice that I had a mostly feathered bird—after only six years of work. I don't have a magic solution to offer except to ask that you have your bird evaluated by your avian veterinarian if he starts to pick, and if the cause isn't physical, please be patient with your feather-picking parrot as you try to distract him away from his feathers.

Freezing

In the wild, birds often "freeze" in position to avoid being seen by predators. If a bird is new to your home, he may react like this the first few times you come in the room, or a longtime pet may react this way to new people. With time and patient conditioning on the owner's part, most birds get over this behavior.

Growling

If your cockatiel or African grey growls, it's because the bird is afraid of something in his environment. The bird growls in an attempt to scare away the frightening intruder.

Don't try to handle a growling bird, but talk to him in a calming voice. Reassure him that you mean him no harm. Examine the bird's environment to try to determine the cause of the growling, and take steps to change whatever seems frightening.

Stress can come from a variety of situations. Some well-meaning pet owners may actually cause their birds to experience stress by overcrowding their birds' cages with toys, food, and other distractions. (PHOTO BY JULIE RACH MANCINI)

If you determine that you or another member of your family are the cause of the growling, work with your bird a little each day to achieve his trust. In time, his growling should subside.

Hissing

Like growling, hissing is an attempt to frighten off something your bird perceives to be threatening. Cockatiels are more likely to hiss than other birds, and some will rock back and forth in addition to hissing. Both are defensive gestures.

As with a growling bird, gentle verbal reassurance and patient daily trust-building sessions may be required to calm your hissing parrot.

Nail Biting

Just as some people bite their nails when they're nervous or worried about something, so do some parrots. Nail biting can be resolved in some cases by working with your bird every day to build his trust in you and his comfort level in his surroundings. Talk to him quietly and move slowly around him because loud noises and sudden movements can be stressful to pet birds. In time, you may notice your bird is biting his nails less often, or he may stop the habit completely after he becomes comfortable in your home.

Panting

Panting can indicate physical problems, such as heatstroke. It can also be an indication of stress. Once you're sure the bird doesn't have heatstroke, evaluate his environment to see what's upsetting your bird, and then take steps to remedy the situation.

Screaming

As mentioned earlier, parrots are great reflectors of their owners' moods. Screaming is one of the most common ways that they express their sense of their owner's stress.

If your parrot suddenly starts screaming, take a moment to assess your own situation. Did you have a bad day at work? Did you just have an argument with your spouse? Did one of your teenagers just test the limits of your patience again? If you answer yes to any of these questions, here's another one: Are you taking the stress you feel at these other situations out on your parrot? Walk away from your parrot, calm down, and take a few deep breaths. After you're calm, go back and see your parrot. Talk to him in a bright and cheery tone. Chances are your bird will sense the change in your mood and will react accordingly.

In other cases, a screaming bird is stressed about something in his environment. It could be that the bird is reacting to a wild bird sitting on the rail of your back porch, or it could be that another bird in the home is misbehaving. In extreme cases, the toaster could be overheating or a pan on the stove may have caught fire. If your otherwise quiet bird suddenly starts screaming, you should investigate to determine the cause before you discipline your parrot.

Finally, birds sometimes need to be reassured that they aren't alone and that you really do still care about them. If your parrot screams to you from one end of the house, simply call back, "I'm here. Are you okay?" Your bird will feel better knowing where you are and will probably go back to his normal routine. Be sure to tell your bird, "I'll be right back," or, "I'm just going in the other room," when you leave his room. This will help your bird understand that you aren't abandoning him.

To prevent screaming from becoming a problem, don't reward your bird for screaming. If you reward him by yelling back or providing him with some other dramatic reinforcement, you will simply be training your intelligent pet to scream again the next time he wants attention. If your bird screams, simply tell him to be quiet in a calm tone. If that doesn't work, a quick dirty look may do the trick. If those solutions don't resolve the problem, simply ignore the bird when he screams 10/29/07

Restraint collars should be applied to feather-picking birds under the guidance of a veterinarian. Before applying a collar, the veterinarian should try to determine the underlying cause for the picking. (PHOTO BY GARY A. GALLERSTEIN, DVM)

and praise him lavishly when he behaves in an acceptable manner. Because parrots like attention from their human companions, they will quickly catch on to this game.

Finally, accept the fact that your bird is going to be a little loud from time to time. He may want to greet the dawn and bid the sunset adieu, or he may just feel very good at some point in the day and want to scream a little. Knowing this from the start will help you accept the occasional outbursts from your pet.

Self-Mutilation

As noted earlier, birds under stress may pick their feathers. In more extreme cases, the birds begin chewing on or picking at their legs, toes, and chests. Veterinary care is often required to help alleviate this condition. Treatment may include the application of an Elizabethan collar to keep the bird from picking itself, surgery to repair skin damage, or behavior-modifying medication.

Sexual Frustration

Some birds become frustrated when they are unable to breed after reaching sexual maturity, and this frustration causes them to become stressed. Frustrated birds may scream, pull their feathers, mutilate themselves, and bite their owners. These birds may be better suited for a breeding program (if you want to set your bird up for breeding or if you can locate a breeder willing to take your bird), or they may need to be sent to a bird retirement facility where they can spend time with other birds, rather than misbehaving and being unhappy in your home. Discuss your bird's sexual behavior with your avian veterinarian, and come up with the solution that's best for your pet.

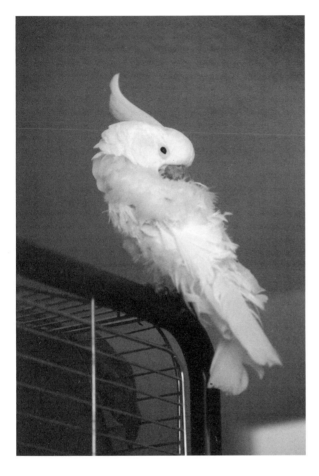

This Eleanora cockatoo was sent to a retirement facility after his sexual frustration became too much for his owners to manage. The bird chewed his feathers, screamed regularly, and was generally unhandleable. (PHOTO BY JULIE RACH MANCINI)

Shaking

Shaking can indicate seizures or other medical problems, or it could simply be a sign of a parrot who's afraid of something in his environment. If your bird is not prone to seizures, you will need to assess his environment to see what could be causing the stress that makes him shake.

Reducing Stress in Your Bird's Environment

One of the easiest ways to prevent stress-related bad behavior in your bird is to reduce the amount of bad stress he feels from his environment. While this may sound like an impossible task, it's really fairly easy if you consider different elements in your bird's environment. Here are some tips:

- **Set a predictable routine for your bird.** Birds are creatures of habit, and they seem to thrive when they settle into a routine with predictable wake-up times, mealtimes, and bedtimes. Pet birds do well after they figure out when people will be home with them and when they will need to entertain themselves with the toys in their cages.

- **Feed your bird familiar foods.** Try to maintain the same healthy diet your bird ate at his breeder's or at the bird specialty store before you brought him home. Introduce new foods to his diet, too, but don't overwhelm him with too many new foods at once, and don't eliminate familiar favorites just for the sake of offering something new and different. Young birds seem to be more open to new tastes and new foods than adult birds, but no bird should be forced into a new diet.

- **Provide your bird with a spacious cage.** Your bird needs to be able to spread his wings and stretch easily in his cage. Smaller birds may even be able to fly from one end of the cage to the other to exercise. If your bird has a crest or long tail feathers, he should be able to perch in his cage comfortably without having either crest or tail feathers touching cage bars.

- **Set up your bird's cage in a secure spot in your home.** This spot should have at least one solid wall behind it because birds like to feel secure, and having a solid wall behind the cage means that your pet won't have to worry that something or someone will sneak up behind his house.

- **Keep your bird out of direct sunlight.** While birds seem to enjoy the warmth of the sun on their feathers and they benefit from exposure to sunlight, they do not do well when left in direct sun. This can lead to overheating and possibly heatstroke, so don't expose your pet to direct sunlight either in his cage or when traveling in a car. If your bird's cage is in a sunny spot in your home, provide a shaded area in the cage by draping his cage cover over one corner of the cage so your bird can move out of the sun to cool off as needed.

- **Locate the bird's cage in the room so that he can see the room's doorway.** By letting your pet see the doorway, he will know when someone is coming into the room, so he won't be surprised or startled by unexpected visitors.

- **Provide your bird with appropriately sized, interesting toys with which he can entertain himself during the day.** Check the toys weekly for signs of wear and rotate them so your bird doesn't become bored with any one toy. Replace worn toys with new ones so your pet doesn't injure himself during playtime.

- **When talking to your bird or servicing his cage, don't hover over the cage.** By the same token, don't hang mobiles or potted plants over your bird's cage. Birds perceive threats when people or things hover over them, so it's best not to stress your pet by spending too much time standing over his cage. If some members of your family are especially tall, they may need to crouch by the cage or sit next to it in order not to stress your bird when they interact with him.

- **Limit access to your bird's room by other pets.** Although you may think it's cute to have your dog run in and greet your bird each morning by sitting in front of the cage, your bird may view the dog as a predator intent on doing harm, even though your dog is the friendliest animal in your neighborhood.

Now that we've looked at some ways you can manage your bird's environment to manage his stress, let's look again at some of the stressors at the beginning of the chapter to see if there are ways to manage your bird's stress even more:

By properly *introducing new people and pets* in the home to your bird, you can help reduce his stress level over them. Proper introductions include supervising all interaction between your bird and other pets to ensure no animals are injured, and you must also monitor all interactions between your bird and other people until the people involved demonstrate that they are capable of handling your bird without causing him harm or distress.

Loud noises and s*udden movements* can be reduced in your home by encouraging people to approach your bird's cage quietly. Say the bird's name to let him know you are approaching his cage so he is not startled. Many parrots seem to react less to loud noises and sudden movements after they have become accustomed to the normal household routine, but it's always a good idea to monitor how your bird reacts to noises and movements. He may enjoy commotion and join in the ruckus, or he may sit on the sidelines and cautiously observe. By knowing how your bird reacts to such situations, you can help lessen his stress if he is suddenly presented with a room full of happy soccer players who just won the city championship or a group of football fans watching the big game and cheering their team to victory.

You can manage your bird's stress over *furniture rearrangement* by talking to him as you move his room around. Sound positive and upbeat about the change, and reassure him that he will be fine. Stay with your bird for a few minutes immediately after the room is rearranged to ensure that he seems comfortable with the new setup. Make sure not to arrange furniture near his cage so that anything hangs over the cage or otherwise seems dangerous or threatening because this setup could lead to stress in your pet.

You will quickly learn that your bird is a good barometer of *your moods*. He may be harder to manage if you've had a difficult day at work or if you've just had a fight with your partner, or he may be a perfect angel if things in your emotional life are on an even keel. When you've had a tough day, take a few minutes to try to relax before handling your bird. Take a few deep breaths and shake off any tension in your arms and shoulders. Reassure your pet that you've had a tough day,

MORE WAYS TO REDUCE
YOUR BIRD'S STRESS

- Relocate your bird's cage to a more active room in your home.

- Bring your bird into the family room or your home office on a portable perch to give him a change of scenery.

- Buy a larger cage.

- Leave the television or radio on for your bird when you leave home.

- Give him more bathing opportunities.

- Give him more opportunities to exercise.

- Change the toys in your bird's cage.

but things are better now that you are home with him, and you'll probably notice how he'll try to make you laugh or smile to cheer you up.

Your bird probably won't have too much trouble with too many other items on the list at the beginning of the chapter because you, as a caring owner, won't allow him to be dirty or become bored or eat unhealthy food. By taking the time to examine the world through your bird's eyes, you can help reduce his stress level, which will help him stay healthy and be better behaved, too.

chapter 6

BEHAVIORS THAT INDICATE BOREDOM

Because birds are such intelligent creatures, they can become bored fairly easily, and they can indicate this in a number of ways, including feather picking, shredding paper, overeating, screaming, or destroying your possessions.

In some cases, parrot owners don't do much to help the situation, keeping their birds in what is essentially solitary confinement. Pet parrots like to be part of the action, so don't put your bird's cage in an isolated part of the house or in a room that you use only occasionally. Breeding birds may need privacy and some peace and quiet, so they can be housed in rooms that aren't used frequently, but single pet parrots should be kept in the family room, living room, or den where they can be a part of family activities.

Chewing

Chewing and destroying things around the home are often the activities of a bored bird. I know a cockatoo who showed how bored he was by destroying his owners' television remote control and two cordless phones in the space of a few weeks. By giving him some discipline and some boundaries for behavior, his owners channeled his energy away from these destructive behaviors. They challenged his mental abilities with new and better toys, supervised his every move when he was out of the cage, and disciplined him when he looked as if he was going to chew on something that was off limits. They gave him a wider variety of foods to entertain him and even made eating a challenge by offering him nuts in the shell that he had to open and peapods that he had to split in order to retrieve the peas.

Birds who live in solitary confinement may develop behavioral problems because of boredom. (PHOTO BY JULIE RACH MANCINI)

Feather Picking

Boredom is one of several reasons that may cause a bird to pick her feathers. If your bird suddenly begins picking her feathers and no medical cause for the picking is found, there is a good chance that your bird is reacting to a lack of interesting things in her life. Feather picking is comforting to the parrot (although the behavior looks painful to us). Some birds pick small areas of feathers, such as their legs, while others start on their chests and pick down to their vents. Regular opportunities to exercise can reduce or eliminate feather picking in some parrots.

As discussed in the previous two chapters, the cause of feather picking must be found before the problem can be resolved. You may need to work with your avian veterinarian and/or avian behaviorist to make this determination.

Overeating

Overeating is a common behavior in parakeets who have been neglected by their owners. These birds never come out of their cages to exercise or interact with their owners, but their owners often ease their guilty consciences by offering the birds lots of treats, including millet.

Oil seeds are a food that parakeets love, but they are high in fat and can make a pet bird obese if she is allowed to indulge in them to her heart's content. If you notice that your bird's breastbone has suddenly disappeared into rolls of fat, she's becoming overweight and needs to exercise and interact with you. Amazons and some species of cockatoos can become overweight easily, so watch these birds for signs of obesity.

Feather picking has many causes, including a monotonous diet, boredom, stress, sexual frustration, and physical illness. Notice the bald spot in the middle of Sindbad's chest. (PHOTO BY JULIE RACH MANCINI)

Consider your bird obese if you can see bald patches in her feathers. These are created by fat deposits under the skin that cause the feathers to part. An overweight bird may stand with her feet wide apart, or you may be able to see rolls of fat across her abdomen, along her flanks and inner thighs, and around her crop. A little fat in these locations is acceptable, but large amounts of fat are not. Ask your veterinarian for more information on how you can determine if your pet bird is overweight.

Obesity can cause a bird to develop heart disease, fatty tumors, respiratory distress during exercise, or egg binding. An overweight bird is also at higher risk to suffer complications if she has to be anesthetized.

Paper Shredding

Another common behavior associated with parrot boredom is paper shredding. Parrots who have access to the paper that lines their cage trays often shred it because they have energy to burn and nothing else to do.

Amazon owners need to monitor the amount of fat that their birds consume because Amazons are natural snackers and can rapidly become overweight. Oil seeds, such as sunflower or safflower seeds, and nuts are common sources of dietary fat for pet birds. (PHOTO BY GARY A. GALLERSTEIN, DVM)

You can make this paper shredding into a game: Provide your parrot with a variety of chewable paper items, including subscription cards from magazines, index cards, or the empty tube from a roll of paper towels or toilet paper. Hold these up for your bird's inspection and destruction. It's a simple way to spend time with your parrot and help her burn off some excess energy. Your pet can perform this shredding routine while she sits on the arm of your chair as you read a magazine or watch TV. Your bird will appreciate the attention, and you'll enjoy watching her chew up the things you offer. You might even be able to train her to shred things over the trash can; if you do, make sure to keep an eye on your pet so she doesn't fall in after an overzealous round of shredding!

If you have a peach-faced lovebird who suddenly starts shredding paper and tucking the strips into her rump feathers, she's not bored. This is an instinctive behavior in females that indicates an interest in nest building. In the wild, female peachies gather twigs and small strips of bark from trees, tuck them into their rump feathers with both ends showing and fly off to a nest site. In your home, your lovebird may gather strips of newspaper, toothpicks, or other small items in an attempt to build a nest in her cage.

Refusing to Eat

Although some bored birds overeat, others become extremely fussy eaters. To help prevent this, you may need to be creative in how and what you feed your bird. You may want to offer your parrot some tempting treats on a skewer or rod feeder, stuff goodies into the openings of a pinecone (some companies offer commercially made versions), or vary the food choices in her dish to encourage her to take an interest in eating again.

Some foods that most parrots find irresistible include the following:

- Fresh peas in the pod

- Peanuts, walnuts, or pecans in the shell (Crack the shells slightly to let your pet see the treat inside before you offer them the first time.)

- Quarter-sections of fresh pomegranates (Be warned that the purple juice from the seeds becomes a permanent part of your wall color after your bird squirts it around her cage, so you may want to hang some clear plastic behind the cage to protect your paint prior to serving pomegranate sections.)

- Sliced whole grapes with the seeds left in (These seeds are not poisonous to your pet.)

Take notice of what your bird enjoys eating so you can try tempting her taste buds if she ever decides to turn up her beak at mealtime.

Restlessness

A bird who is temporarily bored with a situation (for example, she's had enough cuddling and wants to go play on her cage or play gym) will become fidgety and restless. Your relationship with your pet will thrive if you pay attention to signs of restlessness and accommodate your bird. If you don't, she may even bite you out of frustration.

Preventing Boredom

To help keep your bird from being bored and beginning some of these behaviors, you can play games with your parrot. (Be sure to supervise your pet during playtime to protect her health and well-being.) Energy expended in playing, either by itself or with you, is energy that your formerly bored parrot won't channel into otherwise destructive acts. The following games are particularly effective pastimes

Although Sindbad looks as if she's in trouble here, she's not. Hanging upside down is a game she plays to indicate that she is content with the world. (PHOTO BY JULIE RACH MANCINI)

for medium-sized and large parrots, such as Amazons, African greys, cockatoos, and macaws:

- **Shell game:** Play a variation on the old "shell game" from the carnival sideshow. In the avian version, you can hide a favorite treat under a nut cup or paper muffin cup and let your bird guess which shell hides the prize.

- **Great escape:** Offer your bird a clean, knotted-up piece of rope or vegetable-tanned leather and see how long it takes your pet to untie the knots. Give your bird extra points if she doesn't chew through any of the knots to untie them. Be sure to remove the rope or leather after playtime is over so your bird doesn't become entangled in it later, which could lead to injury.

- **Mechanic:** Give your parrot a clean nut and bolt with the nut screwed on and see how long it takes your bird to undo the nut. Make sure the nut and bolt are large enough that your pet won't swallow accidentally either one while playing, and take the nut and bolt away after your bird has finished her playtime.

- **Peek-a-boo:** This is one of my bird's favorites. I put a beach towel loosely over her and her cagetop, then let her work her way out from under the towel and to the edge of the cagetop. She's come to expect the cuddling and lavish praise I use to reward her for being so clever as to find her way out every time. Put the towel away after you're done playing so your bird doesn't become entangled in it, and watch her carefully if she "helps" you fold laundry. She won't know the difference between her peek-a-boo towel and the other towels in your home, and if she tries to hide under your laundry she could get folded up with the rest of the clothes, or even sat upon if someone comes in to talk to you as you're folding the clothes.

- **Tug-of-war:** Give your bird one end of an empty paper towel roll and tug gently. Chances are your parrot won't easily let go, or if she does, she will quickly be back for more. If your bird is naturally aggressive, you shouldn't let her "win" too frequently, but if she's naturally shy, let her "win" often to build her confidence.

In addition to these games, you can take your bird out of her cage and dance with her. Your bird can dance by herself on her cagetop or play gym, or you and your bird can dance together. My parrot especially likes peppy, up-tempo oldies such as "Gimme Some Lovin'," "Your Momma Don't Dance," and "Rescue Me."

You can also hold the bird out at arm's length and let her flap her wings. You may have to lift and lower the bird slowly a few times to give her a hint of what you want her to do. Let your bird flap until she appears to be just a little winded, and build up her stamina by extending the exercise periods slightly each day. This exercise is particularly good for Amazons and rose-breasted cockatoos, who can be prone to obesity. Be sure you are standing away from ceiling fans, low-hanging lamps, and other objects that could harm your bird while she's flapping.

Your bird may have some games of her own to play with you. Many parrots enjoy "accidentally" knocking things off their cagetops to watch their owners bend over to fetch the dropped item. My stepdaughter Rhonda's parakeet, Andre, was a master of this. After she taught him to drop coins in front of chosen people seated at a table, Andre modified the game by running to the edge of the table and dropping the coin over the edge. His little eyes seemed just a bit brighter as he watched Rhonda pick up the coin and place it in front of him for a "do-over" on his trick. She never scolded him for his antics, and he loved the attention she gave him by pretending to be exasperated with him for altering the trick.

Some birds entertain themselves by getting into apparently hazardous situations, such as hanging from their cage ceilings by a single toe, just to be rescued

Some parrots like to play peek-a-boo with their owners. (Photo by Julie Rach Mancini)

by their owners. My parrot used to do this to when she was feeling particularly full of herself. I soon accepted it as part of her normal range of behavior, but it was apparently a bit unsettling to the staff of the veterinary hospital where I used to board her because they called me while I was away on a business trip to make sure this was part of her normal routine and not an indication of stress.

The Importance of Toys

As mentioned in chapter 1, "Flock Behavior in the Wild and How It Applies in the Home," your pet bird needs to have access to appropriately sized, interesting toys that she can play with each day. Pet birds need toys to occupy their minds, bodies, and beaks. Accept that your bird will chew on any toy you buy, and that you will eventually have to replace it. When selecting toys for your pet, keep a few safety tips in mind.

Size

Is the toy the right size for your bird? Large toys can be intimidating to small birds, which makes the birds less likely to play with them. On the other end of the spectrum, larger birds can easily destroy toys designed for smaller birds, and they can sometimes injure themselves severely in the process. Select toys for your pet bird that are marked for her approximate size range to ensure that they are appropriately sized for your pet.

Safety

Is the toy safe? Good choices include sturdy wooden toys (either undyed or painted with bird-safe vegetable dye or food coloring) strung on closed-link chains or vegetable-tanned leather thongs, and rope toys. If you buy rope toys for your pet bird, make sure her nails are trimmed regularly to prevent them from snagging in the rope, and discard the toy when it becomes frayed to prevent accidents.

Unsafe items to watch out for are brittle plastic toys that can easily be shattered into fragments by a pet bird's busy beak (this problem occurs most often when larger birds are given toys designed for parakeets and other small parrots), lead-weighted toys that can be cracked open to expose the dangerous lead to curious birds, loose link chains that can catch toenails or beaks, ring toys that are too small to climb through safely, and jingle-type bells that can trap toes, tongues, and beaks.

Pay attention to the fastener used to attach the toy to your pet's cage or play gym, too. Split-ring key rings are sometimes used on bird toys, and a bird may be able to open the ring with her beak. After she's opened the ring, she may end up with her tongue or her toe caught in the split-ring fastener, which can be a painful situation. To ensure your pet's safety, purchase toys that feature a C-clip fastener, or replace split-ring fasteners with the safer C-clips before offering them to your pet.

Social Concerns

Mirrors are found on many parakeet toys, and most birds are fascinated with and enamored of that handsome bird in the reflection. Some birds become so infatuated with "the other bird" that they seem to lose interest in their owners, so you might want to wait until your parakeet is settled in her surroundings and comfortable with you before adding a mirrored toy to her cage. Mirrored toys may also make a parakeet less likely to talk, a topic I'll discuss in more detail in chapter 11, "Will My Bird Talk?"

Homemade Toys

Some entertaining toys can be made at home. Give your pet bird an empty paper towel roll to chew, or string some Cheerios on a thong of vegetable-tanned leather. You can also offer your bird a dish of raw vegetables or uncooked pasta pieces to destroy, or you can hide special treats inside an empty toilet paper roll with its ends folded over.

Parrot Tricks

Trick training is another way you can alleviate boredom in your pet bird. A bird who regularly learns new tricks and has an opportunity to perform them is less likely to become bored. Look at the situation as your bird would: What could be better than having your attention each day while the two of you work on new tricks? Your bird gets your attention, she gets cuddles and scratches if she behaves well, and she can also be rewarded with treats. What more could she want?

Before you try to trick-train your parrot, you will have to determine if she's a good candidate for learning tricks. Does she enjoy showing off for you and for other family members, or is she a bit more reserved in her personality? Extroverted birds are more likely to enjoy learning and performing tricks than introverted ones.

Does your parrot like to have her head scratched and rubbed? Head scratches often take the place of treats as the training process progresses, so it's ideal to have a bird who enjoys this process, rather than one who doesn't like head rubs.

Has your bird mastered the "up" and "down" commands? These two commands help you keep your feathered star under control when she goes out in public to perform, so it's best to have her learn these two basic commands before she moves on to learning any tricks.

To teach your bird the "up" command, gently press your finger up and into the bird's belly when she's perched on your hand. She will almost automatically step up and onto your finger. As she steps up, say "step up" or "up." Your bird should learn this command rather quickly, along with the "down" command, which you can teach her by saying "down" as you set her on her cage or play gym. These two little words offer a great deal of control over your bird. You can say "up" to put an unruly bird back in her cage, or you can say "down" to a parrot who needs to go to bed as you put her in her cage at night.

Does your bird trust you enough to learn tricks? Parrots who trust their owners come to them willingly and allow their owners to pet them all over their bodies. These birds also seem to enjoy interacting with their owners and easily take food from their owners when it is offered.

Once you've determined that your bird is a good candidate to learn to do tricks, you should watch her normal behaviors to see if there's anything she does routinely that you can make into a trick. For instance, does she raise her wings over her head frequently? If so, you can probably teach her to "pose like an eagle" without much trouble. Does she quickly climb up pants legs when she's on the floor? She may be able to learn to shinny up a rope and ring a bell for a treat. By watching your bird, you can easily come up with some routine behaviors that will turn into tricks with a little refinement from you.

As you begin the training process, keep a couple of things in mind:

- **Respect what your bird likes to do.** This is an outgrowth of watching her normal behaviors to see which ones can become tricks and an evaluation of your pet's overall personality. Please don't force a bird into learning tricks because you think it's a fun thing to do—she must enjoy it, too, or what should be an enjoyable experience for both of you will soon become an ordeal.

- **Make sure you train your bird in short sessions.** Parrots and other pet birds don't have extremely long attention spans, and they may become cranky when you try to keep their attention longer than about ten minutes in length. End your training sessions on a positive note as much as possible, and provide training sessions a few times a day. If you work outside the home, spend a few minutes before you leave for the office with your bird, and repeat the training session in the evening after you've returned home. If you work at home or if you come home for lunch, you may be able to squeeze in an extra training session in the middle of the day.

Before you start training a parrot to do tricks, you'll need to set up a quiet place for training. In this quiet place, you'll need to have a T-stand for your feathered student to sit on during her lessons, some special treats to reward her good behavior, and a clicker or other sound cue that will let your bird know that she has performed a trick correctly. During training, you will use the treats, along with verbal cues or hand signals, to help your bird learn the behaviors you are teaching her.

Ride in a Wagon

To teach a bird to ride in a wagon, you must first get her accustomed to the wagon. Roll the wagon in front of your pet to show her what the wagon will do. After a few days of short sessions of watching the wagon roll by, put your bird in the wagon. Praise her and pet her as she sits in the wagon. Let her practice sitting in the wagon for brief periods of time for a few days.

When your bird seems comfortable sitting in the wagon, pull the wagon a short distance. Praise your parrot for her good behavior if she sits calmly, or comfort and reassure her that everything is okay if she seems panicked by the wagon's movement. Put your bird in the wagon for short rides several times a day, and gradually increase the length of those rides.

Wave Hello

To teach your parrot to wave, put your hand out as if you want your bird to step up onto it. When your bird puts out her foot, pet and praise her lavishly.

After a few sessions of simply having your bird lift her foot, continue the training by stepping away from your bird so that she cannot climb on your hand, but offer your hand just the same. Praise and pet your parrot for raising her foot, and your bird will soon get the idea that you want her to raise her foot.

When your bird has mastered raising her foot at your bidding, raise your hand as you have been, then wave at your parrot. Frequently, she will mimic your actions. Praise and pet her for her ability to follow your lead, and pretty soon, you have a bird who waves.

Some parrots will demon-strate a high level of trust in their owners by learning how to lie on their backs. (PHOTO BY JULIE RACH MANCINI)

Shake Hands

Shaking hands is a simple extension of the waving gestures. Hold out your hand as if you want the bird to step onto it, and let her take hold of your finger with her foot. Begin shaking the parrot's foot gently. Repeat this series of gestures several times, and soon you have a parrot who shakes hands. This trick seems to work better with larger parrots, but it's possible to teach parakeets and cockatiels to shake hands, too.

Play Dead

A parrot who likes to be petted and can be turned over by her owner is a good candidate to play dead. First, you must get the bird accustomed to the feel of your hand on her back while she perches on her cage or play gym. When the bird seems comfortable with your hand on her back, hold her between your hands on her side.

When the bird is accustomed to being held in this way, you can move to holding her between your hands on her back. Once she seems peaceful in this position, remove the hand you have on her feet or belly, and you have a bird playing dead in your hand.

A friend of mine trained her cockatoo to "go to sleep" in this way. She can now flip the bird over in her hand and tell him, "Night-night," to which the bird answers, "Night-night," and closes his eyes. She can then carry him to his cage, where he climbs onto his sleeping perch for the night. She is the only person the bird will allow to do this trick; he doesn't seem to trust anyone else to do it right.

Your bird will have to have an inordinate amount of trust in you before she will allow you to flip her over onto her back. This is not a common parrot posture. Conures are more likely to lie on their backs than other species, but some birds may never be comfortable in this position. If your bird seems distressed when you flip her over on her back, you may have to try to teach her some other trick.

YOUR BIRD'S PLAY GYM CAN
BE A BOREDOM BUSTER!

When your bird seems bored with her cage, take her out for a supervised play session on her play gym. Play gyms can be as simple as a ladder-and-perch combination on a flat tray, or they can provide all sorts of playing possibilities for your pet bird. At the very least, a play gym should provide your bird with a chance to climb a little and flap her wings, but a play gym can also feature different types of dowels and branches for climbing variety, along with bird-safe eye screws from which different toys can be hung.

You can purchase a play gym from your local pet supply story or by mail order, or you can custom-build one for your pet if you're handy with simple hand tools. If you're building your own play gym, remember to use untreated pine or other soft wood for the parts of the gym your pet is likely to chew on. Don't use pressure-treated wood for any part of the gym because the pressure-treating process introduces chemicals into the wood that can poison your bird if she chews on it.

When shopping for a play gym for your bird, remember to select one that's of an appropriate size for your pet. Large birds will become easily bored on a small-bird play gym, and smaller birds may be intimidated by a play gym for larger birds. Make sure the gym's dimensions allow room for your pet's crest or long tail feathers (if she has either or both) and that she won't be crowded by low-hanging perches when she wants to sit upright or flap her wings from the top of the gym. Ideally, the gym should be situated in a tray that has a slight border to help contain dropped treats and other playtime debris. In the case of larger pet birds, having the gym on wheels or casters is ideal for moving it from room to room if your pet wants to spend time with you in your home office during a work-at-home afternoon.

Keep your pet's play gym interesting by providing a regular variety of toys on the gym, and also offer some healthful treats, such as peas in the pod or papaya slices, that offer your pet a little challenge along with her snack time.

It took me a few years of patient training, but my parrot is now comfortable having me flip her over on her back. She will lie in my hand this way, and she will lie on her back on the examination table at the veterinarian's office. Inasmuch as she wasn't hand-tamed when I got her, and she didn't even like to be picked up, held, or cuddled in her previous home, we have made some progress since we've been together.

I conditioned her to this behavior by flipping her over briefly when I had her out of her cage for her evening cuddle session, and I petted her crop and under her wings and told her she was a very good bird. She didn't really care for being flipped over at first, but she did like having her crop and sides rubbed, so she learned to enjoy being flipped over. I don't keep her on her back for long, which she seems to appreciate, too.

The Crossing Guard

My stepdaughter Rhonda has had a way with animals for many years. From her childhood parakeets to the chickens, hogs, and sheep she raised as an FFA member in high school, they all seem to understand her and to try to please her by performing behaviors that are slightly above and beyond the normal.

Rhonda's parakeet, Andre, could do some amazing things, but the most amazing thing he did was what I like to call the "crossing guard" trick. Rhonda worried about Andre's safety as he followed her around her home in southern California because she feared that another family member might accidentally step on him even though we were all warned that Andre was out of his cage. To protect her precious pet from harm, she taught Andre to stop and look both ways as he left a room to ensure he wouldn't be stepped on in the hallway. She began her training by putting her hand in front of Andre as a physical barrier to keep him from walking out into potential danger, but she soon progressed to a simple voice prompt of "Stop!" and "Look both ways, Andre!" He rarely ventured into the hall without checking for oncoming people, and it was quite a sight to see him peek around the doorway and look left, right, left before he would walk into the hall.

If you want to teach your pet more tricks, look for *Parrot Tricks* by Tani Robar and Diane Grindol at your local bookstore. See appendix B, "Resources," for details.

chapter 7

BREEDING BEHAVIORS

All parrot owners eventually learn that birds are governed by their hormones. Some birds get through breeding season without harming themselves or their owners too badly, while other parrots become biting, screaming, feather-picking monsters until their hormones subside.

When parrots reach sexual maturity and breeding season rolls around, most of them are motivated to mate. However, most pet birds have no bird to mate with, so they try to mate with their owners, perches, toys, or other objects. If you see your bird mount an object and rub his vent against it, he's demonstrating mating behavior. Some birds cluck or honk while mating.

The good news is that if your bird feels like mating, you're providing for him well. Mating is something that birds do only when all conditions are right. There must be a sufficient, steady supply of food and water, the bird must be in good health, and he must feel comfortable and secure in his environment. Only healthy birds mate; sick birds don't have the strength or the energy for it.

Signs of Maturity

Most pet bird species are considered to be adult birds when they are about a year old. (African greys take a bit longer to mature and are considered adult birds by the age of 2.) By this time, the birds have reached their full size and have molted into their adult plumages. They are now ready and able to breed, and the transition from young bird to breeding adult can bring some new and different behaviors into play. All these behaviors are perfectly normal for your bird, but they may be a bit alarming to you as your feathered baby suddenly seems to change into an unknown creature.

This cockatoo may be defending his territory. Notice how his crest is raised and his body feathers are fluffed to make him appear larger. (PHOTO BY PAMELA L. HIGDON)

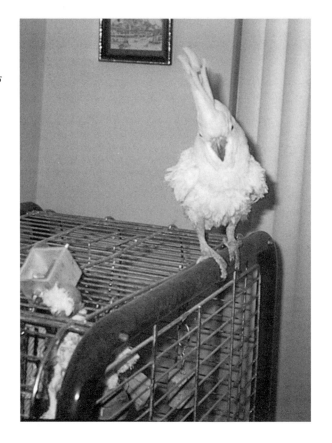

Aggression

Aggression can take many forms. Breeding birds may bite their owners, may defend their cages fiercely, or may become overly protective of their food dishes. In many species, male birds are more aggressive than females, but in eclectus and some types of parrotlets, the female is the more aggressive member of the pair.

Biting

Mature birds may bite their owners to protect their cages and territories. They may also bite their owners' significant others for daring to pay attention to the owner that the bird has selected as his substitute mate, or they may bite their owners for having the nerve to pay attention to a human mate. Mature birds also bite to defend their food bowls. They often give indications—eye pinning, tail fanning, growling—that their owners shouldn't push their luck. However, some owners don't take the hint and they get bitten.

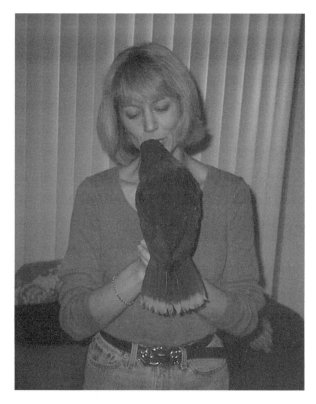

Although most display behavior is credited to male birds, some female birds display by fanning their tail feathers for their favored people during breeding season. (PHOTO BY PAMELA L. HIGDON)

Display Behavior

If it's late winter or spring and your bird suddenly starts strutting, screaming, singing, flapping his wings, and generally trying to draw attention to himself, chances are this is a male bird who's displaying in order to attract a mate and scare off other males. If your bird has a crest, he will raise it frequently during display periods.

Egg Binding

Egg binding is a breeding problem that requires urgent veterinary attention. A hen is egg-bound if she is unable to lay an egg that is stuck in the oviduct. The causes of egg binding can include an oversized or soft-shelled egg, stress, low blood calcium levels, or overbreeding. If left untreated, egg binding can cause kidney, intestinal, or urinary problems. It can also develop into a life-threatening situation.

If you see a hen panting, paralyzed on the cage floor, or straining to lay an egg, or if you see an egg partially out of the cloaca, the hen is egg-bound. She will need to be placed in a small, warm cage (about 85°F) in a humid room, such as a bathroom with a hot shower running. Sometimes heat and humidity are enough to help an egg-bound hen pass the egg, but in other cases, veterinary care is required. Once you have placed your hen in a warm and humid environment, contact your veterinarian for further instructions.

Egg Laying

A single pet bird will lay eggs without a male bird being present. These eggs are clear and will not hatch. If your bird lays eggs, it means that she is healthy and content. Egg laying can be quite a shock to some owners. I know because my parrot presented me with eggs after being a pet in my home for more than eight years. She did not lay eggs in her previous home, so it was a bit unsettling to uncover her cage one morning and see what appeared to be an off-white Ping-Pong ball in her cage.

To discourage egg laying, some experts advise removing the eggs from the cage as they are laid. Others recommend leaving the clutch intact until the hen

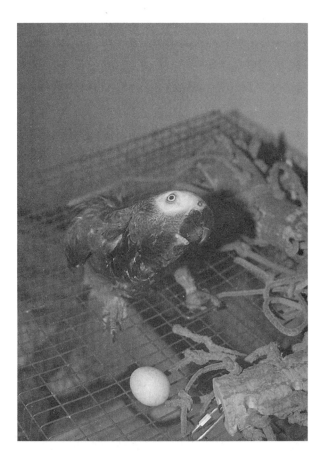

Your bird may demonstrate her interest in breeding by surprising you with an egg.
(PHOTO BY JULIE RACH MANCINI)

completes her laying. In extreme cases of egg laying, hormone treatments may be needed to stop the bird's body from creating the eggs. Consult your avian veterinarian for suggestions on how to stop your parrot from laying eggs.

Feather Picking

Birds who are sexually mature may take out their frustrations at being denied the opportunity to breed by pulling their feathers. In extreme cases, the birds may also indulge in self-mutilation of their chests or feet.

Separated lovebirds may pick their feathers in frustration and loneliness, pining for their mates. When reunited, the birds appear to be pleased to see their formerly missing companion. Lovebirds were, in fact, named for their common practice of clumping or cuddling together as if they were in love with the bird closest to them on the perch or tree branch. Lovebirds groom their neighbors constantly and cuddle or snuggle with them.

Masturbation

If you notice your bird rubbing his vent against a favorite toy or against your hand, he's working off his sexual frustration. You can curb your bird's behavior by removing the toy that is the object of his affections. You can also allow your bird to burn off excess energy by exercising outside his cage, such as by climbing, flapping, or chasing a toy that you're dragging across the floor.

During breeding season, this cockatoo used a lock on the top of his cage to work off his sexual frustration. (PHOTO BY JULIE RACH MANCINI)

These macaws are likely a bonded pair because they regularly engage in mutual preening sessions. (PHOTO BY JULIE RACH MANCINI)

You may also need to change the way you handle your bird during breeding season. Don't rub a bird's lower back or under his wings during this time because you may trigger a breeding response. In many cases, these signals do not cause any harm to bird or owner, but if your bird becomes aggressive during breeding season, be careful about how you handle him during this time.

Mutual Preening

Mutual preening is a behavior that bonded pairs demonstrate. In mutual preening, members of the pair will sit close to each other and one bird will preen the other's neck and the top of the head, areas the bird being preened cannot reach.

Nest Building

Although parrots do not build nests in the traditional sense, they may start looking for small, dark nooks and crannies in your home in which to lay eggs. Some birds like to inspect kitchen cupboards and may start trying to nest in your pots and pans, while other birds will attempt to make nests in the cubbyholes of roll-top desks. Still others may check out your linen closets, looking for a warm, soft place among your sheets and towels. If you notice your bird has developed a sudden preoccupation with dark, out-of-the-way places, he may be indicating his willingness to breed.

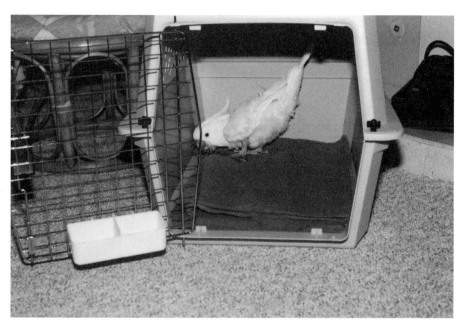

This Eleanora cockatoo is looking at his travel carrier as a potential nest site. (PHOTO BY JULIE RACH MANCINI)

Pair Bonding

Pair bonding helps parrots successfully raise chicks. Indications of pair bonding include mutual preening, mutual feeding, and defense of the mate and of the birds' home territory.

Because parrot chicks generally take several months to raise, there needs to be a bond between the parent birds to ensure that both take an interest in raising the chicks. In some species the male birds share incubating duties, while in others the male feeds the female bird while she sits on the eggs, guards the entrance to the nest, and feeds the chicks after they hatch.

The pair bond is also part of a pet bird's charm because the pair bond fosters loyalty and affection between parrots and their owners. At the onset of sexual maturity, this pair bond between parrot and owner may be trying because the bird may consider his owner as his mate. When he does, he will preen his owner, attempt to feed him or her, and vigorously defend the owner against all interlopers (including spouses and other family members) by biting either the owner or the interloper.

Not all parrots perceive their owners as mates, and not all parrots defend their owners during breeding season. These behaviors are discussed because they *can* occur, not because they *will*.

Bonded pairs of birds often conduct themselves in unison. (PHOTO BY JULIE RACH MANCINI)

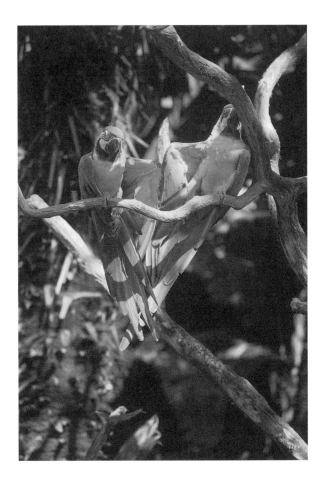

Paper Shredding

Peach-faced lovebirds are particularly prone to this behavior. Females shred long strips of paper, tuck them in their rump feathers, and fly off in search of a potential nesting site.

Regurgitating Food

Regurgitation in a healthy bird is a courting behavior in parrots. Males regurgitate to females and to chicks, and young parrots regurgitate to one another.

If your bird regurgitates to you, you can calmly return him to his cage or play gym to allow him to settle down. You can also distract him with a favorite toy. I generally thank my parrot for her kind thoughts but let her know that I'm fixing my own meal soon. This way, I believe she knows that I appreciate her gesture and am not appalled by it.

Regurgitation can also indicate a variety of physical problems, including crop infections, a blockage in the digestive tract, thyroid gland enlargement, or proventricular dilatation syndrome. If your bird appears ill and regurgitates, contact your avian veterinarian.

Screaming

Parrots under the influence of their hormones are prone to screaming fits during breeding season. If your bird becomes extremely vocal, you can try to distract him with a favored toy, you can cover his cage for about ten minutes to give him a "time-out," or you can expose the bird to new experiences, such as play time in a different room or a ride in the car.

Displaced Affection

On occasion, pet birds treat their human "mates" no differently than they would parrot mates. One spring, a friend of mine who owns a male Eleanora cockatoo showed up at her doctor's office sporting a collection of bruises, slashes, and other marks of potential abuse. The doctor immediately suspected abuse, and she was being abused, but not by any human member of the household. Her cockatoo had chosen her as his mate and he was taking out his frustrations at not being able to breed with her.

In the spring, after the bird reached sexual maturity at about age 5, my friend was subjected to increasing amounts of abuse from her pet. What started as an amusing display of crest raising and tail spreading soon turned into fits of flying at her face in a threatening manner. This behavior lasted about three months.

The following year, the behavior got worse and lasted longer, culminating in the onslaught of bites and scratches that my friend's doctor saw when she sought treatment for an unrelated sinus infection.

Height is power in the bird world. Birds who are allowed to be taller than their owners may be difficult to manage. (PHOTO BY PAMELA L. HIGDON)

After this particular spring, my friend sought the assistance of avian behaviorist Sally Blanchard, who made some suggestions for behavior modification. Now the bird is not allowed to sit on my friend's shoulder. This was once his favorite perch, but he is too difficult to control when he's up there. He also is not allowed to perch on any item higher than my friend's chest level. He used to enjoy sitting on the bar at the top of the shower stall, for example, but the height gives him too much power and makes him even more difficult to control.

The bird has also been reintroduced to the concept of the "up" command, and he comes out of his cage only when he's on his best behavior. Previously, he was allowed out every day when his owners came home from work, whether he was behaving or not. His owners now look him in the eye and calmly tell him "No" when he misbehaves, and they put him back in his cage for "time-out" if he becomes difficult to handle and manage.

Not only did my friend's health and appearance improve after she took control of her cockatoo's behavior, but his behavior and appearance seemed to improve, too. He had a history of picking the tops of his wings every spring, but he stopped pulling those feathers after my friend instituted stronger control over his life.

Breeding Basics

Many parrot species are difficult to sex visually. Males essentially look like females, which can make setting up true breeding pairs impossible. Although some longtime breeders can obtain a fair degree of accuracy by observing their birds, pet owners and novice breeders shouldn't try to visually sex their birds, or you may end up like me, who found my so-called "male" bird laying eggs after being a pet for sixteen years.

If you are going to set up birds for breeding, the following sexing methods are available: observation, DNA sexing, surgical sexing, fecal analysis, and feather sexing. Brief descriptions of these methods follow:

- Observation is generally an unreliable method. I discovered my "male" parrot's gender when "he" laid an egg!

- DNA sexing analyzes red blood cells to determine whether male or female chromosomes are present in your bird. Your veterinarian takes a blood sample from your bird and sends it to a laboratory for examination. Results are available in about three weeks.

- Surgical sexing requires that a small incision is made in the bird's side under anesthesia. A veterinarian inserts an endoscope into the incision to look for either an ovary if the bird is female or a testicle if the bird is male. Although it might seem risky, surgical sexing is quite safe if performed by an experienced avian veterinarian.

Many parrot species cannot be sexed visually, which can make setting up breeding pairs quite challenging. (PHOTO BY GARY A. GALLERSTEIN, DVM)

- Fecal analysis examines a small sample of the bird's droppings for the presence of reproductive hormones. This test is only effective with sexually mature birds.

- Feather sexing looks at feather pulp from a blood feather for the presence of sex chromosomes. The feather is kept on ice and sent to a laboratory by overnight mail for evaluation.

Your avian veterinarian can further discuss these sexing methods with you and help you decide which is the best one to use on your breeder birds.

Breeding Small Parrots

Cockatiels are very popular pet birds and provide a good illustration of what to expect if you would like to breed your birds. They are also one species that you can sex visually. Cockatiels develop their adult plumage at about 6 months of age, and the differences in gender become apparent at that time. Many breeders can distinguish the males from the females before this point, however, since males begin to vocalize when they are about 3 months of age, while females remain relatively quiet.

In traditional gray birds, males will have lemon yellow feathers on their faces, foreheads, cheeks, and throats, and their orange cheek patches will be brighter than those of the female birds. The facial feathers of traditional gray female birds will have a gray wash to them, and the cheek patches will be smaller and duller. Females will also show barred feathers on their backs, rumps, and tails.

In color mutations, male cinnamons and fallows develop their characteristic yellow masks and lose their barred tail feathers, while the females have duller facial feathers and retain their barred feathers. Whitefaced males have (as their name suggests) white faces, while female whitefaces actually have grayish faces and the characteristic barring on their tail feathers.

In lutinos, you can distinguish males by the lack of barred feathers on their wing and tail feathers, but you must examine the birds closely to determine if his feathers are barred or not, since the yellow bars are often hard to see against the lutino's white feather background.

Pearls and pieds are difficult to sex visually because their mutations hide some of the characteristic colors and patterns. Pearl males may or may not lose their spots as they mature, and many ultimately look like standard gray males after their first molts. Pearl females retain gray facial feathers, while pearl males have light faces.

Even more challenging to sex visually are the albinos. Both sexes are pure white and lack the characteristic yellow masks or orange cheek patches used to differentiate males and females of other mutations. In these cases, other methods of determining gender, such as feather sexing, DNA analysis, or surgical sexing may be required.

Once you've established which of your birds are male and which are female, consider their strengths and weaknesses. You want to be sure to create breeding pairs for good reasons, so you may want to put two birds with outstanding pet qualities together, or you may want to try to improve the color or pattern of future generations by pairing two prime examples of a particular mutation.

After you've selected your pairs, you'll need to think about nest boxes for your growing flock. Any nest box larger than 10 inches by 10 inches in the box floor should work well for raising cockatiels. Many breeders set their birds up with boxes that measure 12 inches high by 12 inches wide by 12 inches deep. The box should feature a perch slightly below the box opening on both the interior and exterior of the box. Having a perch on the inside helps parent birds get in and out of the box more easily, and it also offers them a site from which to feed growing chicks.

The box should also have a viewing hole so you can check on the progress of the chicks without disturbing the parent birds too much. If you house your breeding birds in an aviary, be sure to provide two or three more nest boxes than you have pairs. Females will fight over the boxes, which can lead to decreased egg production because the birds are more interested in squabbling over territory than they are in laying eggs.

You can have a definite impact on your birds' breeding success. Aviary disturbances by people or other animals, along with excessive handling of breeding birds, can cause birds not to mate. These activities can also chase nesting birds off eggs or cause parent birds to abandon their chicks in the nest.

Ensure that all perches in the breeding cage are secure. Your birds will likely mate on their perches, and loose perches can result in infertile eggs because your birds are unable to mate successfully on unsteady footing.

You'll know your selections were successful when you hear your male birds whistling and see them flying around or chasing the females. The males may bow, nod, or chirp at their mates, while the females will indicate their readiness to breed by crouching low on perches with their tails up and their crests down. The male will then proceed to mate with the female, and eggs will follow in about seven to ten days. During the interval between mating and egg laying, you will probably notice that the female spends an unusual amount of time in the nest box and devours cuttlebones and other calcium supplements eagerly.

Five eggs is the average cockatiel clutch size, although hens can lay anywhere from two to fifteen eggs. Eggs are laid on an alternate day schedule and will hatch in the order in which they were laid. If you see more than ten eggs in a box, you should suspect that two hens are laying simultaneously in the same box, although some breeders have reported as many as fifteen fertile eggs being produced by a pair in a single clutch.

The parent birds will start to incubate the eggs after the hen has laid at least two. The parents share incubating duties, with the male bird usually setting on the eggs during the day and the female taking the night shift.

While the parents are incubating their eggs, be sure to provide them with a water dish. Although cockatiels aren't usually enthusiastic bathers, many parent birds appreciate the chance to soak their feathers during this time because wet feathers can help raise the humidity in the nest box. Having a humid atmosphere in the box helps chicks hatch more easily by softening the eggshells slightly.

During incubation, parent birds will keep the nest box immaculately clean. Don't be alarmed to see some monstrous droppings from your parent birds because they will wait to eliminate until they are well away from the nest box.

Chicks, however, will eliminate in the box after they hatch, so breeders need to pay attention to nest box lining and to the chicks' toes, which can become damaged from being caked with droppings.

The parents will sit on the eggs for about nineteen days before the chicks start to hatch. Cockatiels turn their eggs about every thirty minutes during the day and about every ninety minutes or so during the night. If you should have to incubate eggs artificially, keep this time frame in mind or else the developing chick could become stuck to the albumen in the egg and die.

When the chicks hatch, they are covered with a yellowish down. Whitefaces and albinos, of course, have white down. Other mutations, such as the lutino and fallow, can be identified by their red eyes, which appear as pink bulges under closed lids.

Chicks take thirty-six to forty-eight hours to hatch. They start by rotating within the eggshell and breaking the shell around the middle from the inside. The chick's head is in the large, rounded end of the egg during hatching, and you can hear him chirp (or pip) as he makes his way into the world.

After the chicks hatch, try not to open the nest box for inspection when the parent birds are inside because they could scramble for cover and injure the chicks inadvertently. To move the parents out of the way, tap lightly on the side of the nest box or offer them a favored treat in the main cage.

The following chronology will help you appreciate how quickly cockatiel chicks mature:

- **1 to 3 days**   Chicks are covered with yellow or white down. They have naked heads and pink feet, skin, beaks, and ceres. Their eyes are closed, and they weigh about 4 grams (.15 ounce) and measure about 3 cm (1.25 inches) in length. They will huddle with their clutchmates for warmth and support with their heads tucked inward and their bottoms pointed up and out.

- **4 days**   Eyes begin to open.

- **5 days**   Chicks begin to vocalize when begging for food.

- **9 days**   Contour feathers begin to appear. First evidence of crest feathers.

- **10 days**   Baby cockatiels hiss when disturbed.

- **12 days**   Chick loses the egg tooth on the end of his beak.

- **15 days**   Upper and lower mandibles of the beak become hard.

- **19 days**   Orange cheek patches are evident in birds who will have them. Chicks also raise crests and spread wings when disturbed.

- **21 days**   Chicks can now be handled daily to develop their pet qualities. Now is the time to start teaching them how wonderful being rubbed lightly on the back of the neck feels! Chicks will also start grasping at things with their feet, so be careful that they don't injure themselves while exploring.

- **30 days**   Chicks will look very much like their parents, having attained adult weight of 90 grams.

- **35 days**   Chicks begin to fledge (grow the feathers they will need to fly). Hen may begin laying next clutch of eggs as the younger chicks prepare to fledge.

- **40 days**   Chicks are usually weaned and eating on their own. Scatter seed on the floor and place extra seed dishes in the cage as chicks make the transition to feeding themselves. Watch the chicks to be sure they are really eating, not just playing with food.

- **50 days**   Large feathers on the chicks have become keratinous.

- **90 days**   First molt. The chick's beak turns dark gray.

- **270 days**   The chick has become sexually mature and attained his adult plumage.

WHY CAN'T I SPAY MY PARROT?

Some parrot owners are probably wondering why pet birds can't be spayed like dogs or cats can. A salpingohysterectomy, or the surgical removal of a bird's uterus (shell gland) and oviduct, is a more complicated procedure in a pet bird than spaying a dog or cat, and it is not routinely recommended. The surgery is indicated, however, to treat excessive cases of egg laying, to relieve an egg-bound hen, or to treat egg-related peritonitis (an infection caused by an egg breaking inside a female bird's body).

To perform a salpingohysterectomy, your avian veterinarian will anesthetize your pet bird. He or she will then cut an incision in the bird's left side and will carefully remove the uterus and oviduct, but the bird's ovary will be left in place. After the uterus and oviduct are removed, the incision will be closed and the bird will move to a recovery area, where she will be monitored for any complications before being released to your care.

If your bird begins laying an excessive number of eggs, you need to have her evaluated by your avian veterinarian. Together, you and your bird's vet may be able to come up with treatments that will lessen the number of eggs she lays so that her health is not endangered by egg overproduction. Treatment options can include hormone injections, reducing the length of daylight in the bird's cage, removing her favorite nesting sites, or relocating her to a new cage.

Adult birds can raise two clutches a year and should be allowed to rest to maintain their good health. Cockatiel hens can lay eggs for eight to ten years, but the fertility decreases as the bird ages. Male cockatiels are fertile for twelve to fourteen years.

Breeding Problems

Excessive egg laying can be a problem in cockatiels, and some female birds will lay eggs without a male bird present. Unfortunately, this problem is not always easy to solve. Some excessive egg layers benefit by being put in breeding programs, while other birds can be "cycled out" of egg laying by allowing them to lay one clutch and incubate it for the normal time period. Still other birds cycle out of egg laying by having the nest "destroyed" by the owner removing all the eggs to simulate predation or other natural disasters.

More persistent egg layers may require a series of hormone shots from a veterinarian to solve the problem. Be aware that repeated series of these injections may cause health problems, such as obesity, increased water intake, increased urination, and diabetes. Finally, some birds may need a surgery to resolve their egg-laying problems. This operation is rather complex and unlike altering pet dogs and cats, it is not recommended as a standard course of action for pet birds.

If you have a hen who lays excessive eggs, make sure to supplement her diet with calcium and have mineral blocks and cuttlebone available to her. Egg-laying hens who do not have access to supplemental calcium will use the calcium in their own bones to create eggshells for their eggs, which can lead to fractures and other complications for the hen.

Infertility is a problem that many breeders face at some point in their careers. Infertility can be caused by parent birds who are too young or too old to breed successfully; unsteady perches in the breeding cage; an underlying health problem, such as a bacterial or fungal infection in the parent birds; pair incompatibility; pet birds who are unable or unwilling to bond with another bird; an inadequate number of nest boxes; a poor diet for the parent birds; or an overly aggressive hen.

Approximate Breeding Ages for Some Commonly Kept Pet Parrots

Budgies, cockatiels, and lovebirds	1 year
Conures	1½ to 2 years
Lories	2 to 3 years
Pionus, small cockatoos, and macaws	2 to 4 years
African greys, Amazons, and large cockatoos	3 to 6 years

Some birds fail to incubate their eggs. Frightening events, such as earthquakes or rodents in the aviary, can cause birds to abandon their eggs. An unbonded pair of parent birds may also fail to incubate.

Some parent birds pick their chicks' feathers. If one of your pairs begins to pick their babies, you may have to foster the chicks out to other pairs. In some cases, the male bird is the culprit, which means that he should be removed from the breeding cage when the chicks start to feather out. The female can usually finish raising the chicks on her own. If this occurs, you may choose to remove the picking parents from your breeding program.

Although it seems odd to us, it is common for parent birds to eat their eggs. If you choose to use an egg eater in your breeding program, you will need to take away each egg as it is laid and replace it with an artificial one. Sometimes the egg-eating desire resolves once the hen starts to brood her clutch. However, birds who are confirmed egg eaters should not be bred.

Breeding Larger Parrots

Conures breed fairly well in captivity and provide a good example of what you will need to do to breed larger parrots. Set up your conures in breeding pairs, one pair per cage. Although the Patagonian conure will breed in a colony setting (several pairs together in a large aviary or flight), other conure species do not do well in colony settings.

Most conure species breed in the spring and summer, and some seem to be stimulated to breed by regular rainfall. Proper light and temperature are also key to breeding success. If your birds are kept indoors, you may have to provide them with supplemental light. One way to do so is to hang a Vitalite over their cage. When the indoor temperature reaches about 75°F and the birds are exposed to about 15 hours of light daily, their breeding cycles should be triggered.

Conures like small nesting spaces. The ideal small conure nest box is a vertical enclosure that measures 10 inches by 10 inches by 18 inches. Larger species favor a nest box that measures 12 inches by 12 inches by 24 inches. The box entrance is at the top, and an inspection panel on the side will allow you to check on the eggs and chicks without overly disturbing the parent birds. Line the box with pine shavings and place it in the upper rear of the cage or aviary to provide security for the breeding pair.

Although it may seem obvious, be sure to select only healthy birds for your breeding program. The process of breeding and raising chicks puts a tremendous strain on a bird's body, so it's important to start with strong, healthy birds. Also, quarantine any new arrivals to your breeding program for at least one month to ensure that no diseases are spread in your aviary. Feed these birds last and with separate food and water bowls from the rest of your flock to prevent transmitting any diseases from the new birds to existing breeders in your collection.

When selecting your breeding pairs, make sure that you have pure pairs of the same species of conure. Conures can and will hybridize (breed with birds outside their own species), but aviculturists discourage such pairings. By mixing species in your breeding program, the resulting chicks will have diluted bloodlines and will not further the preservation of the birds' unique genetic heritage for the future.

To set up your breeding pairs, put all potential mates together in a large aviary, if possible, and let the birds pair off on their own. If you have two birds in a large cage in your living room and they've demonstrated a pair bond (for example, sitting close to each other, preening each other, or feeding each other), they've already established their relationship and are good candidates for going to nest.

Once you've introduced a pair to each other, try not to separate those birds because forming a strong pair bond between the parent birds is crucial to breeding success. Remember that newly paired-up birds may not have viable eggs in their first season together, so you must give your breeding pairs ample time together (more than one breeding season) to determine if the pair will produce young. Although it may be tempting to split up infertile pairs after a fruitless breeding season, you must be patient and give the birds an opportunity to get accustomed to each other before determining their success or failure as parents.

If you will be keeping more than one pair of breeding conures in your home, don't stack the breeding cages on top of each other. Some birds become quite disturbed by the action of cage cleaning above or below them, and this could cause your parent birds to injure themselves by flying into the wire, or they could damage the eggs while scrambling in or out of the nest box.

One of the first steps a breeding pair of conures will take is to begin gnawing at the nest box. The hen will do most of the gnawing, although the male may join in. Some conures will chew on their nest boxes so extensively that they destroy the boxes completely. If your birds are enthusiastic chewers, make sure the nest box has a double floor, or consider giving these birds a metal nest box with a wooden lining.

You can tell when your pair is ready to lay eggs if you see the female staying in the nest box most of the time, if both members of the pair are more aggressive at feeding time, if the male feeds the female more frequently, or if the female's lower abdomen appears swollen. Sometimes you will see the birds mating on a perch in the cage, while at other times they will mate in the nest box. Check the nest box daily using the inspection door to see how many eggs your birds have laid.

To determine if you have viable eggs, you will need to let the female incubate them for five to seven days. Then carefully remove the eggs while the parent birds are out of the nest box (this may be a challenge), and hold a light up to the wide end of the egg. If you see red veins inside the egg, it's fertile. If you don't, the egg is clear (infertile). Clear eggs can indicate a number of things, including an incompatible pair, two female birds masquerading as a true pair, or illness in the parent birds.

Depending on the species, conure eggs take between twenty-two and twenty-six days to incubate. Only the females incubate the eggs during this time. The chicks hatch twenty-four to seventy-two hours after they pip, which means that the air space in the wide end of the egg shifts and the chick starts to break out of the shell in search of oxygen.

Newly hatched *Aratinga* chicks have white down and pink skin. Their eyes begin to open about twelve days after they hatch. When the chicks are about 2 weeks old, their legs and beaks begin to darken and the first hint of feather shafts can be seen under their skin. Feather colors begin to appear when the chicks are about 1 month old, and they are fully feathered when they are about 2 months old. At this time, they are also ready to leave the nest. Their parents continue to feed them for several weeks after the chicks leave the nest.

Some *Aratinga* hens become aggressive during breeding season. If your bird becomes aggressive, try to leave her alone as much as possible. Other *Aratinga* hens may bite at or eat their eggs. If you discover your bird has done this, she may need extra calcium, protein, or vitamins in her diet.

Recently hatched *Pyrrhura* chicks have pink skin and a hint of down. Their eyes begin to open about two weeks after they hatch, and the chicks show the first signs of feather shafts under the skin when they are about 10 days old. After about forty days, the chicks are fully feathered and ready to leave the nest, although the male bird continues to feed them for several weeks after they leave the nest.

Bringing Up Babies

Chicks who are still in the nest box can be handled, but be aware that some hens do not appreciate human intrusion and will take action, including killing the chicks. This is not a common problem in breeding birds, but it does occur.

Parrot parents become anxious if all the chicks are removed from the nest box at the same time and are kept away from the parent birds for any length of time. This shouldn't discourage you from cleaning the nest box occasionally, but you should make an effort to clean quickly and return the chicks promptly to their parents.

How to Hand-Feed Chicks

Although most parrots are reliable parents, occasionally the need to hand-feed chicks will arise. Some hens will reject chicks, or a hen may die. If you do suddenly find yourself with a nestful of chicks to hand-feed, proper heat and extreme cleanliness are crucial.

Chicks must be kept warm but they should not overheat, so you must strike a delicate balance. Recommended starting points are 85°F for feathered birds and 90°F for unfeathered birds. Adjust the temperature down if the birds start to pant and hold their wings away from their bodies, and adjust up if you see them shivering or huddling together.

Clean hand-feeding supplies and fresh formula will lead to healthier chicks. Keep this in mind if the temptation to cut corners should arise. Use a different syringe for each baby you feed, and thoroughly clean and disinfect the syringes between feedings.

Carefully follow the preparation instructions on the package of a good-quality hand-feeding formula. Keep the formula temperature between 100 and 104°F to ensure the chicks can digest it properly. Fill each syringe with the recommended amount of formula (this will vary with the species of bird being fed and the age of the chicks) and place the syringes in a jar of warm, clean water to keep them warm. Get your chicks out of the nest, and place each one in a small, secure container (like an empty margarine tub) with a clean, wadded-up paper towel in the bottom to make cleanup easy.

To hand-feed a chick, put the syringe in the left corner of the bird's mouth and aim the formula into the back right corner of the bird's mouth and throat. Birds have two openings in their throats: one that leads to the lungs (the trachea), located on the left side of the throat, and the other that leads to the stomach (the esophagus), located on the right side of the throat. Obviously, you want the food to go down the esophagus and not into the lungs, where it can cause aspiration pneumonia. Apply firm, gentle pressure to the syringe's plunger and, before you know it, you've hand-fed a bird!

If you take it upon yourself to hand-feed chicks, you must realize that this is a very demanding task. Some chicks will require round-the-clock care, and you must be there to provide it.

Banding Baby Birds

Once your chicks have hatched and are feeding successfully, you will want to band them. Some states require that budgies be banded, and serious breeders want their chicks banded to keep track of bloodlines and successful breeding pairs. Also, bird stores may be reluctant to sell unbanded chicks, so if you plan to do business with a store, you will need to have banded your chicks prior to selling them. You will need to band your chicks when they are about 5 days old. Sometimes you can wait until day 6, but chicks grow quickly, which means you have a very small window of opportunity to get the bands on the chicks.

To band a chick, you will need a clean, dry washcloth to set the chick on during banding, a toothpick, and a band (available from parrot clubs or bird supply stores).

Place the washcloth on a tabletop or other sturdy surface, and place the chick on the washcloth on his right side. Hold the chick's left foot in your left hand and slide the band over the two front toes with your right hand. After you've slipped the band over the first two toes, hold the chick's foot with your right hand and continue moving the band up the chick's leg with your left hand, pulling the toes forward and the band back as you go.

If necessary, use the toothpick to flip the band over the longer back toe. The shorter back toe should follow right along (if not, use your trusty toothpick to gently move the band along), and the chick is banded. Reassure the chick that he's a beautiful, brave bird at this point and return him to the nest.

Chick Development

About four weeks after chicks of smaller species, such as cockatiels or budgies, have been banded, they'll begin to try flying. Be prepared to hear lots of flapping coming from your young birds, and don't be surprised if they first try their wings in their nest box. This will last about a week in most cases, with an adventurous chick finding his way to the nest box opening for his first look at the outside world at the age of 5 weeks. Shortly after, this daring young bird will try his first flight. Make sure to have plenty of perching options available close to the nest box opening because this first flight is traditionally short and weak.

After one chick tests the air, his clutchmates soon follow suit, and breeders are treated to many short, clumsy flights and the chicks' first amusing attempts at perching, side stepping, and turning around on the perches. With practice, though, flying, perching, preening, and other important skills improve.

Shortly after their first tentative flights into the real world, your chicks should discover the food and water bowls in their parents' cage. By watching their parents crack seeds, sample fresh foods, and drink water, the chicks should learn how to eat, but it will probably take them a week or so to perfect their skills. Breeders will enjoy watching their chicks learning to crack seeds because the line between foodstuff and play toy is sometimes quite blurry for a chick! Like any baby, almost anything a parrot chick can get into his mouth is fair game. Keep an eye on curious youngsters so they don't ingest something harmful in these early explorations into the world.

African grey chicks can provide a number of challenges to breeders. Baby greys can be prone to leg and neck problems. Some chicks may have been sat on too tightly by their parents, which can result in their leg bones being deformed. This condition is called spraddle leg, and it is not unique to greys. Consult your avian veterinarian if you notice that your chicks' legs splay out to one side or the other. Splints or even surgery may be needed to correct the problem. A baby with a severely tilted or twisted neck may also be suffering from bacterial or respiratory problems, both of which will require veterinary attention as well.

You may notice that some of your baby greys shake after feeding. Although it may seem that the chick is having convulsions, this behavior is usually not cause for alarm. It often disappears as the babies mature and gain some coordination.

Baby greys' personalities begin to develop when they are about 7 weeks old. They begin by whining for attention and actively seeking affection from their owners. This phase usually passes by the time a bird is weaned (between 12 and

14 weeks of age). Some greys maintain cuddly dispositions, but most become more reserved with age.

Clip a baby grey's wings and nails when he is about 8 weeks of age so he isn't able to fly freely and injure himself or escape and so his nails do not catch on anything as he explores his world. Also, by getting the baby grey used to grooming at an early age, he will accept grooming more readily later on.

When the African grey chicks are about 10 weeks old, they'll begin to try flying. Expect to hear lots of flapping because the chicks will test their wings inside the nest box before actually flying. Baby greys should start sampling grown-up bird food when they are about 12 weeks old.

chapter 8

JUVENILE BEHAVIORS

Young birds have a great many endearing behaviors. They beg for food, they explore nearly everything with their mouths, and they are charmingly clumsy. Most owners adore their birds at this stage and spend a lot of time cuddling with them and fussing over them.

Some particularly clever birds learn how to exploit their situations by using these behaviors, and owners have to be able to determine when the behaviors are genuine and when a bird is trying to work a situation to her advantage.

Many first-time owners with good intentions create behavioral problems in their baby parrots by spoiling them. Because the chicks are so cute and cuddly and helpless, owners often rush to their baby parrots each time the chick screams. In other cases, the owners hold the birds too much and fail to encourage the bird to spend time by herself. These owners do not teach the baby parrot to entertain herself, so the bird doesn't learn how to play. Finally, some owners spend every waking hour with their birds when the birds are chicks, but then try to engage in other activities once the birds grow up. In all these situations, the potential exists for creating spoiled, uncontrollable feathered monsters.

To keep this from happening to you, offer your baby parrot a balance of cuddling, attention, and care from the time you bring her home. Provide her with a safe, secure home, plenty of interesting, nourishing food, and lots of clean water. Make sure she has the chance to take naps and get enough sleep (remember, growing up is tiring work!). Take her to the veterinarian regularly to ensure her good health, and keep her nails and wings trimmed for her safety.

Check on your young parrot when she screams to make sure she isn't cold, hungry, or in danger, but don't rush to pick her up every time she vocalizes. Instead, occasionally pet the bird on the back and tell her she's a good, brave bird,

Many birds enjoy looking at themselves in mirrors. Here Sindbad is playing "find the pretty bird." (Photo by Julie Rach Mancini)

or reward her with your attention by playing with her, feeding her a special treat by hand, showing her a new toy, or introducing her to her play gym. (Be sure your parrot has adequate perching skills before you allow her to sit on a play gym for any length of time).

As your bird grows up, you can reassure her vocalizing from another room with a simple "I'm here. Are you being a good bird?" or some other comment that indicates you have heard the bird's call, but that you aren't going to rush to her side after each vocalization. If the bird continues to vocalize, you may want to check on her to make sure that she did not tip over her food or water bowl, or that she does not have her wing feathers stuck in her cage bars or is in some other uncomfortable situation.

Show your bird around your house when you bring her home, and make sure to take her from room to room regularly. Give your bird a change of scenery by taking her to look for "pretty birds" in the bathroom mirrors. Take her on a room-to-room tour in the morning and in the evening so she can see other areas rather than simply sitting in her cage day after day. When your bird is old enough to perch and play safely, offer her perching opportunities in different rooms of the house.

Approximate Weaning Ages

Budgerigar	6 weeks
Cockatiel	7 weeks
Conure	8 weeks
Miniature macaw	9 weeks
Amazon	11 weeks
African grey	13 weeks
Cockatoo and macaw	14 weeks

Stages of Development

A young parrot goes through several phases of development while she is maturing. She begins life as a **neonate** or hatchling or chick. All of these terms refer to a very young bird who has recently emerged from the egg. At this time her eyes are closed and she has very little down or feathers on her body. Neonates rely on their parents or a hand-feeder to provide them with food.

After the neonate's eyes open, she moves into the second phase of development, called the **nestling** phase. Nestlings start to develop down and begin to notice the world around them, but they still rely on their parents or a hand-feeder for food.

The young parrot remains in the nestling phase of development until she starts to fly. At this time, it moves into the **fledgling** stage of development. Fledglings have developed a full set of feathers. They are learning to fly and to eat on their own, although they still need daily feedings from their parents or a hand-feeder.

After the young birds learn to fly, they become even more independent and wean from their parents' or hand-feeders' daily feedings. The **weanling** phase is discussed in more detail below. It is followed by the **juvenile** phase, in which a young bird continues to learn about the world around her. She is still growing and developing, and her feathers may not yet have attained their full adult coloring. As she continues to grow, she appears to be an adult bird, but she is not yet sexually mature.

These two photos show a female Eclectus at different stages of development. The photo on the left shows a weanling bird. Notice her dark eyes and the light coloration on her beak tip. The photo on the right shows the same bird as a mature adult. Notice her yellow eyes and black beak. There is a pronounced difference in the color of her red and purple feathers. (PHOTOS BY MARY SELBY)

The Weanling Stage

An important part of a young parrot's life is the weanling stage. During weaning, a baby parrot learns to eat solid food rather than the food she receives from her parents or from a hand-feeder. It is a stressful time for both bird and owner as the bird makes the adjustment to an adult diet. Weaning is different from fledging, when a chick starts flying, although some people use the terms interchangeably.

Chicks will often decide for themselves that they no longer want to eat hand-feeding formula, and most will wean between the ages of 5 and 12 weeks. Smaller species, such as budgies and cockatiels, wean more quickly than the larger species, such as macaws and cockatoos.

About three weeks before weaning time, start placing small pieces of fruits and vegetables in low-sided bowls in the chick's brooder to encourage her to play with (and hopefully eat) some of these interesting new foodstuffs. Unsweetened cereals are also popular weaning foods. The chick may play with these foods more than she eats them, but at least your pet is being introduced to foods that look, feel, and taste different from the hand-feeding formula that she is used to.

Change the foods frequently because the environment in the brooder will be warmer than your home environment, which may cause food in the brooder to spoil more quickly. Continue to offer feedings of formula if your chick will take them, and monitor your bird's weight carefully. Expect the bird to lose weight—between 10 and 15 percent of her body weight—as she weans. If your bird loses too much weight or seems unable to eat, immediately consult your avian veterinarian or the breeder from whom you bought the bird.

When you start eliminating formula meals for your chick, begin by terminating the midday hand-feeding. If the bird seems to be comfortable without her midday meal, try eliminating the morning feeding, too. Offer seeds, pellets, and fresh foods during the day to encourage your chick to eat solid food, but still give her an evening feeding of formula so she will have some food in her stomach during the night.

Sometimes a chick will wean more easily if she takes her meals of "real food" with you. Offer your bird her own plate at the table and let her see you and your family eating. If you have other birds in the house, you can enlist them as models of behavior for your chick.

Keep in mind that some chicks in a particular clutch will wean sooner than their clutchmates, and some species, such as cockatoos, wean reluctantly at best.

As parrot chicks grow up in the wild, their parents gradually and gently encourage them to become self-sufficient. Chicks are conditioned from the moment they come out of the egg to beg for food from their parents. They improve their begging skills while their parents are feeding them so that they are true experts by the time they should be weaned. Young parrots in the wild often harass their fathers mercilessly with begging and chasing when they are about to be weaned. However, the parent birds gradually stop giving in to the chicks' begging for food, which forces the chicks to be self-sufficient.

Before the parent birds wean their chicks, they encourage them to explore their surroundings, and many parent birds give their chicks a gentle nudge that gets the young birds started on their first flights. The parent birds continue to encourage their chicks to explore as the chicks are weaned and as they continue to grow. The parents teach the chicks where to find food, which foods are good to eat, how to protect themselves against predators, and other important life lessons.

In the home environment, parrot owners either don't know or forget to give their young birds gentle nudges toward self-sufficiency. They often make huge fusses over their baby birds when the birds first come into their homes. Couples or family members may even compete to see who will hold the little bird while she's being hand-fed. As stated earlier, too much attention will discourage the parrot from learning how to entertain herself. As the bird grows up, she's likely to learn to beg for attention, or simply be baffled by the change in her owner's

CLUMSY GREYS

Although many young birds have trouble with their balance as they are growing up, African greys are particularly noted for being clumsy. If you have a
young grey in your home, take the time to help her feel secure as she learns
about her new home. Make sure she is settled comfortably on your hand or
arm before walking around with her so she doesn't fall. Many young greys feel
even more secure if their owners let them lean into their chests while perching
on their arms.

behavior. The stage is set for this poor, confused little parrot to become a screaming, feather-pulling, attention-craving problem pet who may get bounced from
home to home.

This does not have to happen. Owners need to plan ahead for their parrots
to be mature birds and reward them when they are playing quietly or entertaining themselves. Owners also need to spend consistent amounts of time with their
birds as they mature so the bird doesn't suddenly feel she's been abandoned. By
using a little common sense and by providing a safe, secure environment for your
bird, you should be able to prevent your bird from becoming a spoiled baby who
doesn't know how to entertain herself.

The Terrible Twos

You may have heard the phrase "the terrible twos" used in conjunction with the
behavior of young parrots when they are around 1 year old. These behavioral
changes can occur any time between the ages of 6 and 30 months, depending on
the size of the parrot. Keep in mind that smaller birds mature more quickly than
larger ones.

During this period, the parrot will vocalize and explore her territory more
than ever before, and she may bite her owner and other humans deliberately. She
will also challenge her position in the family, and she may frequently change her
loyalties to people in your family. The person who used to be the parrot's one and
only best friend in the whole world may be shunned or chased away in the morning, only to be wooed back by nightfall. This is a very confusing time for the parrot, and it can make owners crazy, too, as the formerly well-behaved little bird
seems to turn into a monster before their eyes.

It doesn't have to be this way. Yes, your little feathered friend is changing, but
she doesn't have to become a completely unhandleable fiend. If you started your
bird on the road to self-sufficiency correctly by teaching her the "up" and "down"

commands (see chapter 9, "Behaviors Every Bird Should Know") and by encouraging her to play by herself when she was a chick, your adjustment to your parrot's changes will be less stressful than if you had spoiled her as a baby. Still, there will be a period of adjustment as your parrot tries to figure out where she fits in the family flock.

In the wild, this is the time when a young parrot learns about her environment and her flock by exploring her world and testing her independence. She spends time away from her parents, but the young bird also wants to know where they are as she explores. Your young bird will need attention and guidance from you as she explores her new home.

In your flock, your young parrot can test the limits of her environment and find her place in the family's pecking order by climbing, destroying toys, and flapping her clipped wings on a play gym or cage top. All these activities help a growing young parrot expend energy and work off her frustrations at growing up.

This period is a perfect time to start teaching your pet to talk. In fact, your bird might surprise you one morning by greeting you with a "Hi!" or a "How ya doin'?" that you didn't even intend to teach her.

This is also the time to offer your pet a wide variety of toy choices. Be sure to introduce each one to your pet carefully because young birds are a bit skittish about new things. By giving your bird several toys at a time, you are allowing her some control over her life by letting her choose the toy she wants to play with.

Some common household items that can be hazardous to a chewing bird include prescription and over-the-counter medications, matches, pens, pencils, crayons, houseplant fertilizers, and chocolate. (PHOTO BY JULIE RACH MANCINI)

This poor cockatiel fell into a pot of cooking oil. Although she was not burned, the bird still needed immediate veterinary attention so her feathers could be cleaned and so she could be examined for breathing difficulties, potential eye problems, poisoning, and shock. (PHOTO BY GARY A. GALLERSTEIN, DVM)

This is also the time to be sure you have parrot-proofed your home because your bird will be exploring every inch of it, and you don't want to tempt your pet into danger. Be aware of these potential dangers in your home:

- Unscreened windows and doors, which offer potential escape routes

- Mirrors, which can be flown into and cause injury to a bird

- Exposed electrical cords, which can cause electrocution if chewed on

- Toxic houseplants, which can poison a pet bird

- Unattended ashtrays, which can cause burns from lit cigarettes or poisoning from ingesting cigarette butts

- Venetian blind cords, in which a bird can hang herself

- Sliding glass doors, which can provide an escape route if open or a concussion or broken neck if flown into when closed

- Ceiling fans, which can cause broken bones or internal injuries if a bird flies into one while it's on

- Open washing machines, dryers, refrigerators, freezers, ovens, or dishwashers, which can injure or kill a bird if she becomes trapped in one of them

- Open toilet bowls and uncovered fish tanks, which can cause drowning if fallen into

- Leaded stained-glass items or inlaid jewelry, which can poison a bird if chewed on

- Uncovered cooking pots on the stove, which can cause a variety of injuries, including drowning, scalding, or poisoning, particularly by inhaling fumes from overheated nonstick cookware

- Crayons and permanent markers, which can poison a bird if chewed on

- Pesticides, rodent killers, and snail bait, which can poison a bird if eaten

- Untended stove burners, which can cause burns when a bird lands on a hot element

- Candles, which can burn a bird or poison a pet who chews on them

- Sofa cushions, under or between which a parrot can hide

- Afghans or balls of yarn, which can entangle a parrot and possibly strangle it

Take a few minutes to examine your home from your bird's point of view and put tempting items out of reach. By offering your bird a safe environment and appropriate choices about what to chew on, you can help her make the transition through "the terrible twos" without it being such a trial for either of you.

If your bird will spend most of the day by herself, be sure that she has time out of her cage with you in the morning and in the evening, as well as access to interesting toys during the day. (PHOTO BY JULIE RACH MANCINI)

Give your bird a change of scenery by allowing her to visit parts of your home outside her cage—it is important to help your bird explore her world safely. (PHOTO BY JULIE RACH MANCINI)

As your bird enters this transitional period, be aware that this is the time that some serious behavior problems such as biting, screaming, and feather picking can take root. Frequently, the bird engages in these unwanted behaviors because she discovers that you will give her more attention (yelling at her, shaking your finger or fist at the bird, or paying attention to her when she acts up) when she misbehaves than when she behaves. Be careful not to play into your parrot's hand because she will take every opportunity to test you and your patience during this time. Remember that if you've laid the groundwork with your bird by teaching her the "up" and "down" commands and by encouraging her to entertain herself from time to time, you will get through this with your nerves and good humor intact!

If your bird will be spending long periods of time on her own during the day, be sure that she has things to do while you're away. Give your bird interesting foods to eat, challenging toys to play with, and a comfortable environment. By leaving on a radio or television set, your bird will have enjoyable background noise. You should also make an effort to spend some time with your bird before you leave the house—perhaps you can have a cup of coffee as your bird is having breakfast in the morning. Soon after you get home in the evening, you can let her out of her cage for a play session.

SWEET BABY BIRDS

Almost all young parrots are sweet, loving creatures. Remember that these birds' personalities will change and develop over time as they grow into adult birds. You can help your pet stay sweet by handling her regularly and refreshing her training on the "up" and "down" commands each day. Also remember to reward her with verbal praise and attention when she does something you want her to do, because your attention will make her more likely to repeat the behavior.

Juvenile Phobia

If your young bird suddenly displays a fear of absolutely everything, she is having an episode of phobic behavior. Although it will seem as though nothing has changed in your routine, the bird is reacting to changes within her maturing body. She is beginning to feel independent, but if she hasn't been taught how to explore her world safely, she will become phobic and will prefer to stay in her cage all the time because the cage feels safe and secure.

If your bird displays an episode of phobic behavior, all is not lost. You can still help your pet learn how to explore her world safely. Take her to different rooms in your house and talk to her in a positive, upbeat tone. Tell her about her environment, and reassure her that everything will be okay. Make sure your bird has time out of her cage so she doesn't become overly territorial about her cage or feel cagebound.

chapter 9

BEHAVIORS EVERY BIRD SHOULD KNOW

Training a parrot takes a great deal of time and patience on the part of the bird owner. You must first gain your pet's trust, and then you must work never to lose it.

A good first step in taming your parrot is getting him to become comfortable around you. To do this, give your bird a bit of warning before you approach his cage. Don't "sneak up" on your bird, and try not to startle him. Call his name when you walk into the room. Try to be quiet and to move slowly around your pet because these gestures will help him become more comfortable with you. Keep your hands behind you, and reassure the bird that you aren't there to harm him, that everything is all right, and that he's a wonderful pet.

After your bird is comfortable having you in the same room with him, you may want to try placing your hand in his cage as a first step toward taking him out of the cage. Place your hand in your bird's cage and hold it there very briefly. Don't be surprised if your bird flutters around and squawks at first at the "intruder."

Continue this process daily, and leave your hand in the cage for slightly longer periods of time each day. Within a few days, your parrot won't make a fuss about your hand being in his space, and he may come over to investigate this new perch. Do not remove your hand from the cage the first time your parrot lands on it; just let the bird become accustomed to perching on your hand.

After several successful perching attempts on successive days, try to take your hand out of the cage with your bird on it. Some birds will take to this new adventure willingly, while others are reluctant to leave the safety and security of home. (Before taking your bird out of his cage, be sure your bird's wings are clipped and all doors and windows are secured.)

You need to build a bond of trust with your bird in order to train him successfully. Hand-feeding special treats is a good way to reinforce a trusting relationship. (PHOTO BY JULIE RACH MANCINI)

If your bird doesn't seem to respond to this method, you can try an alternate taming method. Take the bird out of his cage and into a small room, such as a bathroom that has been bird-proofed (i.e., the toilet lid is down, the shower door is closed, and the bathroom hasn't been recently cleaned with any strong chemical cleansers). Sit down on the floor, place your bird in front of you, and begin playing with him. Don't be surprised if your bird tries to fly a few times. With clipped wings, however, he won't get very far and will give up trying after a few failed attempts.

Perching on Your Hand

As your bird becomes more comfortable around you, see if you can make perching on your hand a game for your pet. Once he masters perching on your hand, you can teach him to step up by gently pressing your finger up and into the bird's belly. This will cause the bird to step up. As he does so, say, "Step up" or "Up." Before long, your bird will respond to this command without much prompting. If you aren't comfortable with having your bird climb on your finger, you can use a stick to substitute for your finger during training.

Teaching your bird the "up" and "down" commands will give you a way to control your pet. (PHOTO BY JULIE RACH MANCINI)

Along with the "up" command, you may want to teach your bird the "down" command. When you put the bird down on his cage or play gym, simply say, "Down," as the bird steps off your hand. These two simple commands offer you a great deal of control over your bird because you can say, "Up," to put an unruly bird back in his cage, or tell a parrot who needs to go to bed, "Down," as you put him in his cage at night.

As you are teaching the "up" and "down" commands, be alert to your bird's moods. If he seems unusually alert and on edge, you may want to stop the session because he may be trying to tell you he's had enough for now. On the other hand, if your bird seems relaxed and content to continue climbing, it's okay to continue the session, but be sure not to extend a session longer than about ten minutes.

After your bird has mastered the "up" and "down" commands, encourage him to climb a "ladder" by moving him from index finger to index finger (the "rungs"). Keep taming sessions short (about ten minutes is the maximum parrot attention span), and make the taming process fun because it will be much more enjoyable for both of you. Build up your bird's stamina by having him climb the ladder several times a day. Have him climb the ladder in the morning while he's out for a little playtime after breakfast, then climb again when you come home from work and again just before bedtime. Build up the number of repetitions at each playtime until your bird climbs the ladder at least twenty times a day.

After your pet has become comfortable sitting on your hand, try petting him. Birds seem to like to have their heads, backs, cheek patches, under-wing areas, and eye areas (including the closed eyelids) scratched or petted lightly. Quite a few like to have a spot low on their backs at the bases of their tails (over their

On occasion, parrots need their owners' help to scratch itchy spots they can't reach. Petting your parrot is a good step toward gaining his trust. (PHOTO BY JULIE RACH MANCINI)

preen glands) rubbed. Many birds do not enjoy having their stomachs scratched, although yours may think this is heaven. You'll have to experiment to see where your bird likes to be petted. You'll know you're successful if your bird clicks or grinds his beak, pins his eyes, or settles onto your hand or into your lap with a completely relaxed, blissful expression on his face.

Some people think that you need to wear gloves while taming your parrot. However, gloves will only make your hands appear more alien, and more frightening, to your bird. If your pet is frightened, he will take more time and patience on your part to tame, which is likely to make the process less enjoyable for you.

Toweling a Parrot

Every parrot should be able to tolerate being wrapped in a towel. Towels make pet birds easier to handle, and they give the birds something to chew on other than an owner's fingers or clothes.

Avian veterinarians often wrap their patients in a towel to handle them, and groomers will towel parrots during wing and nail trimming. If you groom your parrot yourself, you will find the procedure is easier if the bird is toweled. Your avian veterinarian can give you a demonstration on how to towel a parrot.

Use a towel appropriate to your bird's size. Budgies, canaries, and lovebirds can be toweled with washcloths, and kitchen dish towels work well for medium-sized birds. Bath towels are suitable for larger parrots.

WHERE TO PET A PARROT

- Ears
- Nares
- Eyelids
- Cheeks
- Under the wings

- Base of the tail
- Belly
- Wing fold
- Under the crest
- Under the chin

Many birds like to be petted on their cheek patches and under their chin. (PHOTO BY PAMELA L. HIGDON)

To towel a parrot, drape the towel over your hand loosely and reach into your parrot's cage. Catch the parrot's head with your toweled hand and lift the bird off his perch. As you bring the bird out of his cage, support his body with your other hand as you wrap the loose ends of the towel around the parrot's wings and feet, but don't confine the parrot too tightly.

When you've completed the toweling process, your parrot should be secure in the towel, but not wrapped so tightly that he is unable to breathe. Birds need to be able to inhale and exhale easily, and they don't have diaphragms as we do to help them breathe. Keep the towel off your bird's face.

Toweling a parrot can make him easier to handle. Gently grasp your parrot's neck with your toweled hand, and wrap the towel around the wings and body to contain him. Be sure not to constrict the bird's chest; you want him to be able to breathe easily. (PHOTO BY JULIE RACH MANCINI)

To towel a macaw, it is important to catch the bird on the ground and in a corner. Use a folded, thick terry-cloth bath towel and keep your hands behind the towel. (PHOTO BY GARY A. GALLERSTEIN, DVM)

Your bird may be less fearful of a towel if you use one that's similar in color to his feathers. My African grey seems to tolerate gray, black, or pastel towels with equal levels of comfort. Any neutral, solid-colored towel should suffice for toweling a parrot. Be sure that the towel you use does not have loose threads hanging off it—you don't want your bird's feet entangled in the towel.

To make toweling easier on your parrot, turn it into a game. You can play peekaboo with a young parrot to make the towel seem less threatening. Move slowly to envelop your parrot loosely in the towel, and reassure him often that he's a brave bird and that toweling is fun!

Housetraining Your Parrot

Although some people don't believe it, parrots can be housetrained so they don't eliminate on their owners. If you want to housetrain your bird, you will have to choose a phrase that will indicate the act of eliminating to your pet, such as "go

Parrots can be trained to eliminate on command. Owners need to pay attention to their birds' behaviors to ensure that the birds do not hold in their droppings for long time periods. (PHOTO BY JULIE RACH MANCINI)

poop" or "go potty." You will have to observe your pet in order to identify how he indicates that he is about to eliminate. Your bird may shift around or squat. When you have mastered your pet's body language, use the chosen phrase at the appropriate time so the bird associates the phrase with the action.

Once your bird seems to associate "go potty" with eliminating, you can try picking him up and holding him until he starts to shift or squat. Tell the bird, "Go potty," while placing him on his cage, where he can eliminate. Once he's done, pick him up again and praise him for being such a smart bird! Expect a few accidents while you are both learning this trick, but soon you'll have a housetrained bird. You will be able to set the bird on his cage about every 20 minutes, give him the command, and expect the bird to eliminate.

Don't be surprised if your bird occasionally seems to take longer than usual to eliminate. Sometimes my parrot goes right away when I hold her over the trash can, while other times she preens, grooms my bangs, clicks her beak, pins her eyes—in short, she does whatever she can to postpone the inevitable trip back to her cage.

If I try to put her back into her cage after eliminating and she's not ready to go, she will flap her wings furiously as if to make herself larger than the opening of the cage door.

Disciplining Your Parrot

When disciplining your parrot, you must be careful not to lose your temper, and never hit your bird. Birds are very sensitive, intelligent creatures who do not deserve to be hit, regardless of how angry you are.

A cage cover can be used to calm a noisy parrot, or it can help a bird settle down for bedtime. (Photo by Julie Rach Mancini)

Although parrots are clever creatures, they are not linear "cause-and-effect" thinkers. If a parrot commits action A (chewing on some molding under your kitchen cabinets, for example), he won't associate reaction B (being yelled at, being locked in his cage, or being otherwise punished) with the original misbehavior. As a result, most forms of discipline are ineffective with parrots.

So what do you do when your parrot misbehaves? When you must discipline your pet, look at him sternly and tell him "No" in a firm voice. If the bird is climbing on or chewing something he shouldn't, remove him from the source of danger and temptation as you tell him "No."

When I discipline my parrot, usually all I have to do is say her name sharply or tell her, "Be quiet," in a firm tone and she gets the message. She often answers my verbal reprimand with an indignant little huff or a series of small squeaks, but she usually settles down after being disciplined verbally. If a verbal reprimand isn't enough, I cover her cage with a dark beach towel for a few minutes to settle her down.

If your bird has wound himself up into a screaming banshee, sometimes a little "time-out" in his covered cage (between five and ten minutes) does wonders to calm him down. Once the screaming stops and the bird is settled enough to play quietly, eat, or simply move around his cage, the cover comes off to reveal a well-behaved, mellower pet.

Ignoring your pet briefly is another discipline method that can be effective. Parrots crave attention and need to feel like they are members of your family flock, so ignoring your bird for misbehaving may cause him to behave better just so you will pay attention to him. However, you must make sure your pet is safely in his cage and out of danger to use this discipline method.

These cockatoos are in a suitable cage for traveling, but this cage is too small for these birds to live in full-time. Cockatoos need large cages and plenty of toys to keep their active minds entertained. (PHOTO BY GARY A. GALLERSTEIN, DVM)

On the Road

If you are thinking of traveling with your bird, consider the following issues:

- Does your bird like new adventures?
- Is there a trusted relative or friend with whom you can leave the bird while you are away?
- Does your avian veterinarian's office offer boarding?
- How long will you be gone?
- Is it illegal to bring your bird to your destination?

If you are going on a family vacation, it is usually best to leave the bird at home in familiar surroundings with his own food, water, and cage or in the care of a trusted friend, relative, pet-sitter, or avian veterinarian.

Birds who will be shipped via air cargo need to travel in airline-approved pet carriers. Check with your airline to determine which carrier is best for your bird. (PHOTO BY JULIE RACH MANCINI)

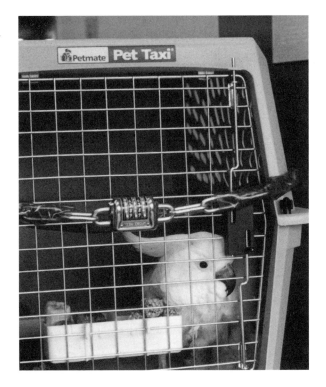

Generally, travel is stressful for birds because many birds are creatures of habit who like their routines. Moreover, taking birds across state lines or international boundaries poses some risk. It is illegal to bring some species into certain states. For example, California and some other states prohibit the entry of Quaker (also known as monk) parrots, on the grounds that the birds are considered a threat to local crops. Some foreign countries have lengthy quarantine stays for pet birds. Although it might be difficult to leave your bird behind, staying at home is usually better for the bird.

Some parrot behavior consultants believe the exact opposite, however; many think travel is a broadening experience for parrots and that it helps them become less territorial and less bonded to their cages and homes. With the advent of pet-friendly superstores, birds have more opportunities to get out and about with their owners than ever before.

Despite my belief that pet birds should stay home, there are still times that they will need to travel, such as when they visit the veterinarian or if you move.

If a car trip is in your pet's future, you will need to acclimate your bird to traveling in the car. Some pet birds take to this new adventure immediately, while others become so stressed out by the trip that they get carsick. Patience and persistence are usually the keys to success if your bird falls into the latter category.

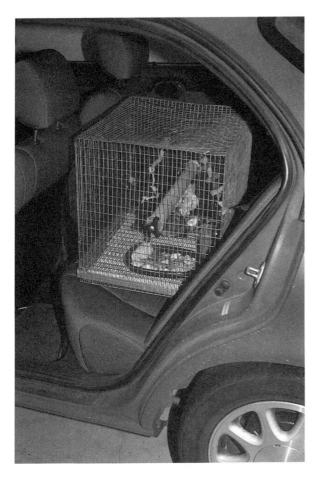

Car rides can be used to reward birds for good behavior, or they can be used as distractions for pets who like to pick their feathers. (PHOTO BY JULIE RACH MANCINI)

To get your pet used to riding in the car, start by taking his cage (with door and cage tray well secured) out to your car and placing the cage inside. Make sure that your car is cool before you do this because your bird can suffer heatstroke if you leave him in a hot car.

When your bird seems comfortable sitting in his cage in your car, take him for a short drive, such as around the block. If your bird seems to enjoy the ride (he eats, sings, whistles, talks, and generally acts like nothing is wrong), then you have a willing traveler on your hands. If he seems distressed by the ride (he sits on the floor of the cage and shakes, screams, or vomits), you have a bit of work ahead.

Distressed birds often need only to be conditioned to traveling in the car. You can do this by talking to your bird throughout the trip. Praise him for good behavior and reassure him that everything will be fine. Offer special treats and juicy fruits (grapes, apples, or citrus fruit) so your pet will eat and will also take in

Acrylic travel carriers allow birds to see where they are going, which may help them enjoy car rides more. (PHOTO BY JULIE RACH MANCINI)

water. (On long trips, you may want to remove your pet's water dish during travel to avoid spillage. If you do take out the dish, make sure to stop frequently and give your bird water so he doesn't dehydrate.)

As your bird becomes accustomed to car travel, gradually increase the length of the trips. When your bird is comfortable with car rides, begin to prepare him for the trip by packing your car as you would on the first travel day. If, for example, you plan to place duffel bags near your bird's cage, put the bags and the cage in the back of the car for a "practice run" before you actually begin the trip so your bird can adjust to the size, shape, and color of the bags. A little planning on your part will result in a well-adjusted avian traveler and a reduced stress level for you both.

My parrot enjoys car trips immensely. When we first began traveling together, I would put her cage on the front passenger seat of my car so she could see me and I could talk to her during the trip. She could climb up into the corner of her cage closest to me and hang on to the cage bars, watching me drive, whistling her own tunes to accompany the music from the radio, grinding or clicking her beak, and pinning her eyes at me. I think she also enjoys the feeling of the air-conditioning blowing through her feathers because she made sure to position herself so that the vents could blow on her full force, even on only slightly warm days. However, after giving the matter some thought, I decided she is safer riding in the back seat of my compact sedan, so that's where she has traveled for the past five years. I try to place her cage behind the passenger seat so she can still see me and I can keep an eye on her, too.

You may be tempted to have your pet ride in your car without being confined to his cage. You may have seen pictures in magazines of birds perched on car headrests or have been intrigued by the concept of an avian car seat. Please resist these temptations because your bird could easily fly out of an open car window or be injured severely in the event of an accident if he is not in a secure carrier or cage while traveling in your car.

chapter 10

MANAGING UNDESIRABLE BEHAVIORS

Parrots are wonderful pets, but they do have some behaviors that owners find puzzling, troubling, or downright dangerous. These behaviors include biting, chewing, screaming, feather pulling, self-mutilation, excessive egg laying, and dominance. In many cases, these behaviors make perfect sense to the parrot, but they can frustrate even the most patient and understanding parrot owner. The good news is that many of them can be managed effectively or even prevented.

Although parrots are tame, they are not domesticated to the same degree as dogs and cats. Some captive-bred parrots are only a few generations away from life in the jungle, and people whose parrots were originally wild caught essentially have a tame wild animal living with them. Part of the parrot's initial appeal and charm to her new owner is the bird's independent nature, but that same nature often causes friction between pet and owner, particularly as the pet matures.

Avoid Instigating Problem Behaviors

In some cases, owners cause their birds to behave in inappropriate ways. For example:

- An Amazon owner who is roughhousing with his parrot shouldn't be surprised when the bird gets excited and bites him while in the throes of emotional overload, but the owner gets both his hand and his feelings hurt when he is nipped by his pet.

- In another case, an African grey owner who is playing with her bird's beak stimulates the bird to begin regurgitating her last meal to her.

- In still another instance, an evening cuddle between a male cockatoo and his owner causes him to initiate breeding behaviors, including displays and masturbation.

In all these situations, the birds are exhibiting normal, natural reactions to the stimuli presented by their owners. It's the owners' perceptions of how their birds should behave that are the problems, and certainly the owners' behavior that needs to be modified to prevent these situations from occurring again.

When your parrot misbehaves, rather than getting angry with her, take a moment to see what caused the bird to misbehave. Parrots are not just "dumb animals" who misbehave for no reason; often the behavior is motivated by something the owners have done or a factor in the environment. Did your bird bite you because you provoked her with frightening body language, or did a large bird just swoop by your sliding glass door? Did your bird scream because she saw a squirrel on the balcony that needed to be chased away, or did you cause the bird to scream by "abandoning" her?

By taking a moment to consider your bird's motivation for misbehavior, you can often prevent the problem from recurring.

Many cases of apparent parrot misbehavior are really a reflection of misguided owners. Their expectations are too high, or they want the parrot to be something she cannot be. Bonnie Munro Doane and Thomas Qualkinbush put it very well in their book *My Parrot, My Friend* (see appendix B, "Resources,") when they said: "To live happily with a parrot requires patience and tolerance for behavior that is normal to the bird. Acceptance of a certain amount of mess, noise, and destruction of property will go a long way in preventing the development of relationship difficulties between person and parrot. If the parrot has been properly socialized, her

Beak wrestling can be viewed as a greeting, as a challenge to fight, or as a prelude to mating. An owner who plays with his or her bird's beak could be setting the bird up to bite. (PHOTO BY JULIE RACH MANCINI)

Birds who bite have often learned this behavior as a response to the behavior of their owners. (PHOTO BY PAMELA L. HIGDON)

natural tendencies to boisterousness and self-expression should not be unpleasant for the owner. Occasionally 'accidents' will happen, as they do with small children. But they should be the exception, not the rule. As long as the owner understands that there is no such thing as perfection with a parrot, the parrot/owner relationship should be mutually pleasant and satisfying."

Some unpleasant behaviors can become more than an annoyance, and correction is essential for a happy relationship between bird and owner.

Biting

Getting bitten by your pet parrot hurts. If you happen to have a large bird, such as a macaw or a cockatoo, the potential exists for serious injury.

Biting is not a natural parrot behavior. In the wild, parrots use their beaks to climb, eat, wrestle, or preen, but they rarely bite each other. If a parrot wants to intimidate an opponent, she's likely to scream, strut, posture, or fluff feathers to look larger instead of biting another bird.

Captive parrots are most likely to bite in order to survive or in order to control their situation. Birds who have been severely frightened or badly injured will bite to protect themselves in order to survive. Birds who have been rewarded for

PROBLEM BEHAVIORS AT A GLANCE

Why does my bird scream?

- The bird is stressed about or afraid of something in her environment.
- The bird is reflecting some stress felt by her owner.
- The bird's owner has rewarded the bird for screaming in the past.
- The bird learned how to scream from another bird.
- Screaming feels good.
- The bird is tired.
- The bird is being fed an all-seed diet.
- The bird is protecting her flock and family.
- The bird is sexually mature and wants to breed.
- The bird does not know how to entertain herself.
- The bird is hungry or thirsty and has run out of food or water.
- The bird needs more exercise.
- The bird feels isolated from her family.

What can I do to prevent her from screaming?

- Check to make sure the bird isn't in danger, and then reassure her that she's okay.
- Offer the bird opportunities to interact regularly with her owner or family.
- Let the bird out of her cage for daily exercise and playtimes.
- Make sure the bird has ample opportunities to sleep.

- Feed the bird a balanced diet.
- Offer your bird a combination of care, guidance, and discipline.
- Don't reward the bird for screaming by yelling at her, storming into her room, or shaking your finger or fist at her.

Why does my bird bite?

- She is afraid.
- You are rushing the bird through her usual routine.
- She is overstimulated by you.
- The bird is being fed an all-seed diet.
- She is a baby who is exploring her environment.
- She is trying to get her "mate" to flee from a perceived threat.
- She wants to be the dominant creature in her relationship with you.

What can I do to prevent her from biting?

- Avoid roughhousing with your bird because you may excite her and cause her to bite.
- Offer your bird safe opportunities to explore her environment.
- Offer your bird a variety of interesting toys and foods to chew on.
- Slow down when you're interacting with your bird.
- Don't reward the bird for biting by pulling your hand away each time she reaches out to you.

Why does my bird pull her feathers?

- The bird has a physical problem, such as a *Giardia* infestation, psittacine beak and feather disease syndrome, a thyroid deficiency, or an infection.
- The bird is stressed by something in her environment.
- The bird is nervous.
- The bird's owner rewards her with attention when she pulls her feathers.
- The bird is sexually frustrated.
- The humidity in the bird's environment is too low.
- The bird is being fed an all-seed diet.
- The bird is bored.
- The bird learned how to pull her feathers from another bird.

What can I do to prevent her from pulling her feathers?

- Take the bird to your avian veterinarian for an evaluation.
- Look at your bird's environment to see what's causing her to feel stress.
- Offer your bird a varied diet.
- Offer your bird many interesting chew toys.
- Play with your bird regularly.
- Set up a comfortable routine for your bird.
- Don't reward her for pulling her feathers with extra attention.

Why does my bird throw up?

- She is regurgitating food to show affection for her chosen human.
- Something has frightened her.
- She has a crop infection and needs medical attention.
- She has a blockage in her digestive tract and needs medical attention.

How can I help her to stop throwing up?

- Be careful how you pet your bird, particularly her beak.
- Have your bird evaluated by an avian veterinarian if she shows other signs of illness.

Why does my bird get quiet around strangers?

- Having strangers around frightens your parrot.
- Your parrot is trying to determine whether the stranger is friendly or unfriendly; when she does, she'll probably start making her normal noises.

How can I help her be more comfortable around strangers?

- Introduce your bird to new people and places early in her life.
- Have more than one person handle your bird regularly.
- Have more than one person be responsible for daily bird care.

biting in the past will bite again in order to try to control their owners and environment. Although yelling, cursing, or shaking your bitten hand in the air may not seem to be positive reinforcement to you, your bird sees all these actions as rewards and will bite you to see you do them again.

Parrots have a few natural instincts that may cause them to bite, such as occasional mood swings, a need to protect their territory from intruders, and aggression during breeding season. If you add in provocative human behavior, unintentional reinforcement, and misunderstanding of how a bird uses her beak, voilà!—you have a biting parrot.

If your parrot bites you while she's perched on your hand or she begins chewing on your clothing or jewelry, you can often dissuade her from this behavior by gently rotating your wrist about a quarter turn. Your bird will quickly associate the rocking of her "perch" with her misbehavior and will stop biting or chewing. Don't rock your arm if you have a young parrot on your arm, however. Young birds are unsteady on their feet, and a rocking arm could shake their confidence greatly. Some behaviorists recommend ignoring initial nips from baby birds because in many cases the birds are just trying to maintain their balance the only way they know how.

If your bird bites you, do not thump her on her beak as punishment. It's easy to react to your bird's behavior with a quick thump on the beak, and this was a gesture encouraged by some bird tamers who worked with wild-caught parrots. However, parrot behavior consultants have since discovered that birds do not understand this kind of punishment, and such a gesture will encourage your bird to want to bite you that much harder the next time she gets a chance.

Similarly, don't grab your bird's beak to discipline her. Grabbing a bird's beak can say several things to a bird: It can be a greeting, it can indicate sexual behavior, or it can issue a challenge to fight. If your bird enjoys having her beak touched and gently wrestled with, you can reward her with these gestures, but don't try this as a form of discipline. Your parrot will not perceive your actions as punishment.

To prevent your bird from biting, make sure she has access to plenty of acceptable chew toys, an interesting variety of foods, and opportunities to exercise outside her cage.

Don't encourage your bird to bite by pulling your hand away when your bird tries to test the strength of the perch you're offering. Very clever parrots soon learn to intimidate people in this way, and they quickly become biters. In other cases, birds learn to bite if owners offer toys or treats each time the birds reach out with their beaks toward their owners' hands or clothing.

Bird bites tend to hurt more than a finger or hand: They also hurt the bird owner's feelings. I've heard people say things such as, "My bird must not like me any more because he bit me," or "Why did my bird turn on me? I hand-raised her." Although birds are intelligent creatures capable of a wide range of emotions, they don't equate liking or not liking a person with their ability to bite this person.

Frequently, the bird really does like the person she bit and is showing her affection in this way. If a bird owner is bitten on the face, the bird may have been trying to encourage the person to flee from some perceived danger. (Birds relate most closely to our faces—they don't seem to know quite what to do with the rest of us.) In other cases, the bird is expressing her hormonal surges or feelings of frustration at being unable to breed.

You are well advised not to take a bird bite personally. This is a normal part of bird ownership that's to be expected. You can take some steps to minimize your chances of being bitten (for example, by exercising caution when handling a sexually mature parrot during breeding season), but you cannot realistically eliminate biting from your parrot's repertoire of behaviors.

Don't stop handling a bird who bites, because a lack of physical contact could create additional problems and result in a relationship that neither you nor your bird enjoys very much. A parrot who is never handled or played with will be "in control," but is also likely to become phobic. She may become overly attached to her cage, or cagebound, which makes her even more prone to bite because she feels compelled to defend her territory. In addition, the parrot feels neglected and may start other behavioral problems, such as feather picking or screaming, while the owner feels hurt and unloved by the bird.

Avoid this problem by offering your bird consistent discipline and guidance from the time you bring her home. Also pay attention to your pet's body language and the signals she sends out. Often, a bird gives plenty of warning before she bites—as long as you know how to interpret her body language.

If your bird has started to become cagebound, you must take steps to prevent her from becoming increasingly attached to her home. Take the bird out of her cage and take her into another room in your home—a room that is not as familiar to the bird as the room her cage is in. Play with the bird in this room and teach her (or give her a refresher course in) the "up" and "down" commands. Let the bird explore this new room and other rooms in your house in the course of your play sessions.

When you return your bird to her cage, give her another refresher session in the "up" and "down" commands (see chapter 9, "Behaviors Every Bird Should Know") before putting her back in her cage. After a few play sessions away from her cage and diligent work with the "up" and "down" commands, you should be able to handle your formerly cagebound bird with ease. Again, remember to watch your pet for signs that she wants to bite you, and take steps to prevent this from happening. You can still enjoy your pet, even when she's sexually mature, if you use a little common sense.

BRINGING A CAGEBOUND BIRD
OUT OF HER CAGE

My stepdaughter, Rhonda, kept two parakeets from the time she was about 9 through high school. She handled one bird, Andre, almost from the moment she got him, while the other bird, Jewel, came to her as a second-hand pet. Jewel was timid and reluctant to come out of her cage because of the way she had been mistreated in a previous home. She sat quietly in a corner of her cage most days, hoping no one would notice her, while Andre took his place as the star of the show, learning tricks and a few phrases under Rhonda's patient teaching.

Rhonda took the time to talk quietly to Jewel while she played with Andre. She explained what she was doing as she cleaned Jewel's cage and told her about the food or treats she offered her. As Jewel became accustomed to the routine Rhonda set up for the birds, she became less fearful and eventually allowed Rhonda to take her out of her cage. Rhonda did this by putting her hand into Jewel's cage and allowing Jewel to get adjusted to Rhonda's hand, rather than just reaching in and grabbing her. She let Jewel proceed at her own pace, rather than Rhonda imposing her plans on the bird.

Rhonda made sure to take Jewel out only when Andre was also out of his cage; she believed this made Jewel feel more at ease. If Jewel started to act uncomfortable at being out of her cage, Rhonda would reassure her with quiet words and gentle pats, or she would hold Jewel at chest level so Jewel could hear Rhonda's heartbeat.

Although Jewel never learned to say a lot or to do many tricks, she did become a handleable little parakeet, thanks to a lot of patient handling by Rhonda.

Chewing

Parrots chew to keep their beaks in condition. Chewing becomes a problem behavior in pet situations when the owner does not provide ample opportunity for a parrot to chew on acceptable items. The bird then turns her chewing needs loose on whatever she can find, such as furniture, wallpaper, or paneling.

Bird owners can prevent episodes of problem chewing simply by anticipating a bird's need to chew and providing acceptable items for this purpose. These can include wooden or leather toys, cardboard rolls from paper towels, toilet paper rolls, or nuts in the shell. Some birds are wild about chewing on seemingly indestructible things, such as manzanita perches or Plexiglas toys. You may want to

Your parrot won't know the difference between your jewelry and acceptable chew toys. It's up to you to provide your pet with appropriate things to chew on. (PHOTO BY JULIE RACH MANCINI)

save some of your bird's favorite kinds of chew toys to use as a distraction when she seems determined to chew on anything she can get her beak on.

Although it may seem incredibly simple, you can control a parrot's chewing tendencies by limiting her access to chewables in the home. In addition to stringent housekeeping, you will need to supervise your bird when she's out of her cage. If your bird can't get her beak on your antiques, your answering machine, or your prized houseplants, she can't chew on any of these items.

Screaming

Screaming is another behavior that makes perfect sense to a parrot but may cause an owner to wonder why he or she didn't adopt a nice quiet hamster instead of a bird.

All parrots will make noise during the day. They often greet the dawn and say goodnight to the sun by being especially vocal early in the morning or late in the day. This is normal psittacine behavior that can be curbed somewhat but not completely eliminated.

Sometimes parrots are just a little lonesome and in need of reassurance, so they scream to see where their people are. In these cases, simply call back to your bird, "I'm here. Are you okay?" or another reassuring phrase. In many cases, the bird will quiet down quickly after hearing your voice.

In other cases, a bird screams because she feels isolated from her family. My own bird demonstrated this conduct. I put her cage on the far side of the living room, thinking that she would benefit from the sunshine and the view afforded by the patio door on that side of the room. However, she screamed almost every night around suppertime. I thought she was saying good night to the sun, that she was hungry or tired, and I really didn't think much more about it.

An infestation of ants made it necessary to move her cage away from the patio door and about 10 feet closer to the dining room and kitchen area in my town house. I sprayed the area with Camicide, and I moved her cage to make spraying safer for her and easier for me.

Originally, I had planned to make the move temporary, but she was so much quieter and seemed so much more content in the new location that I left her alone. I believe she felt she was too far away from the center of activity (the dining room table that sat in the middle of a large open living room/dining area/kitchen) and was letting me know that by screaming.

At other times, birds may scream because something in the environment frightens them. In these cases, you will have to work with your bird over time to desensitize her to whatever she finds scary. If your bird screams at you when you wear a hat, for example, set the hat on a table far away from the bird's cage and gradually (over a period of a few days or a week), bring the hat closer to your bird's cage. Tell your bird how brave she is as the hat gets closer to the cage, and cuddle and pet her to further reward her bravery.

Still other birds scream because they think they have to "protect" their home and families. This type of vocalizing clearly hearkens back to the wild, where parrots alert each other to danger in the area by screaming or calling to one another. In these cases, before disciplining your helpful watch-parrot, it's a good idea to check to see that your toaster isn't smoking or there isn't a crow perched on the balcony railing.

Screaming—a normal parrot behavior—can easily get out of control. (PHOTO BY JULIE RACH MANCINI)

Other birds will scream when they are tired. In these cases, covering the cage for a few minutes will invariably have a soothing effect. If your bird seems to be consistently tired and cranky, you may have to adjust her bedtime. Remember that birds need about twelve hours of sleep a night. If your bird is in the living room with you as you watch television or as your children do homework under a bright desk lamp, her natural sleep rhythms may be disturbed. You may ease the situation by providing a heavier cage cover or by relocating the bird to another part of the house. But remember—don't banish your bird to some far-flung, seldom-used part of your house, because feelings of neglect or isolation can also cause screaming.

Some screaming birds learn how to scream from other parrots in the home. If you have one screaming bird in your flock, don't be surprised if other birds adopt the behavior, especially if you reward the screaming bird by making large outbursts of emotion whenever she screams. Birds love this stuff and will do whatever they can to receive more of this kind of attention!

If your bird likes to scream, you may be able to train her to whistle or say "hello" instead of screaming. To do so, in response to the screaming you'll have to whistle or say whatever you want the bird to say. Reward your parrot with attention when she whistles back or repeats the phrase you're trying to teach her, and ignore her when she screams in response to you. Your bird should quickly catch on to what you want her to do, and you'll have resolved the screaming problem.

Once again, the fundamentals of good care will help to prevent or alleviate problem screaming. Give your bird consistent attention (at least two hours a day); allow her ample opportunities to exercise outside of her cage by flapping or climbing; provide her with an interesting environment, complete with a variety of toys and a well-balanced diet; and leave a radio or television on when you're away to provide background noise. If you treat your bird right, she shouldn't become a screamer.

Other Problem Behaviors

Feather picking, self-mutilation, egg laying, and dominance are all behaviors that cause problems for parrots and their owners. As I've said in other parts of the book, many things can cause a bird to pull her feathers or mutilate herself, including illness, boredom, stress, and the desire to breed. The desire to breed may also cause a female bird to lay eggs, and some species may be prone to laying a large number of eggs during breeding season. I have heard reports of cockatiels who lay more than twenty eggs in a single season.

Some owners have inadvertently encouraged their birds to be dominant because the birds have unlimited access to their owners' shoulders or to high places in the home, or they live in large, tall cages that allow them to frequently have their heads higher than their owners' heads.

When setting up their birds' homes, owners need to remember that height is power in the parrot world. If your bird's cage allows her to be taller than most family members when she is atop the cage, you may want to lower the cage height slightly or provide steps or other means for shorter family members to gain height when dealing with your bird. Make sure to hold and carry your parrot at mid-chest height to allow you some control over your parrot and her behavior.

Patience Is a Must

Although you want to solve your bird's behavior problems promptly, don't settle for quick-fix solutions, such as putting the bird in a dark closet or spraying her in the face with water. Remember that birds don't think in cause-and-effect terms, so they won't understand why you are punishing them. Such quick fixes will actually do more damage to the long-term relationship you have with your pet, which could lead to even more behavior problems in the future. You can't resolve your bird's problem behaviors without taking the time to learn the cause(s).

Moreover, your bird's misbehavior probably didn't start overnight, so why should you expect an instant solution to the problem? It would be nice if things worked that way, but unfortunately they don't.

Consult Professionals

If the solutions suggested in this chapter don't help you resolve your bird's behavior problems, it's time to seek expert help. Your avian veterinarian can evaluate your bird's behavior to see if there's a physical cause behind it, and he or she can recommend bird behaviorists who may be able to help you have a better-behaved pet.

An avian behaviorist will consult with you in person and over the telephone to determine the cause of your parrot's behavior problems. He or she may be able to quickly identify some triggers for your bird's behaviors, or the problem may take several consultations before the behaviorist begins to see a pattern of behavior.

The behaviorist may come to your home to consult with you about the location of your pet's cage and her daily routine, or you may meet with the behaviorist in an office as you meet with your avian veterinarian. Avian behaviorists have put a lot of time and energy into studying bird behavior, so they can be valuable resources as you work toward solving behavior problems in your pet.

Drug Therapy

In extreme cases of psittacine behavior problems that cannot be resolved through behavior modification, an avian veterinarian may prescribe psychotropic (mood-altering) drugs. These drugs have successfully treated some cases of feather picking or self-mutilation.

If your avian veterinarian recommends drug therapy for your parrot, you must still continue with behavior modification methods, such as offering toys, playing with your bird, or varying her diet. In addition to the behavior modification, you will need to watch your parrot closely to see if the drugs help stop her behavior problems. You must also watch for side effects because these drugs can cause liver and kidney problems in pet birds.

Drug therapy is not a step that should be taken lightly or quickly. Discuss drug therapy options fully with your avian veterinarian. The two of you know the status of your bird's health and which options you have explored regarding behavioral modification. Together, you can make the best decision for your pet.

chapter 11

WILL MY BIRD TALK?

A talking bird—what could be more remarkable than that? Imagine the looks on the faces of your family and friends as your bird says clever things on cue. You will be the envy of all your pet-owning friends, won't you?

I'm sure the appeal of a talking bird was one of the reasons my parents bought my childhood pet, a parakeet named Charlie. My mother talked to him daily. She spoke to him in a bright, happy voice as she changed his cage paper and she talked to him throughout the day as she did chores around the house. She was a patient teacher, sticking to a simple phrase to start with in the hopes Charlie would talk back.

Later in this chapter we'll see how Charlie's speech lessons turned out, but I must begin this chapter with a warning: Most bird owners should not expect their birds to talk. Birds who talk are unusual, and birds who willingly perform in front of strangers are rare birds, indeed. If you are lucky enough to have a bird like this, you are truly a special bird owner.

Remarkable Talkers

A bird's ability to talk has been one of the most appealing aspects of pet bird ownership since the days of the ancient Romans. A description of parrots written by the Greek historian and physician Ctesias tells of the talking ability of a parrot he called Bittacus, whom experts now believe was a plum-headed parakeet. This bird could speak both Greek and an Indian language.

Some species are more prone to talking than others. African greys, Amazons, budgerigars, and mynahs are considered among the best talking birds, but none of them is guaranteed to talk. With persistence and patience on the owner's part,

You will be more successful in training a bird to talk if you keep a single pet. Birds kept in groups are more likely to bond with one another and to speak "birdese" rather than bond with humans and learn to speak our language. (PHOTO BY GARY A. GALLERSTEIN, DVM)

a bird from a species not noted for talking may learn a few words or even a few phrases.

Three parrots have amassed particularly noteworthy vocabularies. Puck, a budgie in northern California, holds the Guinness World Record for the largest vocabulary of an animal. Puck's owner estimates that her bird has a 1,728-word vocabulary! Another parrot, an African grey named Prudle, reportedly had a 1,000-word vocabulary when he retired from public life in 1977.

Sparkie, a budgie who lived in Great Britain from 1954 to 1962, held the record for a talking bird in his time. He won the BBC's Cage Word Contest in 1958 by reciting eight four-line nursery rhymes without stopping. At the time of his death, Sparkie had a vocabulary of 531 words and 383 sentences.

Sometimes, a parrot will surprise you with his ability to say just the right thing at just the right time. While watching a movie one night, my bird surprised me by saying "Good-bye!" in a rather loud voice as one of the characters in the film exited a scene. Another parrot I know yells "Night-night!" to get slow-moving dinner guests out the door so that he can go to bed.

The tips offered here will help you teach your pet bird to talk, but please don't be disappointed if your pet never utters a word.

You may notice that your parrot is more vocal early in the morning or at dusk. Your bird may be more receptive to speech lessons at these times of day.

Remember that language, whether bird or human, helps members of a species or group communicate. Most baby birds learn the language of their parents because it helps them communicate within their family and their flock. A pet bird raised with people may learn to imitate the sounds he hears his human family make, but if you have more than one bird, the birds may find communicating with each other easier and seemingly more enjoyable than trying to learn your language.

Although most birds raised around humans do learn to talk, some choose to make other sounds. Calvin, a physically challenged budgerigar I used to bird-sit, had ample opportunity to learn human speech from his owner and other people who saw him regularly in her office. Instead of speaking English, though, Calvin chose to imitate the computer printer, modem, and other machines found in his owner's office!

Tips for Talking Success

Teaching a bird to talk is a process that involves regular effort on your part with little obvious reward, at least at first. Once you hear your bird repeat something you've taught him, you'll begin to reap the rewards of your work. Here are some tips to keep in mind as you begin the training process.

As mentioned above, you will be more successful in training a bird to talk if you keep a single pet rather than a pair or group. By the same token, don't give your bird toys with mirrors on them if you want the bird to learn to talk, since

Mirrored toys may make a bird less likely to talk because your pet may try to bond with the handsome bird he sees in the mirror. (PHOTO BY JULIE RACH MANCINI)

If you want to teach your bird to talk, start with one phrase and make sure that you have the bird's attention. Train your bird in a quiet place, speak positively, and keep the training sessions short. (PHOTO BY PAMELA L. HIGDON)

your bird will think that the bird in the mirror is a potential cagemate with whom he can bond.

It is best to start speech training with a young bird because younger birds are more likely to want to mimic human speech. It is also best to start with one phrase. Keep it short and simple, such as the bird's name. Say the phrase slowly so that the bird learns it clearly. Some people teach their birds to talk by rattling off words and phrases quickly, only to be disappointed when the bird repeats them in a blurred jumble that cannot be understood.

Be sure to say the chosen phrase with emphasis and enthusiasm. Birds like a "drama reward" and seem to learn words that are said emphatically—which may be why some of them pick up bad language so quickly! Make sure to watch your language around your bird, or you may be surprised to find out that he learns words you had no intention of teaching him.

Try to have phrases make sense. For example, say "Good morning" or "Hello" when you uncover the bird's cage each day. Say "Good-bye" when you leave the room, or ask "Want a treat?" when you offer your pet his meals. Phrases that make sense are also more likely to be used by you and other members of your family when conversing with your bird. The more your bird hears an interesting word or phrase, the more likely he is to say that phrase someday.

Don't change the phrase. If you're teaching your bird to say "Hello," for example, don't say "Hello" one day, then "Hi" the next, followed by "Hi, Petey!" (or whatever your bird's name is) another day.

Keep training sessions short. Most bird behavior experts seem to recommend 10- to 15-minute sessions.

Train your bird in a quiet area. Think of how distracting it is when someone is trying to talk to you with a radio or television blaring in the background. It's hard to hear what the other person is saying under those conditions, isn't it? Your bird won't be able to hear you any better or understand what you are trying to accomplish if you try to train him in the midst of noisy distractions. Be sure to keep your bird involved in your family's routine, though, because isolating him completely won't help him feel comfortable and part of the family. Remember that a bird needs to feel comfortable in his environment before he will draw attention to himself by talking.

Be patient with your pet. Stop the sessions if you find that you are getting frustrated. Your bird will sense that something is bothering you and will react by becoming bothered itself. This is not an ideal teaching and learning environment. Try to keep your mood upbeat. Smile a lot and praise your pet when he does well.

Graduate to more difficult phrases as your bird masters simple words and phrases. Consider keeping a log of the words your bird knows. This is especially helpful if more than one person will be teaching your pet to talk.

When you aren't talking to your pet, try listening to him. On occasion, birds mumble to themselves to practice talking as they drift off to sleep. Because some birds have very small voices, you'll have to listen carefully to see if your pet is making progress.

You may be curious about the efficacy of the talking tapes and compact discs sold in pet stores and through advertisements in bird magazines. Some birds do learn from the repetition of the tapes and CDs that, fortunately, have gotten livelier and more interesting to listen to in recent years. Other birds benefit from having their owners make tapes of the phrases the bird is currently learning and hearing those tapes play when their owners aren't around. I would not recommend playing taped phrases for your bird during the day. The repetition is likely to bore your bird, and if he's bored, the bird will be more likely to tune out the tape—and tune out the training in the process.

No Guarantees for Talking

If your consistent, patient training seems to result in no progress, you may have to accept the fact that your bird isn't going to talk. We finally had to do so with my childhood bird, Charlie. Despite my mother's most patient attempts to teach him to say "Pretty bird," he never learned to talk. My mother did things by the

TALKING PROBLEMS AT A GLANCE

Why does my bird refuse to talk?

- The bird has yet to learn to talk.

- The bird is receiving too much information—too many people are trying to teach the bird to talk or too many phrases are being taught at the same time.

- The bird doesn't feel well physically.

- Something in the bird's environment is causing him to feel uncomfortable.

How can I get my bird to talk?

- Keep training sessions short.

- Start with one phrase and stick to it.

- Be positive and upbeat in the training sessions.

- Be patient.

book, too. Charlie was a budgie, which meant that he was more likely to talk than other psittacine species. My mother spoke in a bright, cheerful voice; she kept the training sessions short; she kept a positive attitude and tone when talking to the bird; and she displayed patience that rivaled Job's, but Charlie remained silent. Perhaps he was too old, perhaps he was too isolated, or perhaps he just wasn't interested in the phrase.

As I've said before, don't be too disappointed if your pet doesn't learn to talk. As one *Bird Talk* reader stated, "Talking should be the icing on the cake," rather than the primary reason for owning a bird. If your pet never learns to talk, continue to love him for the unique creature that he is rather than wishing for what you want him to be.

chapter 12

BEHAVIORS EVERY BIRD OWNER SHOULD KNOW

Bird keeping isn't particularly difficult to do. In fact, if you do only ten things for your bird for as long as you own her, your bird should have a healthy, well-adjusted life.

Ten Steps to Better Bird Care

1. Provide a safe, secure cage that is appropriate for your bird's size in a secure yet active location in your home. Clean the cage regularly to protect your pet from illness and to make her surroundings more enjoyable for both of you.

2. Clip your bird's wings regularly to ensure her safety. Bird-proof your home and practice bird safety by closing windows and doors securely before you let your bird out of her cage, keeping your bird indoors when she isn't caged, and ensuring that your pet doesn't chew on anything harmful or become poisoned by toxic fumes from overheated nonstick cookware, cleaning products, and other household products.

3. Offer your pet a varied diet that includes pellets (if your pet is a parrot, canary, or finch), nectar (if she's a softbill), fresh vegetables and fruits cut into appropriate-sized portions, and healthy people food. Provide the freshest food possible, and remove partially eaten or discarded food from the cage before it has a chance to spoil. Your bird should also have access to clean, fresh drinking water at all times.

Setting up your bird's cage in your living room or family room will help her feel as if she's part of your family. (PHOTO BY JULIE RACH MANCINI)

4. Establish a good working relationship with a qualified avian veterinarian early on in your bird ownership (preferably on your way home from the pet store or breeder). Don't wait for an emergency to locate a veterinarian.

5. Take your pet to the veterinarian for regular checkups, as well as when you notice a change in her routine. Illnesses in birds are often difficult to detect before it's too late to save the bird, so preventive care is a must.

6. Set and maintain a routine for your bird. Make sure that your bird is fed at about the same time each day, that her playtime out of her cage occurs regularly, and that her bedtime is well established.

7. Provide an interesting environment for your bird. Make her feel that she's part of your family. Entertain and challenge your bird's curiosity with a variety of safe toys. Rotate these toys in and out of your bird's cage regularly,

and discard any that become soiled, broken, frayed, worn, or otherwise unsafe.

8. Leave a radio or television on for your bird when you are away from home. A too-quiet environment can be stressful for many birds, and stress can cause illness or other problems for your pet.

9. Provide consistent discipline for your bird. Your bird is not a cause-and-effect thinker, so she won't understand being punished for misbehaving. She also won't understand if you discipline her some of the time by putting her in her cage for a time-out, while not disciplining her at other times. Consistent discipline is one of the easiest ways to prevent behavior problems in your pet bird, so be sure you're sending a clear, consistent message whenever you correct your bird's behavior.

10. Pay attention to your pet on a consistent basis. Don't lavish abundant attention on the bird when you first bring her home and then gradually lose interest in her. Birds are sensitive, intelligent creatures who do not understand such a mixed message. Set aside a portion of each day to pay attention to your bird—you'll both enjoy it, and your relationship will benefit from it. Besides, wasn't companionship one of the things you were looking for when you picked a bird as a pet?

A varied diet featuring fresh fruits and vegetables can help maintain your pet bird's health. (PHOTO BY JULIE RACH MANCINI)

Change the toys in your bird's cage regularly to keep your pet's environment interesting. (PHOTO BY JULIE RACH MANCINI)

A Daily Care Routine

Along with daily attention from and interaction with you, her owner, your bird requires a certain level of care each day to ensure her health and well-being. Here are some of the things you'll need to do each day for your pet:

- Observe your bird for any changes in routine, and report any changes to your avian veterinarian immediately.

- Offer fresh food and water and remove old food and water bowls. Wash dishes thoroughly with detergent and water. Rinse completely and allow to dry.

- Provide fresh paper in the cage tray.

- Cover your bird's cage at about the same time every night to indicate bedtime. All pet birds seem to enjoy a familiar routine. When you cover the cage, you'll probably hear your bird rustle around for a bit, perhaps getting a drink of water or a last mouthful of food before settling in for the night. Keep in mind that your pet will require eight to ten hours of sleep a day, but you can expect that she will take naps during the day to supplement her nightly snooze.

- Check your pet's droppings. Although it may seem a bit unpleasant to discuss, your bird's droppings require daily monitoring because they can tell you a lot about her general health. Budgies produce small, flat droppings that appear white in the center with a dark green edge, while larger parrots produce tubular droppings. These droppings are usually composed of equal amounts of fecal material (the green edge), urine (the clear liquid portion), and urates (the white or cream-colored center). Softbills produce more liquid droppings that are consistent with their fruit-based diets.

  Texture and consistency, along with frequency or lack of droppings, can let you know how your pet is feeling. For example, if a parrot eats a lot of fruits and vegetables, her droppings are generally looser and more watery than those of a bird who eats primarily a pelleted diet. But watery droppings can also indicate illness, such as diabetes or kidney problems, that cause a bird to drink more water than usual.

The color of droppings can also give an indication of health. Birds who have psittacosis typically have bright, lime-green droppings, while healthy birds have avocado or darker green and white droppings. Birds with liver problems may produce droppings that are yellowish or reddish, while birds who have internal bleeding produce dark, tarry droppings. Be aware, however, that a color change doesn't necessarily indicate poor health. For example, parrots who have splurged on a certain fresh food soon have droppings with that food's characteristic color. Birds who overindulge on beets produce bright red droppings that can look for all the world as though the bird has suffered some serious internal injury. Birds who eat a large quantity of sweet potatoes, blueberries, or raspberries produce orange, blue, or red droppings, respectively. During pomegranate season, birds who enjoy this fruit develop violet droppings that can look alarming to an unprepared owner.

As part of your daily cage cleaning and observation of your feathered friend, look at her droppings carefully. Learn what is normal for your bird in terms of color, consistency, and frequency, and report any changes to your avian veterinarian promptly.

Weekly Tasks

Your weekly bird-related chores will include the following:

- Remove old food from cage bars and from the corners of the cage where it invariably falls.

- Remove, scrape, and replace the perches to keep them clean and free of debris. (You might also want to sand them lightly with coarse-grained sandpaper to clean them further and improve perch traction for your pet.)

- Rotate toys in your bird's cage to keep them interesting. Discard any toys that show excessive signs of wear, such as frayed rope, cracked plastic, or well-chewed wood.

- Clean the bird's cage thoroughly. You can simplify the process by placing the cage in the shower and letting hot water from the showerhead do some of the work. Be sure to remove your bird, her food and water dishes, her toys, and the cage tray paper before putting the cage into the shower. Let the hot water run over the cage for five to ten minutes, and then scrub at any stuck-on food with an old toothbrush or some fine-grade steel wool. After you've removed

Scrubbing your bird's cage with a kitchen sponge that has a pot-scrubbing abrasive side can help remove stuck-on food. Keep the cage-cleaning sponge separate from your other sponges and use it solely for this purpose. (PHOTO BY JULIE RACH MANCINI)

This is how your cage's tray should look after it has been cleaned. Don't allow stuck-on food or other debris to remain in the cage or on the cage tray after your weekly cleaning. (PHOTO BY JULIE RACH MANCINI)

the food and other debris, disinfect the cage with a spray-on disinfectant, which you can purchase at your pet store. Make sure to choose a bird-safe product, and read the instructions fully before use.

Rinse the cage thoroughly and dry it completely before returning your bird and her accessories to the cage. (If you have wooden perches in the cage, you can dry them more quickly by placing the wet dowels in a 400°F oven for 10 minutes. Let the perches cool before you put them back in the cage.)

Weather-Related Concerns

Warm weather requires a little extra vigilance on your part to ensure that your pet remains comfortable. To help your pet stay cool, keep her out of direct sun, offer her lots of fresh, juicy vegetables and fruits (be sure to remove these fresh foods from the cage promptly to prevent your bird from eating spoiled food), and mist her lightly with warm water from a clean spray bottle that is used solely for birdy showers. Offer showers frequently, and be sure that your pet has adequate time to dry off completely before bedtime. (There's more on grooming your bird in the next section.)

Warm weather may also bring out a host of insect pests to bedevil you and your bird. Depending on where you live, you may see ants, mosquitoes, or other bugs around your bird's cage as the temperature rises. Take care to keep the cage scrupulously clean to discourage pests, and remove fresh foods promptly to keep insects out of your bird's food bowl. Finally, in cases of severe infestation, you may have to use Camicide or other bird-safe insecticides to reduce the insect population. (Remove your bird from the area of infestation before spraying.) If the problem becomes severe enough to require professional exterminators, make arrangements to have your bird out of the house for at least 24 hours after spraying has taken place.

You'll also need to pay attention to your bird's needs when the weather turns cooler. You may want to use a heavier cage cover, especially if you lower the heat in your home at bedtime, or you may want to move the bird's cage to another location in your home that is warmer and less drafty.

At least once a year, your bird will lose her feathers. Don't be alarmed; this is a normal process known as molting. Typically, a bird will molt annually, but many pet birds seem to be in a perpetual molt, with feathers falling out and coming in throughout the summer.

You can consider your bird in molting season when you see a lot of whole feathers in the bottom of the cage and you notice that your bird seems to have broken out in a rash of stubbly little aglets (those plastic tips on the ends of your shoelaces). These are the feather sheaths that help new pinfeathers break through the skin, and they are made of keratin (as are our fingernails). The sheaths also help protect growing feathers from damage until the feather completes its growth cycle.

You may notice that your bird is a little more irritable during the molt; this is to be expected. Think about how you would feel if you had all these itchy new feathers coming in all of a sudden. However, your bird may actively seek out more time with you during the molt because owners are handy to have around when a bird has an itch on the top of her head that she can't quite scratch! (Scratch these new feathers gently because some of them may still be growing in and may be sensitive to the touch.) Some birds may benefit from special conditioning foods during the molt; check with your avian veterinarian to see if your bird is a candidate for a special molt diet.

Good Grooming

Your bird has several grooming needs. First, she must be able to bathe regularly. She will also need to have her nails and flight feathers trimmed periodically to ensure her safety.

Bathing Your Bird

You can bathe your bird in a variety of ways. You can mist her lightly with warm water from a clean spray bottle, as mentioned earlier, or you can allow her to bathe in the kitchen or bathroom sink under a slow stream of water. Many smaller birds prefer to bathe in their cages, either in a small, flat saucer of warm water, a plastic bathtub, or an enclosed birdbath that you can purchase at your local pet store. Some birds will roll in damp fresh greens in their food bowls, while others want to jump right in the shower with their owners! Bathing is important to birds to help them keep their feathers clean and healthy, so don't deny your pet the chance to bathe.

Bathing is a regular part of your bird's routine in the wild. Some parrots enjoy taking a dip under the bathroom faucet. (PHOTO BY JULIE RACH MANCINI)

AVOID MITE PROTECTORS

In pet product catalogs or in your pet store, you may see mite protectors that hang on a bird's cage. Well-cared-for pet birds don't have mites and shouldn't be in danger of contracting them. The fumes from some of these products are quite strong and can be harmful to your bird's health. If your pet does have mites, veterinary care is the most effective treatment method.

Unless your bird has gotten herself into oil, paint, wax, or some other substance that elbow grease alone won't remove and that could harm her feathers, she will not require soap as part of her bath. Under routine conditions, soaps and detergents can damage a bird's feathers by removing beneficial oils, so don't use shampoo during your bird's normal cleanup routine.

Let your bird bathe early in the day so she has an opportunity for her feathers dry completely before bedtime. In cooler weather, you may want help the process along by drying your pet off with a blow dryer to prevent her from becoming chilled after her bath. To do so, set the blow dryer on low and keep it moving so that your bird doesn't become overheated. Your bird may soon learn that drying off is the most enjoyable part of her bath!

Conditioners, anti-picking products, and other substances that are applied to your bird's feathers will serve only to encourage your bird to overpreen. Birds do not care to have these products on them and will respond by preening themselves so thoroughly that they might even remove all of their feathers in a particular area. If you want to encourage your bird to preen regularly and help condition her feathers, simply mist the bird regularly with clean, warm water or hold her under a gentle stream from a kitchen or bathroom faucet. Your bird will take care of the rest.

Trimming Your Bird's Nails

Trimming your bird's nails is a fairly simple procedure. Parrots need their nails clipped occasionally to prevent the nails from catching on toys or perches. Some parrots have light-colored nails, which makes it easier for owners to see where the nail stops and the blood and nerve supply (or quick) begins. In these birds, the quick is generally seen as a pink color inside the nail. If your pet has dark nails, you will need to trim them carefully to keep from cutting them to the quick. An alternative is to file dark nails. You will have to experiment with your pet's likes and dislikes in this area. Some birds don't mind having their nails clipped, but they hate to have them filed. Others are better suited to the file than the

Nail clipping is an important part of parrot grooming. To clip a parrot's nails, recruit an assistant who knows how to restrain the bird properly.
(PHOTO BY GARY A. GALLERSTEIN, DVM)

clippers, and still others probably wish that their owners would forget the whole nail-trimming idea!

If your pet is reluctant to have her nails done, you may be able to provide her with a concrete or terra-cotta perch in her cage that will gently file her nails. If you do provide one of these perches for your bird, be sure to watch closely for signs of lameness and remove the abrasive perches if you see that your bird's feet are sore or that she seems to be favoring one foot.

To keep your pet's nails trimmed, you need to remove only tiny portions of the nail. Generally, a good guideline to follow is to remove only the hook on each nail, and to do so in the smallest increments possible. Stop well before you reach the quick. If you do happen to cut the nail short enough to make it bleed, apply cornstarch or flour, followed by direct pressure, to stop the bleeding.

Trimming Your Bird's Wing Feathers

The goal of a proper wing trim is to prevent your parrot from flying away or flying into a window, mirror, or wall while she's out of her cage. An added benefit of trimming your pet's wings is that her inability to fly well will make her more dependent on you for transportation, which should make her more handleable. However, a bird still needs enough wing feathers so she can glide safely to the ground if she is startled and takes flight from her cagetop or play gym.

Wing trims are not usually recommended for finches, softbills, and canaries because these pets are usually confined to aviaries, flights, or cages. Moreover, the stress of catching these birds for wing trimming generally outweighs the value of the wing trim.

The first time you trim your parrot's wings, you may want to enlist the help of your avian veterinarian to ensure that you do a good job. Wing trimming is a task that must be performed carefully to avoid injuring your pet, so take your time if you're doing it yourself. Please *do not* just take up the largest pair of kitchen shears you own and start snipping away. I have had avian veterinarians tell me about parrots whose owners cut off their birds' wing tips (down to the bone) in this manner.

The first step in wing feather trimming is to assemble all the things you need ahead of time and find a quiet, well-lit place to groom your pet. Your grooming tools include:

- A well-worn towel in which to wrap your bird

- Small, sharp scissors to do the trimming

- Needle-nosed pliers (to pull any blood feathers you may cut accidentally)

- Flour or cornstarch to act as styptic powder in case a blood feather is cut

- Nail trimmers (while you have your bird in the towel, you might as well do her nails, too)

Most parrots also require an assistant trimmer to hold the bird while the trimmer clips the wing feathers.

I encourage you to groom your pet in a quiet, well-lit place because grooming excites some birds and causes them to become wiggly. Good light to work under will make your job easier, and a quiet work area may calm your pet and make her a bit more handleable.

Once you've assembled your supplies, drape the towel over your hand and catch your parrot with your toweled hand. Grab your bird by the back of her head and neck and wrap her in the towel. Give her to your assistant and have her hold

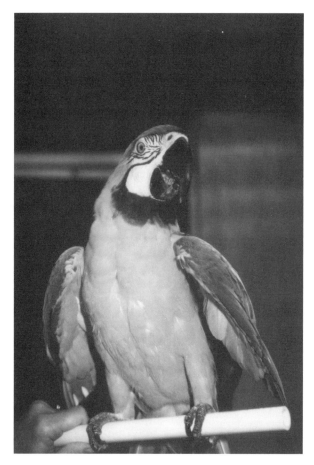

This macaw is testing her balance following a wing trim. Owners need to monitor the growth of their birds' wing feathers regularly to be aware of when it's time for another trimming. Fully feathered birds are more likely to escape than their clipped counterparts. (PHOTO BY GARY A. GALLERSTEIN, DVM)

your bird's head securely with her thumb and index finger. (Having the bird's head covered by the towel will calm her and will give her something to chew on while you clip her wings.)

Lay the bird on her back, being careful not to constrict or compress her chest (remember, birds have no diaphragms to help them breathe), and spread her wing out carefully to look for new feathers that are still growing in, which are also called blood feathers. You can identify these feathers by their waxy, tight look (new feathers in their feather sheaths resemble the end of a shoelace) and their dark centers, or quills, which are caused by the blood supply to the new feather.

If your bird has a number of blood feathers, you may want to put off trimming her wings for a few days because older, fully grown feathers act as a cushion to protect those just coming in. If your bird has only one or two blood feathers, you can trim the rest accordingly.

To trim your bird's feathers, separate each one away from the other flight feathers and cut it individually. (Remember, the goal is to have a well-trimmed bird who's still able to glide a bit if she needs to.) Use the primary coverts (the set of feathers above the primary flight feathers on your bird's wing) as a guideline as to how short you can trim.

Cut the first five to eight flight feathers starting from the tip of the wing, and be sure to trim an equal number of feathers from each wing. Chunky birds such as African greys need to have only about five feathers trimmed, while cockatiels and other sleek parrots need to have about eight flight feathers trimmed. Although some people think that a bird needs only one trimmed wing, this is incorrect. A bird who tries to fly with one trimmed wing and one untrimmed wing may injure herself. It is far better to trim both wings equally.

Now that you've successfully trimmed your bird's wing feathers, congratulate yourself. You've just taken a great step toward keeping your bird safe. But don't rest on your laurels just yet; you must remember to check your bird's wing feathers monthly and retrim them periodically (about four times a year at a minimum).

IF A BLOOD FEATHER IS CUT

If you do happen to cut a blood feather, remain calm. You must remove it and stop the bleeding to ensure that your bird doesn't bleed to death, and panicking will do neither you nor your bird much good.

To remove a blood feather, use a pair of needle-nosed pliers to grasp the broken feather's shaft as close to the skin of your bird's wing as you can. With one steady motion, pull the feather out completely. After you've removed the feather, put a pinch of flour or cornstarch on the feather follicle (the spot from which you pulled the feather) and apply direct pressure for a few minutes until the bleeding stops. If the bleeding doesn't stop after a few minutes of direct pressure, or if you can't remove the feather shaft, contact your avian veterinarian for further instructions.

Although it may seem like you're hurting your parrot by removing the broken blood feather, consider this: A broken blood feather is like an open faucet. If left in, the faucet stays open and lets the blood out. Once removed, the bird's skin generally closes behind the feather shaft and shuts off the faucet. While some birds may squawk or indicate pain when a feather shaft is removed, removing a blood feather shaft is not a particularly painful procedure for your bird.

Be particularly alert after a molt because your bird will have a whole new crop of flight feathers that need attention. You'll be able to tell when your pet is due for a trim when she starts becoming bolder in her flying attempts. Right after a wing trim, a parrot generally tries to fly and finds that the attempt is unsuccessful. She will keep trying, though, and may surprise you one day with a fairly good glide across her cage or off her play gym. If this happens, get the scissors and trim those wings immediately.

Although some people contend that a bird's beak also needs trimming, I would argue that a healthy bird who has enough chew toys seems to do a remarkable job of keeping her beak trimmed. If, however, your bird's beak becomes overgrown, please consult your avian veterinarian. A parrot's beak contains a surprising number of blood vessels, so beak trimming is best left to the experts. Also, a suddenly overgrown beak may indicate that your bird is suffering from liver damage, a virus, or scaly mites, all of which require veterinary care.

What's on the Menu?

The importance of a varied diet cannot be overstressed. Despite some people's long-held ideas, parrots can't prosper on a diet of seeds and water. Think how dull and unhealthy a monotonous diet would be for you. It isn't any more interesting or any healthier for your parrot.

An improper diet causes a number of health problems (respiratory infections, poor feather condition, flaky skin, and reproductive problems, to name a few) and is one of the main reasons some parrots live fairly short lives. Poor diets have also been implicated as causes for some behavior problems in pet birds that have cleared up when the birds were fed well-balanced, healthier diets.

Here's what the Association of Avian Veterinarians recommends as a healthy parrot diet:

- Fifty percent pellets, grain, and legumes
- Forty-five percent dark green or dark orange vegetables and fruits
- Five percent meat (well cooked, please), eggs (also well cooked), or dairy products

This diet should also serve the needs of finches and canaries well, although finch owners may need to add live food, such as insects, to the menu during breeding season.

The pellets, grain, and legumes portion of your parrot's diet can include items in the bread category such as unsweetened breakfast cereals, whole-wheat bread, cooked beans, cooked rice, and pasta.

Dark green or dark orange vegetables and fruits contain vitamin A, which is an important part of a bird's diet and is missing from the grains and legumes

Seed-only diets can contribute to behavioral problems, including screaming, feather picking, and biting. (PHOTO BY JULIE RACH MANCINI)

group. This vitamin helps fight off infection and keeps a bird's eyes, mouth, and respiratory system healthy. Some foods rich in vitamin A are carrots, yams, sweet potatoes, broccoli, dried red peppers, dandelion greens, and spinach.

If you've adopted an older bird who eats primarily seeds, try offering your pet some of the fruits and vegetables that are popular with many parrots, such as peeled and seeded apple slices, sliced-open grapes (you can leave grape seeds in), and corn on the cob. Although these fruits and vegetables are not as rich in important vitamins as their dark green or dark orange counterparts, they can help bridge the gap between seeds and a more varied diet for fussy eaters. To ease the stress of relocating to your home, start by feeding your parrot a diet similar to the one she ate in her previous home. Introduce new foods gradually.

You may be wondering whether to offer frozen or canned vegetables and fruits to your bird. Some birds will eat frozen vegetables and fruits, while others

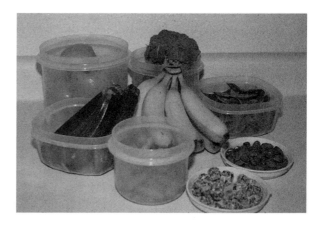

Offering your pet bird a varied diet is a good way to maintain her health, which in turn can have a positive effect on her behavior. (PHOTO BY JULIE RACH MANCINI)

turn their beaks up at the somewhat mushy texture of these foods. The high sodium content in some canned foods may make them unhealthy for your pet. Frozen and canned foods will serve your bird's needs in an emergency, but offer only fresh foods on a regular basis.

Along with small portions of the well-cooked meat mentioned earlier, you can also offer your pet bits of tofu, water-packed tuna, fully scrambled eggs, cottage cheese, unsweetened yogurt, or low-fat cheese. Note, however, that a bird's digestive system lacks the enzyme lactase, which results in an inability to fully process dairy foods. Accordingly, it's best to feed dairy products in relatively small quantities.

Whatever healthy fresh foods you offer your parrot, be sure to remove food from the cage promptly to prevent spoilage, discourage bugs, and help keep your bird healthy. Ideally, you should change the food in your bird's cage every two to four hours (or as frequently as every thirty minutes in warm weather). Your bird should have a tray of food to pick through in the morning, another to select from during the afternoon, and a third fresh salad to nibble on for dinner.

Formulated Diets

Supplement your bird's fresh foods with a pelleted diet. Pelleted diets are created by mixing a variety of healthful ingredients into a mash and then forcing (or extruding) the hot mixture through a machine to form various shapes. Some pelleted foods have colors and flavors added, while others are fairly plain. These formulated diets provide more balanced nutrition for your pet bird in an easy-to-serve form that reduces the amount of wasted food. They also eliminate the chance for a bird to pick through a smorgasbord of healthy foods to find her favorites and reject the foods of which she isn't particularly fond. Some birds accept pelleted diets quickly, while others require some persuading.

If you want to convert your pet to a pelleted diet, offer her pellets mixed in with her current diet or as a side dish. (Make sure the bird recognizes that pellets are food before proceeding.) Once you see that your bird is eating the pellets, begin to gradually increase the amount of pellets you offer at mealtime while decreasing the amount of other food you serve. Within a couple of weeks, your bird should be eating her pellets with gusto.

If your parrot seems a bit finicky about trying pellets, you may have to act as if you are enjoying the pellets as a snack in front of your pet. Really play up your apparent enjoyment of this new food because it will pique your pet's curiosity and make the pellets seem exceedingly interesting.

Whatever you do, don't starve your bird into trying a new food. Offer a variety of new foods consistently, along with familiar favorites. This will ensure that your bird is eating and will also encourage her to try new foods. Don't be discouraged if your parrot doesn't dive right into a new food. Be patient, keep offering your bird new foods, and praise her enthusiastically when she is brave enough to sample something new.

Parrots on pelleted or formulated diets should have all their vitamin and mineral needs met by these special foods, so additional supplements are unnecessary. If you have an older bird who eats mostly seeds, however, you may want to sprinkle a good-quality vitamin-and-mineral powder onto your pet's fresh foods, where it has the best chance of sticking to the food and being eaten. Vitamin-enriched seed diets may provide some supplementation, but some of these products have the vitamins and minerals added to the seed hull, which your pet will remove and discard while she's eating. Avoid adding vitamin and mineral supplements to your pet's water dish because they can act as a growth medium for bacteria. They may also cause the water to taste different to your bird, which may discourage her from drinking.

Opting for Organics

Some pet bird owners prefer to feed their birds organic produce to offer maximum nutrition without pesticides and other additives that could be harmful to a bird. Look for organic produce at your local grocery store or farmer's market. Some manufacturers offer organic bird food, so be sure to check the product label on your conure's formulated diet or seed mix to see if it's organic.

Food Can Be Fun!

For your pet bird, mealtime can double as playtime with just a little effort on your part. By providing your pet bird with new and unusual ways to serve her food, you are helping challenge her mind, which is one way to help ensure she doesn't become bored and misbehave.

DIETS FOR SOFTBILLS, LORIES, AND LORIKEETS

Diets for softbills should include a variety of fruits, some vegetables, a good source of protein, and plenty of fresh water. Suitable fruit choices include apples, pears, papayas, and grapes. Limit the amount of citrus fruits and berries you feed your softbill because the higher acid content of these foods can lead to hemachromatosis (iron-storage disease).

Cut up any fruit before serving because your birds will likely swallow the food whole. You can add chunks of raw dark orange and dark green vegetables to the fruit mixture to provide some variety in your softbill's diet. Protein sources include commercial mynah bird pellets or insects, such as mealworms or crickets.

Some softbills can develop iron-storage disease, in which high levels of iron accumulate in the bird's liver. Limit the iron content in your softbill's diet to less than 150 parts per million. Avoid foods with high iron content, such as commercial dog and cat foods, monkey biscuits, raisins and other dried fruits, and spinach. Some softbills require nectar as a primary part of their diet, while others enjoy it as an occasional treat.

Lories and lorikeets are specialized feeders. These brush-tongued parrots rely on pollen, nectar, and fruit in the wild, and they will not do as well as pet birds will on a typical parrot diet.

To maintain good health, a lory or lorikeet needs a special lory diet, supplemented with fruit. When lory keeping first became popular, these special diets were liquid, which caused the birds to create liquid droppings that they squirted out of their cages. This made lories and lorikeets less popular pets than other parrot species. Fortunately, today's lory diets are available in powdered form, which makes feeding and cleanup easier and helps make these brightly colored parrots more appealing pets.

One way to challenge your pet at mealtime is to offer her nuts in the shell. Medium- to large-sized pet birds love peanuts, walnuts, pecans, filberts, or macadamia nuts served in their shells. You may have to crack the nuts slightly the first time you serve them so your pet will know there's a treat inside, but she should soon get the hang of opening the shells herself.

Another way to make mealtime into playtime is to offer some fresh foods on a skewer. Any firm fruit or vegetable, including corn cobbettes, apple slices, or tomatillos, can be threaded onto a skewer and served to your bird. By making a kabob of new and familiar fresh foods, you may tempt a finicky eater into trying something new, especially if the new food is touching one of her favorites—she may get a biteful by accident and discover something new and tasty!

Another way to entertain your pet with food is to string sugar-free breakfast cereal or uncooked pasta onto a clean piece of string or vegetable-tanned leather and offer it to your bird as a toy. She may just mouth the foods as she plays, or she may eat some of the cereal or pasta. Uncooked pasta is not harmful to your bird, and unsweetened cereals are recommended because your bird doesn't need the processed sugar found in some cereals any more than we humans do. You can try the same approach by making a garland for her cage similar to those made to decorate holiday trees with popped popcorn and fresh cranberries, or you can customize the garland, using your bird's favorites.

FOODS YOUR BIRD *SHOULDN'T* EAT

Now that we've looked at foods that are good for your bird, let's look briefly at those that aren't. Among those foods considered harmful to pet birds are alcohol, rhubarb, avocado (the skin and the area around the pit can be toxic), as well as highly salted, sweetened, and fatty foods.

You should especially avoid chocolate because it contains the chemical theobromine, which birds cannot digest as completely as people can. Chocolate can kill your pet bird, so resist the temptation to share this snack with her.

You also want to avoid giving your bird seeds or pits from apples, apricots, cherries, peaches, pears, and plums, because they can be harmful.

Let common sense be your guide in choosing which foods can be offered to your bird: If it's healthy for you, it's probably okay to share. However, remember to reduce the size of the portion you offer to your bird—a smaller, bird-sized portion will be more appealing to your pet than a larger, human-sized portion.

While sharing healthy people food with your bird is completely acceptable, sharing something that you've already taken a bite of is not. Human saliva has bacteria in it that are perfectly normal for people but that are potentially toxic to birds, so please don't share partially eaten food with your pet. For your bird's health and your peace of mind, give her a portion of her own, on her own plate.

Household Hazards

The phrase "Curiosity killed the cat" could easily be rewritten to reflect a pet bird's curious nature. These inquisitive birds of ours seem to be able to get into just about anything, which means they can get themselves into potentially dangerous situations rather quickly. Because of this natural curiosity, pet bird owners must be extremely vigilant when their birds are out of their cages.

Part of this vigilance should include bird-proofing your home. Remember that the intellect of some of the larger parrots may be on par with that of a toddler. You wouldn't let a toddler have free run of your house without taking a few precautions to safeguard the child from harm, and you should extend the same concern to your pet birds.

Let's go room by room and look at some of the potentially dangerous situations you should be aware of.

Bathroom

This can be a pet bird paradise if the bird is allowed to spend time with you as you prepare for work or for an evening out, but it can also be quite harmful to your bird's health. An open toilet could lead to drowning, the bird could hurt herself chewing on the blow-dryer cord, or she could be overcome by fumes from perfume, hairspray, or cleaning products, such as bleach, air freshener, or toilet bowl cleaner. The bird could also become ill if she nibbles on prescription or nonprescription drugs in the medicine chest, or she could injure herself by flying into a mirror. Use caution when taking your bird into the bathroom, and make sure her wings are clipped to avoid flying accidents.

Kitchen

This is another popular spot for birds and their owners to hang out, especially around mealtime. Here again, dangers lurk for curious pet birds. An unsupervised

Know where your bird is at all times when she's out of her cage. This will help reduce the chance of her being injured accidentally. (PHOTO BY RHONDA MANCINI)

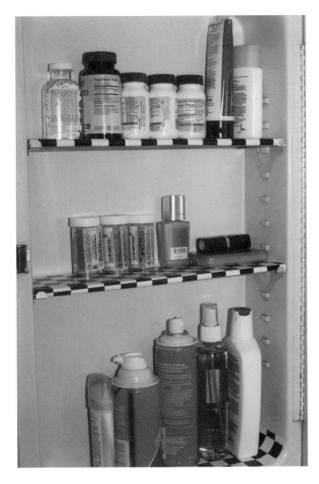

A bathroom medicine cabinet holds many potential dangers for your pet bird. Supervise her carefully whenever she is near any medications to ensure she isn't accidentally poisoned. (PHOTO BY JULIE RACH MANCINI)

bird could fly or fall into an open trash can, or she could climb into an open oven, dishwasher, freezer, or refrigerator and be forgotten when your back is turned briefly. Your bird could also land on a hot stove element, or fall into an uncovered pot of boiling water or sizzling frying pan on the stove. The bird could also become poisoned by eating foods that are unsafe for her, such as chocolate, avocado, or rhubarb (see the earlier sidebar).

Living Room

Are you sitting on your couch or in a comfortable chair as you read this book? Although it probably seems safe enough to you, your pet could be injured or killed if she decides to play hide-and-seek under pillows or cushions and is accidentally sat on. Your pet bird could become poisoned by nibbling on a leaded glass lampshade, or she could fly out an open window or patio door. By the same token, she could fly into a closed window or door and injure herself severely. She could

The area under the kitchen sink is another potentially hazardous area for pet birds due to the number of household chemicals stored there. To protect your bird from ingesting something harmful, do not allow her to play in the area under your kitchen sink. (PHOTO BY JULIE RACH MANCINI)

become entangled in a drapery cord or a venetian blind pull, she could fall into an uncovered fish tank and drown, or she could ingest poison by nibbling on ashes or cigarette butts in an ashtray.

Home Office

This can be another pet parrot playground, but you'll have to be on your toes to keep your pet from harming herself by nibbling on potentially poisonous markers, glue sticks or crayons, or impaling herself on push pins.

Other Areas of Concern

If you have a ceiling fan in your house, make sure it is turned off when your bird is out of her cage. Make sure you know where your bird is before turning on your washer or dryer, and don't close your basement freezer without checking first to be sure your bird isn't in there.

This doesn't mean you should keep your bird locked up in her cage all the time. On the contrary, all parrots need time out of their cages to maintain physical and mental health. The key is to be aware of some of the dangers that may exist in your home and to pay attention to your bird's behavior so you can intervene before the bird becomes ill or injured.

Unfortunately, potential dangers to a pet bird don't stop with the furniture and accessories. A variety of fumes can overpower your pet, such as those from cigarettes, air fresheners, insecticides, bleach, shoe polish, oven cleaners, kerosene, lighter fluid, glues, active self-cleaning ovens, hairspray, overheated nonstick cookware, paint thinner, bathroom cleaners, or nail polish remover. Try to keep your pet away from anything that has a strong chemical odor, and be sure to apply makeup and hair care products far away from your pet. If your pet enjoys grooming your hair or eyelashes, it may be best not to even wear makeup, hairspray, or hair gel around your pet to protect her from accidentally ingesting your cosmetics.

HOW SAFE ARE HOUSEPLANTS
FOR YOUR BIRD?

Poisonous	Safe
Amaryllis	African violets
Bird-of-paradise	Aloe
Calla lily	Burro's tail
Daffodil	Christmas cactus
Dieffenbachia	Coleus
English ivy	Edible fig
Foxglove	Fern (asparagus, Boston, bird's nest, maidenhair, ribbon, staghorn, squirrel's foot)
Holly	
Juniper	
Lily of the valley	Gardenia
Mistletoe	Grape ivy
Oleander	Hen and chicks
Philodendron	Hibiscus
Rhododendron	Jade plant
Rhubarb	Kalanchoe
Sweet pea	Palms (butterfly, cane, golden feather, Madagascar, European fan, sentry, pygmy date)
Wisteria	
	Pepperomia
	Rubber plant
	Spider plant
	Yucca

To help protect your pet from harmful chemical fumes, consider using some "green" cleaning alternatives, such as baking soda and vinegar to clear clogged drains, baking soda instead of scouring powder to clean tubs and sinks, lemon juice and mineral oil to polish furniture, and white vinegar and water to clean windows. These products keep the environment a little friendlier for your bird, and these simple solutions to cleaning problems often work better than higher-priced, name-brand products.

If you're considering a remodeling or home improvement project, think about your bird first. Fumes from paint or formaldehyde, which can be found in carpet backing, paneling, and particleboard, can cause pets and people to become ill. If you are having work done on your home, consider boarding your pet at your avian veterinarian's office or at the home of a bird-loving friend or relative until the project is complete and the house is aired out. You can consider the house safe for your pet when you cannot smell any trace of any of the products used in the remodeling.

Having your home fumigated for termites or other pests poses another potentially hazardous situation for your pet bird. Ask your exterminator for information about the types of chemicals that will be used in your home, and inquire if pet-safe formulas, such as electrical currents or liquid nitrogen, are available. If your house must be treated chemically, arrange to board your bird at your avian veterinarian's office or with a friend before, during, and after the fumigation to ensure that no harm comes to your pet. Make sure your house is aired out completely before bringing your bird home, too.

Bird First Aid

It is always a good idea to be prepared for an emergency situation. With quick thinking and even quicker action, you may be able to help save your bird from serious injury or death.

No matter what the situation, there are a few fundamentals to remember when facing a medical emergency with your pet. First, keep as calm as possible. Your bird is already excited enough from being injured, and an agitated response from you will not help your pet get well. Next, stop any bleeding, keep the bird warm, and try not to handle the bird more than is necessary.

After you've stopped any bleeding and made sure that your bird is warm, call your veterinarian's office for further instructions. Describe what happened to your pet as clearly and calmly as you can. Listen carefully to the instructions you are given and follow them. Finally, transport your bird to the veterinarian's office as quickly and safely as you can.

Here are some urgent medical situations that bird owners are likely to encounter, the reason that they are medical emergencies, the signs and symptoms your bird might show, and the recommended treatments for the problem.

Animal Bite

If your bird is bitten or clawed, infections can develop from bacteria on the biting animal's teeth or claws. Also, a bird's internal organs can be damaged by the bite.

SIGNS THAT INDICATE A PROBLEM

Often there are no signs of injury, but on occasion you will actually be able to see the bite marks.

STEPS TO TAKE

Call your veterinarian's office and transport the bird there immediately. Antibiotics and treatment for shock are often the courses of action veterinarians take to save birds who have been bitten or clawed.

Beak Injury

A bird needs both her upper and lower beak (also called the upper and lower mandible) to eat and preen properly. Infections can set in rather quickly if a beak is fractured or punctured.

This unfortunate budgie lost her beak to the wrath of a larger bird. Be careful when allowing birds, particularly those of different species, to interact. (PHOTO BY GARY A. GALLERSTEIN, DVM)

SIGNS THAT INDICATE A PROBLEM

The bird is bleeding from her beak. This often occurs after the bird flies into a windowpane or mirror or if she has a run-in with an operational ceiling fan. Bird may also have a cracked or otherwise damaged beak, and portions of the beak may be missing.

STEPS TO TAKE

Control the bleeding. Keep the bird calm and quiet. Contact your avian veterinarian's office.

Bleeding

Uncontrolled bleeding can become a life-threatening situation.

SIGNS THAT INDICATE A PROBLEM

In the event of external bleeding, you will see blood on the bird, her cage, and her surroundings. In the case of internal bleeding, the bird may pass bloody droppings or bleed from her nose, mouth, or vent.

STEPS TO TAKE

For external bleeding, apply direct pressure. If the bleeding doesn't stop with direct pressure, apply a coagulant, such as styptic powder (for nails and beaks) or flour or cornstarch (for broken feathers and skin injuries). If the bleeding stops, observe the bird to make sure she does not start bleeding again and for signs of shock. Call your veterinarian's office if the bird seems weak or if she has lost a lot of blood, and arrange to take the bird in for further treatment.

In the case of broken blood feathers, you may have to remove the feather shaft to stop the bleeding. To do so, grasp the feather shaft as close to the skin as you can with a pair of needle-nosed pliers and pull out the shaft with a swift, steady motion. Apply a bit of flour or cornstarch to stop the bleeding, and then apply direct pressure to the skin.

Breathing Difficulty

Respiratory problems in pet birds can be life-threatening.

SIGNS THAT INDICATE A PROBLEM

The bird wheezes or clicks while breathing, bobs her tail, breathes with an open mouth, has a discharge from her nares, or has swelling around her eyes.

STEPS TO TAKE

Keep the bird warm, place her in a bathroom with a hot shower running to help her breathe easier, and call your veterinarian's office.

A BIRD FIRST-AID KIT

- Appropriate-sized towels for catching and holding your bird

- A heating pad, heat lamp, or other heat source

- A pad of paper and pencil to make notes about the bird's condition

- Styptic powder, silver nitrate stick, flour, or cornstarch to stop bleeding (use styptic powder and silver nitrate stick on beak and nails only, not on broken feathers)

- Antibiotic cream or spray

- Blunt-tipped scissors

- Nail clippers and nail file

- Needle-nosed pliers to pull broken blood feathers

- Blunt-end tweezers

- Hydrogen peroxide or other disinfectant solution

- Eye irrigation solution

- Bandage materials such as gauze squares, masking tape (it doesn't stick to a bird's feathers like adhesive tape does), and gauze rolls

- Pedialyte or other energy supplement

- Eyedropper

- Syringes to irrigate wounds or feed sick birds

Keep all these supplies in one place, such as a fishing tackle box. This will eliminate having to search for supplies in emergency situations, and you can take the kit along to bird shows or on trips, or leave it for the bird-sitter if your bird isn't a traveler.

Burns

A sufficiently severe burn can cause your bird to go into shock and die.

SIGNS THAT INDICATE A PROBLEM

A burned bird has reddened skin and burnt or greasy feathers. The bird may also show signs of shock (described later in this section).

STEPS TO TAKE

Mist the burned area with cool water. Lightly apply an antibiotic cream or spray. Do not apply any oily or greasy substances, including butter. If the bird seems shocky or the burn is widespread, contact your veterinarian's office for further instructions.

Concussion

A concussion results from a sharp blow to the head that can cause injury to the brain.

SIGNS THAT INDICATE A PROBLEM

Birds sometimes suffer concussions when they fly into mirrors or windows. They will seem stunned and may go into shock.

STEPS TO TAKE

Keep the bird warm, prevent her from hurting herself further, and watch her carefully. Alert your veterinarian's office to the injury.

Cloacal Prolapse

When a cloacal prolapse occurs, you will see the bird's lower intestines, uterus, or cloaca protruding from her vent.

SIGNS THAT INDICATE A PROBLEM

The bird has pink, red, brown, or black tissue protruding from her vent.

STEPS TO TAKE

Contact your veterinarian's office for immediate care. Your veterinarian can usually reposition the organs.

Egg Binding

When an egg becomes bound, the egg blocks the hen's excretory system and makes it impossible for her to eliminate. Moreover, eggs can break inside the hen, which can lead to infection.

SIGNS THAT INDICATE A PROBLEM

An egg-bound hen strains to lay eggs unsuccessfully. She becomes fluffed and lethargic, sits on the floor of her cage, may be paralyzed, and may have a swollen abdomen.

STEPS TO TAKE

Keep the hen warm, because this may help her pass the egg. Put her, in her cage, into a warm bathroom with a hot shower running to increase the humidity, which may also help alleviate the problem. If your bird doesn't improve shortly (within an hour), contact your veterinarian.

Eye Injury

An untreated eye problem may lead to blindness.

SIGNS THAT INDICATE A PROBLEM

Swollen or pasty eyelids, discharge, cloudy eyeball, increased rubbing of the eye area.

STEPS TO TAKE

Examine the eye carefully for foreign bodies. Contact your veterinarian for more information.

Fractures

In addition to the obvious problems attendant to a broken bone, a fracture can cause a bird to go into shock. Depending on the type of fracture, infections can also set in.

SIGNS THAT INDICATE A PROBLEM

Birds most often break bones in their legs, so be on the lookout for a bird who is holding one leg at an odd angle or who isn't putting weight on one leg. Sudden swelling of a leg or wing or a droopy wing can also indicate fractures.

STEPS TO TAKE

Confine the bird to her cage or a small carrier. Don't handle her unnecessarily. Keep her warm and contact your veterinarian.

Frostbite

A bird can lose toes or feet to frostbite. She can also go into shock and die as a result.

SIGNS THAT INDICATE A PROBLEM

The frostbitten area is very cold, dry to the touch, and pale in color.

STEPS TO TAKE

Keep the bird warm and contact your veterinarian's office for further instructions.

Ingested Foreign Object

SIGNS THAT INDICATE A PROBLEM

There may not appear to be anything wrong with your bird, but if you notice that you cannot locate a small toy or other item with which the bird was playing, she may have mistakenly eaten the object.

Steps to Take

Contact your veterinarian's office immediately.

Inhaled Foreign Object

Birds can develop serious respiratory problems from foreign objects in their bodies.

Signs That Indicate a Problem

Wheezing and/or other difficulty breathing.

Steps to Take

If you suspect that your bird has inhaled something she shouldn't have, contact your veterinarian's office immediately.

Lead Poisoning

Lead poisoning can be lethal to birds.

Signs That Indicate a Problem

A bird with lead poisoning may act depressed or weak. She may become blind, or she may walk in circles at the bottom of her cage. She may regurgitate, or may pass droppings that resemble tomato juice.

Steps to Take

Contact your avian veterinarian immediately. Treatment for lead poisoning must begin shortly after exposure for the bird's best chance of survival. It may require several days or weeks to complete successfully.

Note: Lead poisoning is easily prevented by keeping birds away from common sources of lead in the home. These include stained-glass items, leaded paint found in some older homes, fishing weights, drapery weights, and some parrot toys (some are weighted with lead!). Note that "lead" pencils will not cause lead poisoning—they're actually graphite.

Overheating

An overly high body temperature can be lethal to a bird.

Signs That Indicate a Problem

An overheated bird will hold her wings away from her body, open her mouth, and roll her tongue in an attempt to cool herself. Birds don't have sweat glands, so they must try to cool their bodies by exposing as much of their skin's surface as they can to moving air.

STEPS TO TAKE

Cool the bird off by putting her in front of a fan (make sure the blades are screened so the bird doesn't injure herself further), spraying her with cool water, or having her stand in a bowl of cool water. Let the bird drink cool water if she can (if she can't, offer her cool water with an eyedropper) and contact your veterinarian.

Poisoning

Obviously, any animal that consumes a poisonous substance is in danger. A poisoned bird can die quickly.

SIGNS THAT INDICATE A PROBLEM

Poisoned birds may suddenly regurgitate, have diarrhea or bloody droppings, and have redness or burns around their mouths. They may also go into convulsions, become paralyzed, or go into shock.

STEPS TO TAKE

Put the poison out of your bird's reach. Contact your veterinarian for further instructions. Be prepared to take the poison with you to the doctor's office in case he or she needs to contact a poison control center for further information.

Seizures

Seizures can indicate a number of serious conditions, including lead poisoning, infection, nutritional deficiency, heatstroke, and epilepsy.

SIGNS THAT INDICATE A PROBLEM

The bird goes into a seizure that lasts from a few seconds to a minute. Afterward, she seems dazed and may stay on the cage floor for several hours. She may also appear unsteady and unable to perch.

STEPS TO TAKE

Keep the bird from hurting herself further by removing everything you can from her cage. Cover the cage with a towel and darken the room to reduce the bird's stress level. Contact your veterinarian's office immediately for further instructions.

Shock

Shock indicates that a bird's circulatory system cannot move the blood supply around the bird's body. This is a serious condition that can lead to death if left untreated.

HEALTH INSURANCE FOR BIRDS?

Did you know that pet birds can now qualify for health insurance? Health insurance has been available for pet dogs and cats since the early 1980s, and bird owners began to be able to take advantage of the benefits of pet health insurance in the late 1990s.

Pet bird health insurance coverage can cover major medical treatments and surgeries, laboratory fees, prescriptions, X-rays, and hospitalization. Birds may also be covered for self-mutilation and feather picking as well as routine care. Ask your avian veterinarian for more information about health insurance for your pet bird.

SIGNS THAT INDICATE A PROBLEM

Shocky birds may act depressed, breathe rapidly, and have a fluffed appearance. If your bird displays one or more of these signs in conjunction with a recent accident, suspect shock and take appropriate action.

STEPS TO TAKE

Keep your bird warm, cover her cage, and transport her to your veterinarian's office as soon as possible.

Alternative Health Treatments

Homeopathic treatments, herbal remedies, and acupuncture have become commonplace alternative medical treatments for people today, but did you know they can also be used to treat pet birds? Veterinarians began investigating alternative health treatments for pets in the 1980s, and today pet bird owners may be able to choose such treatments for their birds.

Birds may be good candidates for alternative medical treatments because of their physical and emotional makeup. Their natures are well suited to a holistic approach, which takes into account the bird's whole environment and routine when evaluating her health or illness. A bird owner who practices a holistic approach to bird care will carefully evaluate the bird daily for signs of illness while feeding her a top-quality diet and ensuring that the bird has an interesting and varied routine each day. If the owner finds something out of the ordinary during the daily evaluation, he or she contacts an avian veterinarian for an appointment as soon as the change is noted, rather than waiting to see what might happen to the bird.

Look in the Yellow Pages for veterinarians in your area who include holistic or alternative treatments in their practice, and call the office to find out whether the doctor treats birds. If you don't have a holistic veterinarian in your area, discuss alternative treatment options with your avian veterinarian to see if they are an option for your conure when she is ill or injured.

A good resource for more information on alternative health treatments for pet birds is *Holistic Care for Birds: A Manual of Wellness and Healing* by David McCluggage, DVM, and Pamela L. Higdon. Look for it at your library or bookstore (see appendix B, "Resources," for details).

Bird Showing

You've really come to enjoy your pet bird and other bird owners you've met through visits to your favorite bird supply store and your avian veterinarian's office. You want to take the next step—showing your bird—but you're unsure of how to go about it.

Most of the birds shown in competition are canaries, finches, and softbills and the smaller parrots, such as budgies and cockatiels.

The first step a novice bird exhibitor should take is to join a bird club. Attend meetings of your local bird club to meet exhibitors who are willing to help people new to showing birds, like you. Go to bird shows as an observer and watch the judging. Talk to the breeders of winning birds after the show to see if they have chicks available for purchase. Ask the breeder of your birds, as well as other breeders in the club, to help you start training your birds for the show season. Bird showing is most active in the fall.

Once you have obtained some promising show birds, locate shows through bird magazines, club newsletters, and even bulletin boards in pet stores and veterinary offices. Announcements usually include a contact person's name, address, and phone number along with the date and location of the event. Call or write this person to obtain a show catalog, which is your guide to the particulars of the show you've chosen to enter.

The show catalog will contain the judging standard for the birds who will be shown. The standard describes an ideal of perfection for each type of bird being shown. So far, this ideal bird does not yet exist, but breeders keep trying.

Once you have an idea of the qualities that the judges are looking for, how do you get your bird to live up to her own standard of perfection? You train her and groom her and show her off in a proper show cage.

Show birds must demonstrate grace under pressure during judging. They must appear calm but alert, and comfortable in their show cages (which may or may not be their regular cages). They must also be able to accept and adjust to a stranger looking closely at them and tapping on their cages. Finally, they must be in perfect feather and tip-top overall condition. Sounds like a tall order? It is, but it can be done!

To train your bird for the show circuit, get her accustomed to her show cage well before show season starts. Several months before the first show, put your pet's show cage where your bird can see it. Gradually move the show cage closer to your bird's home. When your bird appears curious about, but not afraid of, the show cage, put her in the show cage with the cage door open. Allow your pet to explore the new cage, but encourage her to stay on her perch.

After your bird has learned to stay on the perch, invite some friends over to simulate a show. Reinforce your pet's good behavior (staying on her perch and not showing signs of panic) with praise and a small treat after "the show."

Next, ask a friend to "judge" your bird. Have this person get close to the cage and give your bird a thorough visual inspection. Ask the "judge" to tap lightly on the show cage with a pointer or pencil and to poke gently at the bird with this object. Praise your bird for her good behavior. (If, however, your bird seems uncomfortable with this added attention, you may want to reconsider the show circuit for this bird.)

After you have trained your bird, you'll need to work on her grooming. To show successfully, she will need to be fully feathered, have her wings and nails trimmed, and have her feet clean. Her eyes will need to be bright and clear, and her nares will need to be free of dust and debris. If your bird suddenly breaks out in pinfeathers, you may want to reconsider showing her at that time, or you may still want to enter the show as practice.

Parrots and Children

Children and parrots may be a natural mix, or they may lead each other into temptation. Children's sudden movements, outbursts of energy, and loud voices may excite a boisterous cockatoo or macaw into joining into the fun. On the other hand, quieter parrots may suffer stress by being around children and may start to demonstrate problem behaviors, such as feather picking or screaming.

Children may be startled by a parrot's loud squawks. If they poke their fingers into a bird's cage they could be unintentionally injured because the bird may bite them to defend her territory. Explain to the child that the cage is the bird's home and that she doesn't like being annoyed by being poked at. Tell the child that bird bites hurt and that a bird's beak is capable of doing damage, particularly if the beak belongs to a cockatoo or macaw. Other birds have a tendency to pinch when they bite, which means the bite hurts, but it doesn't cause a particularly serious injury.

If you notice your child is becoming more curious about your bird as she begins crawling or walking, take precautions to protect your baby and your bird from each other. Consider raising the height of your bird's cage so that your child

---

PARROTS AND ALLERGIES

Cockatoos, African greys, and cockatiels are among the "dustier" parrots and should probably be avoided if a family member has allergies. In the course of daily grooming and preening, parrots can raise a small cloud of dust and dander that may be irritating to some allergy sufferers' sinuses and respiratory systems.

---

cannot accidentally put her fingers in the cage or pull the cage over as she toddles around your home.

Children and parrots can interact well under the right conditions. Friends of mine began training their grandson when he was a toddler about which birds in their flock are child-friendly and which ones bite. He quickly learned which ones could be gently petted and which ones were just to be admired from afar. One of the veterinarians who used to care for my bird would let his children hold her, but only if they sat very still and held her carefully on their laps. Because her previous interactions with children were not this well supervised, I was impressed with her progress regarding children and pleased with their ability to handle her so gently and carefully.

Common sense and parental guidance are the keys to allowing children and birds to interact safely. Remind your children that birds are intelligent creatures worthy of respect and that birds should never be teased or poked. Above all, you as a responsible adult must try to prevent problems before they occur and be ready to intervene to keep both children and birds safe from each other.

Some simple rules for children to follow will greatly enhance the child-bird relationship. Parents should make sure children know to:

- Approach the cage quietly. Birds don't like to be surprised.

- Talk softly to the bird. Don't scream or yell at her.

- Avoid shaking or hitting the cage.

- Avoid poking at the bird or her cage with fingers, sticks, pencils, or other items.

- Handle the bird gently if the child is allowed to take the bird out of her cage.

- Keep the bird inside. In unfamiliar surroundings (such as the outdoors), birds can become confused and fly away from their owners. Most are never recovered.

- Respect the bird's need for quiet time.

Children and birds can get along nicely if the initial introductions are properly handled. (PHOTO BY PAMELA L. HIGDON)

In *My Parrot, My Friend* (see appendix B), Bonnie Munro Doane and Thomas Qualkinbush offer the following guidelines about parrots and children:

- The parrot should be the sole responsibility of the adult who acquired her. It is unfair to expect a child to provide the care these birds require without ongoing supervision in the adult's presence.

- Never leave a child alone with any parrot, regardless of how tame the bird is.

- If you wish to allow your child to pet the parrot, the bird should be perched on the adult's arm, and the adult should have full control of the bird's head.

- Young hand-reared parrots may be allowed to perch on a child's arm, but only after the adult has made a decision about safety for both child and bird.

- Practice good hygiene in handling birds and children. Do not touch your child after cleaning the cage unless you have first washed your hands. Conversely, do not handle the parrot after changing an infant's diapers without first washing your hands.

Parrots and Other Pets

In addition to people in the home, a parrot may be exposed to other pets. Practicing some basic safety guidelines will help keep the peace in your animal kingdom.

Supervise all interactions between pets. Do not allow your bird to be out on the floor of your home unattended. Not only does this protect your bird from other pets, but it also keeps her from being stepped on by humans or from injuring herself.

Cats may be attracted to the quick movements of smaller birds, such as canaries, budgies, and cockatiels. We've all seen Sylvester in the Warner Bros. cartoons try to catch Tweety Pie, and I can attest to the fact that cats like to watch budgies from watching my own childhood pets. Fluff, our Manx cat, thought parakeet watching was great fun, and he even managed to knock over my parakeet Charlie's cage and stand. Larger parrots, such as Amazons, macaws, and cockatoos, may be less threatened by cats, but I would not recommend leaving any bird alone with a cat. Although clipped wings are generally regarded as a safety precaution for birds, in the case of interactions with cats, clipped wings can be a decided disadvantage. For the safety of all pets, closely watch your cat when she's around your birds. Regardless of your bird's size, a curious cat could claw or bite your pet.

Many experts believe that a dog and a parrot can be taught to coexist peacefully, especially if the bird is one of the larger parrots. You may even find the relationship beneficial if your dog helps you clean up the vegetables your bird throws out of her food bowl and onto the floor in the course of a day. Keep in mind, though, that some sight hounds and other hunting breeds may want to hunt or chase your bird as part of an instinctive behavior.

I know of an Ibizan Hound who could visit my veterinarian only on bird-free days. Before the dog arrived, the office mascot (an Amazon parrot) had to be caged—the dog had quite strong hunting instincts. Yet a Greyhound I know has lived peacefully with a ringnecked parrot and a kakariki for many years. She has never shown any desire to hunt these birds.

A PET IS *NOT* A GOOD GIFT

Please do not give *any* live pet as a present. Birthdays, Christmas, Hanukkah, and other holidays are exciting but stressful times for both people and animals.

A pet coming to a new home is under enough stress just from joining her new family; don't add to her stress by bringing her home for a holiday. Instead, give the child pet-care accessories for the actual celebration and a gift certificate that will allow the child to select his or her pet (with proper parental permission and supervision, of course) after the excitement of the special day has tempered.

Careful supervision of your bird will help protect her from injury whenever she is out of her cage. Never let your bird out of her cage without supervising her carefully. (PHOTO BY RHONDA MANCINI)

Owners should supervise interactions between dogs and parrots at all times because a dog could step on the bird accidentally or bite it. Make sure to keep an eye on your dog around your bird's cage, too, so that your enthusiastic canine pet doesn't send bird, cage, and stand flying as she gallops through the living room. In many cases, parrots will learn how to take control of a relationship with a dog, and your bird may take special joy in calling for your dog as you do or imitating your dog's barking.

Small exotic mammals may or may not make good companions for pet birds. Pocket pets, such as hamsters, gerbils, or guinea pigs, tend not to bother birds or be bothered by them, but some bird experts believe that ferrets do not make good bird companions because ferrets have a highly developed hunting instinct that they cannot overcome.

Most reptiles and amphibians should leave medium-sized to large pet birds alone. Small lizards and frogs or toads probably won't pay much attention to your bird, but you may want to watch how your bird reacts to the lizard, frog, or toad for the safety of your reptile or amphibian pet. Large snakes, however, are another matter. For the safety of your pet bird, monitor any interactions between her and medium-sized to large snakes carefully because the snake could consider her a likely meal and try to consume her. Also monitor interactions between large frogs and small birds because many larger frogs commonly eat small birds as part of their diets.

Finally, if your bird tangles with another pet in your home, contact your avian veterinarian immediately. Emergency treatment (for bacterial infection from a puncture wound or shock from being stepped on or suffering a broken bone) may be required to save your feathered friend's life.

Tips for a Well-Behaved Bird

Don't inadvertently encourage your bird to misbehave. Take some time to analyze your bird's setup and how you interact with her to ensure that you haven't unwittingly created some potential behavior problems.

First, check the height of the cage. Is it high enough so the bird feels secure, but not so high that you can't easily reach the bird? Does the bird have a height advantage over you and other members of your family? Remember, birds behave for those they look up to and mistreat those they look down upon.

If you have a high cage and your family is vertically challenged, you may have to raise the height of your family by building a step for shorter people to stand on. This will equalize their height with the bird's and equalize their status in the flock with that of your bird.

Next, do you swoop down on your bird from above? Swooping your hands down on your bird without warning imitates the action of a predatory bird in the wild, which can cause a bird to try to defend herself. Also, many species feel threatened if they are picked up in such a way that their wings are constricted or held against their bodies. Be sure to warn your bird that you are in the area, and allow her to step on your hand by using the "up" and "down" commands rather than just whisking her out of her cage or off her play gym at your whim.

Another problem behavior owners demonstrate toward their birds is to poke or gesture at them. Finger-pointing and extensive gesturing are threatening to people—your bird feels the same way and will react by trying to defend herself from you. She interprets fingers being poked in her face as an invitation to fight and will do so by striking at or biting the offending fingers.

Many bird owners unintentionally antagonize their birds with big gestures, and then they act surprised when their pets bite them. Consider your body language when you're spending time around your bird. Some birds react badly to acrylic fingernails or brightly colored polish, while others will try to preen their owners' nails. If your bird suddenly starts acting strangely about your hands, you may have to get rid of your artificial nails or change the color of your polish. Discourage your pet from preening polished nails because she can possibly poison herself by ingesting some of the polish.

Owners who do not respect their birds' need for privacy and quiet can create a variety of bad bird behaviors. If you want to stay up and watch television after your bird has been put to bed, you may have to move into another room to give your bird a chance to settle down and sleep. If you don't give your bird an opportunity to have time to herself and get adequate amounts of sleep, don't be surprised if she starts to scream or bite. She may simply be trying to tell you she needs a dark, quiet time in which to rest and sleep in order to maintain her health and good humor.

While we're on the subject of rest, be sure to let your bird have adequate periods of rest throughout the day as well as at night. Remember that if your bird doesn't get all the rest she needs, she may be irritable and more prone to misbehaving when she's tired. Also consider your bird's feelings during times of stress, such as breeding or molting. Your bird's body is going through changes during these periods, and she may become somewhat nippier during them.

If your parrot misbehaves and you laugh at her, you may be rewarding the misbehavior without meaning to. The important thing to do when your bird misbehaves (no matter how cute the misbehavior is the first time you see it) is to provide appropriate discipline for your pet to discourage her from behaving badly. To do so, look sternly at your pet and say "Stop it!" in a firm tone or put the bird in time-out for a few minutes. You have to determine which form of discipline will work better with your parrot.

Owners may also unintentionally reinforce bad behavior in their pets in other ways. If a young bird reaches out with her beak to test the perching potential of her owner's arm (remember that young birds like to taste or test things with their beaks) and the owner pulls away, the bird will soon learn that her beak has the power to intimidate people, and she will use that power for her own ends. By pulling away, the owner may also be telling the bird that owners can't be trusted when they put out their hands for the bird to step up on.

Don't allow your pet to become overly bonded to a single person or a single area in your home. Cagebound parrots will defend their homes viciously, and people who are perceived as the parrot's mate will suffer greatly during the parrot's breeding season. To discourage the bird from bonding too closely with any one member of the family, all family members should take part in caring for the bird. Also, in order to keep her from perceiving any one place in the home as her territory that requires defending, the bird should have a variety of locations in the home she can consider her own: her cage in one room, her play gym in another, and perhaps a portable perch on wheels that can move from room to room.

Make sure that you are clear and consistent with your discipline, or your bird will be confused and may be tempted to misbehave so that she can seehow you respond. When you want the bird to step up onto your hand, for example, simply say "Up" or "Step up." Don't sputter and putter out a string of "ups" that sound like a misfiring motor. Birds understand simple, clear direction.

THE DO'S AND DON'TS OF DISCIPLINING YOUR PARROT

- DO cover her cage for no more than 10 minutes to quiet her down.

- DO look sternly at her and tell her "No."

- DO reward her—lots of verbal praise, petting, or occasional food treats—when she behaves in a way that pleases you.

- DO put her in her cage and ignore her for no more than 10 minutes.

- DO rotate your wrist gently to put your adult bird slightly off balance if she bites you while she's on your hand.

- DO be consistent in your disciplinary measures.

- DON'T yell at her.

- DON'T hit her.

- DON'T lock her in a dark room for hours.

- DON'T throw her on the ground.

- DON'T throw her cage around.

- DON'T throw things at her cage.

- DON'T spray water on her.

- DON'T handle her roughly.

- DON'T send mixed messages of discipline.

Don't overdiscipline your pet. For example, if you put your bird in time-out because she was screaming, make sure to uncover the cage within ten minutes of covering it, or the discipline will be ineffective. Your parrot needs quick, effective correction when she misbehaves. A brief denial of your attention and affection is often quite effective. A few minutes under a cage cover or a stern look from a beloved owner go a long way toward modifying your pet's behavior.

Finally, how many birds do you have in your home? How many do you want? How many do you really have time for? Granted, parrots are attractive, interesting pets, and many people want several of them in their homes. I'd love to have more than the one bird I presently own, but I learned early on that I have a one-bird limit. My parrot requires a great deal of time and attention from me, and it wouldn't be fair either to her or to me to try to add more birds to our household—the relationship I have with my bird would suffer greatly.

Remember that each parrot is an individual that requires a certain amount of time and attention from her owner each day. You may be unintentionally setting yourself up to be a disappointed owner if you end up with a flock of parrots who misbehave because they are all vying for your attention. Keep in mind, too, that more parrots means more parrot food, parrot cages, parrot toys, and avian vet bills, all of which can drain your resources considerably.

Most of all, appreciate your pet bird for the wonderful creature that she is. Don't become overly stressed when your bird acts like a bird, even if she bites or screams from time to time. If you become stressed about these infrequent episodes, your bird will sense it, and you will create a vicious cycle that neither of you will enjoy and that will be difficult to modify.

Both you and your bird will enjoy your relationship far more when you accept that neither of you is perfect, but you are both terrific individuals that make an even better pair!

PET BIRD PERSONALITIES

African Greys

As their name suggests, African greys come from Africa and are predominantly gray birds with red tails. These highly intelligent parrots are regarded throughout the bird-keeping world for their talking abilities, although no bird is guaranteed to talk.

On the negative side, greys are prone to feather picking and produce powder down, which can cause allergic reactions in some people.

Greys may become bonded to one person in the home. They are also prone to becoming stressed if they sense tension in the home or if a routine is not established for them. Greys can be high-strung, and they are often suspicious of new people, although they become accustomed to strangers rather quickly.

Greys need good-sized cages, plenty of toys, and ample time out of their cages with their owners. Their diet should consist of a good-quality seed mix or pellets supplemented with a variety of fresh foods. Greys may need more calcium in their diets than other parrots. You can provide your grey with calcium by sprinkling a supplement on his fresh foods, offering a cuttlebone in his cage, or adding calcium-rich foods, such as broccoli, almonds, soybeans, tofu, and collard greens, to your grey's diet.

Amazons

Amazons are medium-sized, chunky green parrots from Latin America. They are noted for their talking and singing skills and can be quite outgoing birds, singing opera or performing tricks for people outside the family flock.

Amazons are playful birds who enjoy human companionship, and they will tolerate cuddling on their terms.

Amazons may be aggressive during breeding season. They can also bond to a single person in the home. They can be strong-willed and stubborn and enjoy being the dominant creature in the parrot-owner relationship.

Amazon owners need to watch the amount of fat their birds consume because Amazons are natural snackers and can become obese. A pelleted diet supplemented with a variety of fresh fruits and vegetables should help keep an Amazon in shape. These parrots need roomy cages with interesting toys and time out of their cages on play gyms or with their owners to keep mentally and physically fit.

Brotogeris

The *Brotogeris* (pronounced bro-toe-JER-us) genus includes grey-cheeked, bee bee, and canary-winged parakeets. These small green birds from Mexico and South America have also been described as "pocket parrots" because of their small sizes and their fondness for hiding in the pockets of their owners' shirts.

Brotogeris make bold pets. They can become very attached to their owners, and they can learn to be noisy if this behavior is reinforced. *Brotogeris* like to climb and are strong fliers, so be sure to keep a pet *Brotogeris*'s wings clipped.

Some grey cheeks can be nippy if they are not handled regularly. Grey cheeks frequently bathe in their water bowls and can bathe themselves right out of drinking water. Their diet should include a good-quality seed mix or pellets supplemented with fresh foods. They need medium-sized cages and ample time out of their cages to interact and play with their owners.

Budgerigars

The budgerigar, commonly called a parakeet, hails from Australia. It has been kept in captivity since the 1840s and has been raised in captivity for more than a hundred years because Australia stopped exporting their perky little parrots in the 1890s. The budgie is the most commonly kept pet bird in the world.

Budgies are noted for their talking ability, but owners may have to listen carefully to hear their birds' small voices. Budgies can be kept singly, in pairs, or in community aviaries. They are good pets for novice bird owners because of their small size and their relatively uncomplicated care regimens.

Despite their small size, budgies need a good-sized cage in order to exercise properly, or they need out-of-cage time every day during which they can play and interact with their owners.

A balanced budgie diet includes seeds or pellets supplemented with an assortment of fresh fruits and vegetables. Budgies are particularly fond of millet sprays as a treat.

Caiques

Caiques (pronounced ky-EEKs) are small, highly active parrots from South America. These intelligent little parrots have good appetites and a tendency to taste almost anything and everything around them. Noted chewers, caiques need to have plenty of toys to destroy. They are also known to be strong-willed and may get out of control quickly unless their owners set guidelines. They are not shy about making themselves heard when the situation presents itself.

Caiques need good-sized cages and time to interact regularly with their owners outside of the cage. Their diets should include fresh foods along with a good-quality seed mix or pellets.

Canaries

Canaries are small cage birds originally from the Canary Islands off of Africa. They have been kept in captivity since the 1400s and are thoroughly domesticated.

Breeders concentrate on different attributes in their canary lines. Some breed canaries for shape and stance, while others breed canaries for their colorful

Canaries have been kept in captivity since the 1400s.
(Photo by Eric Ilasenko)

feathers (along with the familiar yellow, canaries are available with white, red, orange, and brownish feathers). Still others breed song canaries for their lovely singing abilities.

If you want a singing canary, you will have to locate a male bird. Make arrangements with the breeder or store to return the bird if it proves to be a non-singer. Keep in mind that males sing to attract females. If canaries are kept in pairs, males won't sing.

Cockatiels

Second in popularity only to budgies, cockatiels are also from Australia. These slender, crested parrots are known for their whistling ability and their gentle natures. The cockatiel's small size and fairly quiet voice make it a good option for apartment dwellers who want a pet bird.

Cockatiels like to interact with their owners, but on the bird's terms, not the human's. They are good candidates for community aviaries and may be ideal choices for people seeking their first birds.

Cockatiels can be prone to night frights or thrashing episodes and feather picking. They also produce powder down, which can cause allergic reactions in some people.

Cockatiels need a varied diet that includes a good-quality seed mixture or pellets along with fresh fruits and vegetables. Some cockatiels are notorious for being seed-only eaters, so start your young birds off right! A cockatiel's cage should be roomy enough to allow the bird to exercise, or you should make arrangements for your pet to have regular out-of-cage play sessions, because these active little parrots need their exercise.

Cockatoos

Cockatoos originated in Australia. With their striking appearance and cuddly personalities, these crested white or pink birds are sure to attract attention.

Be warned that these feathered teddy bears are not necessarily the "loves" they appear to be. Male cockatoos can kill mates during breeding season. They can demonstrate sexual frustration with people during breeding season, biting the person whom they perceive as their mate. Cockatoos are also prone to screaming, feather picking, and self-mutilation. Moluccans may experience night frights or thrashing episodes.

Cockatoos require a great deal of attention from, interaction with, and guidance from their owners or they are likely to become downright unmanageable. First-time bird owners may be surprised, or even disappointed, in the amount of attention cockatoos demand. Cockatoos produce powder down, which can cause allergic reactions in some people.

Cockatoos need large, secure cages. These intelligent parrots are natural escape artists, so you may have to provide additional locks on your bird's cage besides the latch on the cage door. Cockatoo diets should include good-quality seeds or pellets supplemented with fresh fruits and vegetables.

Conures

Conures are small parrots from South America. Ranging in color from muted greens to brilliant oranges, they are inquisitive little birds who offer something for almost everyone. Some species are quite talkative; others are known to be cuddlers; and still others are playful clowns.

Conures are notorious chewers, and many have quite loud voices. They enjoy regular baths. Some species are noted for sleeping on their backs with their feet in the air, while others tend to be feather pickers.

Conures need roomy cages in which to exercise and play. Of course, they need out-of-cage time, too, which can be spent on a play gym or with their owners. A good-quality seed mix or pellets supplemented with fresh foods makes an adequate conure diet.

Diamond Doves

Diamond doves are native to Australia. They take their name from the pattern of small white dots found across their otherwise gray wings. About a dozen color forms exist besides the wild gray form, including cinnamon, red diamond, yellow diamond, and snow white.

Diamond doves can be housed with small finches in community aviaries. A pair of birds can also be kept in a roomy cage. They eat a variety of grass seeds, supplemented with moistened cornbread or well-cooked hard-boiled eggs. Diamond doves will also eat chopped green food if it is offered.

Diamond doves are prolific breeders in captivity. Chicks hatch after a two-week incubation period, and they can leave the nest ten days after hatching. Sexes can be determined when the chicks are about 6 weeks old, and the young birds are capable of breeding when they are about 5 months of age.

Eclectus

Eclectus are large, solid parrots from the South Pacific. They are not usually cuddly parrots and seem to prefer sitting on their owners' hands or on a perch near their owners.

Some eclectus may pick their feathers. Females can be moody during breeding season after they become sexually mature at about 4 years of age. Females are traditionally more aggressive than males.

Eclectus have different vitamin A requirements than other parrot species. Ask your avian veterinarian for suggestions on the best diet for your eclectus. Provide these parrots with large cages and time-out on a play gym or with you to keep them content.

Finches

Finches are small, active cage birds from Asia, Africa, and Australia. They are well suited to community aviaries or flights, although a pair or a single pet finch can easily be kept in a cage.

Some species are noted for their colorful feathers, while others sing pleasant songs. Finches are often admired from afar rather than being cuddled and held by their owners, although some may learn to enjoy sitting on their owners' shoulders.

In aviary settings, finches may have their feathers picked by cagemates. If you find a picked finch, you may have to remove him from the aviary in order to allow his feathers to grow back.

Grass Parakeets

Grass parakeet is a term used to describe several genera of small, colorful Australian parrots that make good candidates for aviary living. They can be kept with finches and small, nonaggressive parrots. Commonly kept species include the Bourke's parakeet, the Princess of Wales parakeet, and the red-rumped parakeet.

Grass parakeets are noted for their high activity levels and their quiet voices. They do not need regular interaction with people to feel content. Because they are strong fliers and need to exercise their wings, grass parakeets need large flights or aviaries.

Grass parakeets enjoy a mixture of grass seeds in their diet. These seeds can be supplemented with greens, apples, corn, broccoli, and carrots. Some species also relish a bean-and-rice mixture.

Many species of grass parakeets are sexually dimorphic, meaning the males generally display brighter, more colorful plumage than the females.

Hawkheaded Parrots

Hawkheaded parrots are colorful, medium-sized parrots from South America. They are playful, somewhat shy parrots prone to feather picking if stressed.

The hawkhead's plumage is the most notable feature. The birds have brown faces, green wings, and red chest and neck feathers that are tipped in blue. These birds have the ability to raise their neck feathers to the point that the feathers form a ruff around the face. Experts theorize that this behavior developed as a defensive mechanism in the wild. The ruff may also be raised when the birds are exceptionally happy.

Hawkheads are capable of mimicking sounds and whistles, and some may learn to say a few words. They require a varied diet of seeds and fresh foods, daily attention, and mental stimulation, such as toys, to be content pets. They should be housed in good-sized cages.

Kakarikis

Kakarikis (pronounced kak-uh-REE-kees) are small, highly active parrots from New Zealand. Their name derives from a Maori word for "little parrot." They are bold birds with no real fear of people. They are not naturally cuddly, and some individuals may be high-strung.

Two kakariki species are available in the United States: the red-fronted kakariki and the yellow-crowned kakariki. In both species, the birds are predominantly green with either red or yellow feathers on their heads.

Kakarikis are also highly curious birds. They will investigate their environments completely, so care must be taken to parrot-proof any area to which a kakariki has access.

Because of their active natures, kakarikis need large cages. Unlike other parrots, their food bowls should be placed on the bottom of their cages because kakarikis will dig around in their food bowls. Their diets should include a good-quality seed mix supplemented with fresh foods.

Lories

Lories are active, lively parrots from the South Pacific. They are available in a variety of sizes and colors to suit almost anyone's taste. Keep in mind that these brush-tongued parrots are specialty feeders, favoring a diet of nectar and fruit over seeds or pellets.

Some lory species are likely to talk, and all are willing and able to play. Lories like to sleep in nest boxes even when they aren't breeding, so they need to have an enclosed sleeping space attached to their cages. A play gym or a cagetop play area is also recommended for these acrobatic birds.

Lories enjoy frequent baths and may bathe in their water bowls. Their fruit-and-nectar-based diets cause them to produce messy droppings, although powdered forms of diet are available that make lory keeping easier. They are not recommended for first-time bird keepers.

Lovebirds

Lovebirds are energetic little parrots from Africa and Madagascar. They are available in a variety of colors, including blue, green, and yellow and green.

Despite their seemingly cuddly name, lovebirds can be downright aggressive toward other birds and people. Hand-fed birds, which are easier to tame than parent-raised birds, require daily handling to retain their sweet pet qualities. Bird owners who want to admire their pets from afar may fare better with a less-tame pair in an aviary or flight.

Lovebirds are prone to chewing and particularly enjoy ripping up paper. They may also pick their feathers.

Although they're little birds, lovebirds need good-sized cages because they like to climb and exercise. You'll also have to provide your lovebirds with toys, which are another outlet for these parrots' seemingly endless energy. Feed your lovebirds a good-quality seed mix supplemented with fresh fruits and vegetables.

Macaws

Macaws are the largest commonly kept cage birds. They hail from South America and are available in a rainbow of colors, including green, blue, and red.

Macaws are highly intelligent, outgoing birds who can learn to talk or perform tricks. They can be quite destructive in their chewing habits, so be sure to provide these large parrots with plenty of destroyable toys. They are also prone to fits of screaming that makes them unsuitable for apartment living.

Macaws can be aggressive during breeding season and can intimidate some owners with their beaks and their strong wills. Macaws require large cages in order to be healthy and mentally well adjusted. The larger macaws are not recommended for first-time bird owners.

Diets for macaws should include a good-quality seed mix or pellets supplemented with fresh fruits and vegetables. Nuts can be offered as treats, and they will keep your macaws entertained and busy as the birds crack the nuts.

Mynahs

Mynahs are social birds who need regular human companionship. They are among the most renowned mimics in the avian world and are capable of imitating a wide range of voices, intonations, and sounds. In keeping with these charming characteristics, however, they can also be quite loud, especially before bedtime.

Mynahs require large cages in order to exercise regularly. They are not always good candidates for a community aviary because they may not get along well with smaller birds.

As a softbill, a mynah relies on a large amount of insects and fruits in its diet, as opposed to the seed-based diet that most parrots eat. Mynahs are not among the neatest eaters in the animal kingdom and, as a result, require a regular post-meal cleanup to keep your home and their health in tip-top shape. Their fruit-based diets cause them to produce liquid droppings that can be messy. They may be prone to iron-storage disease (hemachromatosis), an often fatal liver problem caused by feeding the birds a diet containing too much iron.

Mynahs can be trained to sit on their owners' hands, but they prefer to sit on a flat palm rather than a pair of fingers or a loosely clenched fist. Mynahs need to have their nails trimmed regularly, but wing trimming is not recommended because mynahs can crash and injure themselves if their wings are clipped. As a result, you must be extremely careful that all windows and doors are closed tightly whenever your mynah is out of his cage.

Mynahs like to sit on their owners' shoulders and preen their owners' hair and faces. During the course of a normal day, a mynah is liable to yawn, stretch, scratch, sneeze, preen, nap, eat, and drink.

Parrotlets

Parrotlets are small, predominantly green birds from Latin America. These spunky little birds have large personalities and are well suited to living in small spaces, such as apartments or mobile homes.

Parrotlets are bold little birds. They enjoy human companionship and are very active. If allowed out of their cage, the birds will play busily on a play gym.

Because parrotlets are so bold, they need close supervision when they are out of their cages to ensure their safety. They can be prone to feather picking. They can be housed in medium-sized cages and should be fed a good-quality seed mixture supplemented with fresh fruits and vegetables.

Pekin Robins

Pekin robins, also called Chinese nightingales, are softbills who are often kept in aviaries or community flights. They are found in the wild in several countries in Asia, and they were introduced to Hawaii, where they can now be found in the wild.

Pekin robins are rather drab in their plumage, but they sing beautiful songs. The male's song has been described as lilting, strong, and sweet. They are active, inquisitive birds who should be kept in pairs because they practice contact sitting and roost close to one another.

In captivity, the pekin robin's diet should include commercial softbill diets—greens and live food, such as mealworms, aphids, and white worms. You can also offer apples, oranges, bananas, grapes, and blueberries. These birds should be housed in large cages or put into community flights with finches.

Pionus

Pionus (pronounced pie-OH-nus) are generally quiet, curious birds from Latin America. These medium-sized, chunky parrots enjoy bathing and climbing, and they are noted for their chewing abilities. Pionus have gentle, even temperaments.

Pionus enjoy human companionship, but they do not need to be handled and cuddled in order to be content. Their size and quiet natures make them ideal for apartment dwellers.

Pionus may wheeze when excited, and they can be high-strung and somewhat nervous. They do not tolerate heat or humidity well and may become stressed easily.

Pionus socialize well and are good choices for first parrots. They need to be housed in large cages and fed a good-quality seed mixture or pellets supplemented with fresh foods.

Quaker Parrots

Quaker or monk parrots are small parrots from South America, available in a variety of colors, including green, lutino (yellow), and blue.

Quakers can develop large vocabularies, and they are capable of learning to do tricks. They are chunky, active little birds who need adequate space in which to exercise. Quakers enjoy a daily bath.

Quakers can be aggressive toward other birds and humans who invade their space. They can also become possessive of their favorite person in the home. Keeping Quakers is illegal in some states because they are perceived as an agricultural threat if they escape.

Quakers should be housed in large cages and provided with plenty of toys. They should be fed a good-quality seed mix or pellets, supplemented with fresh fruits and vegetables.

Ringnecked Parakeets

Ringnecked parakeets are slender, long-tailed birds hailing from Africa and Asia. They take their name from the thin ring of feathers around their necks. Most birds are bright green, but blue and lutino (yellow) mutations are available.

The personalities of ringnecked parakeets differ slightly among the species. Indian ringnecks are comical, while Alexandrines are more serious. Plumheads are talkative little scamps, while slatyheads are sweet, quiet birds. Some species are sexually dimorphic, which means the males and females have different plumage, while others are not.

Broadly, ringnecks enjoy attention more than they like being handled. Ringnecks can develop sizable vocabularies, and they can learn to perform tricks. These active parrots need large cages in which to exercise and to protect their plumage from damage. Their diets should include a good-quality seed mix supplemented with fresh fruits and vegetables.

Rosellas

Rosellas are small, colorful parrots from Australia. They are predominantly known as aviary subjects, but they can also be kept as single pet birds. Rosella owners must realize that these birds are not naturally cuddly birds and like their space. Some birds can be pugnacious.

Eight species of rosella have been recognized in aviculture. Each species has well-defined white or yellow cheek patches and a scalloped pattern on the back.

Rosellas need to be housed in large cages or aviaries. They are active fliers and need regular opportunities to exercise. Offer them a good-quality seed mix and some fresh foods to eat.

Senegals

Senegals are small African parrots from the *Poicephalus* genus that also includes Jardine's, Meyer's, and red-bellied parrots. Senegals may learn to talk and can perform tricks. They are noted for their chewing ability.

Some Senegals may become nippy after they are weaned, and they can be strong-willed pets. Their small size and relatively low noise level make them good candidates for apartment living.

Senegals can be housed in medium-sized cages, and they should be provided with a variety of toys. Their diet should include a good-quality seed mix or pellets supplemented with fresh foods.

Tanygnathus

Tanygnathus (pronounced tan-IG-nay-thus) parrots are found in the Philippine Islands and Indonesia. The genus includes the great-billed parrot, the Muller's parrot, and the blue-naped parrot.

Tanygnathus are predominantly green birds with reddish or coral-colored beaks. In this genus, females tend to be more dominant than males; therefore, male birds may make better pets.

Tanygnathus love frequent baths, so owners must provide opportunities for their birds to bathe. They are also noted for their chewing ability, and they need an ample supply of chewable toys.

A good-quality seed mix and some fresh foods should provide an adequate diet for *Tanygnathus*. They need to be housed in large cages.

Toucans

Toucans are medium-sized softbills from Latin America. Some birds are highly territorial. Their calls, which have been compared to howler monkeys at the zoo, can be irritating to some people.

The toucan's most striking feature is the bill, which is surprisingly light-weight and contains a honeycomb-like structure inside it. Toucans are unable to use their beaks to chew, but with some work they can crush grapes in their beaks. Although the beak is not as useful as a parrot's, it still presents a formidable weapon. If a toucan bites, his beak can be hard to remove from a finger or an ear.

Some toucans require live food, such as small rodents, but much of their diet is made up of fruit. Toucans are prone to hemachromatosis, an often fatal liver disease that results from being fed a diet too rich in iron.

These birds also need to live in large aviaries or flights because they require a lot of exercise. Toucan keepers should know that these birds are infinitely curious about their surroundings and will explore an enclosure thoroughly. Toucans will try to eat almost anything they can get their beaks on, so their aviaries or flights need to be toucan-proofed for their safety. Toucans are not recommended for first-time bird keepers.

Touracos

Touracos are fruit eaters from Africa. These crested softbills can be housed in community aviaries, but, because they are very active, they need a large aviary or flight.

Touracos are seldom aggressive toward other bird species, but they can treat their mates roughly during breeding season. They build flimsy nests and lay two eggs. Parent birds share incubation duties, and the eggs hatch after a twenty-one-day incubation. Hand-fed chicks make devoted pets. These birds are demanding and are not recommended for first-time bird keepers.

RESOURCES

Books
About Bird Behavior
Alderton, David. *A Birdkeeper's Guide to Budgies.* Blacksburg, VA: Tetra Press, 1988.

———. *A Birdkeeper's Guide to Cockatiels.* Blacksburg, VA: Tetra Press, 1989.

———. *A Birdkeeper's Guide to Cockatoos.* Blacksburg, VA: Tetra Press, 1990.

———. *A Birdkeeper's Guide to Finches.* Blacksburg, VA: Tetra Press, 1988.

———. *A Birdkeeper's Guide to Parrots and Macaws.* Blacksburg, VA: Tetra Press, 1989.

———. *A Birdkeeper's Guide to Pet Birds.* Blacksburg, VA: Tetra Press, 1987.

———. *The Complete Guide to Bird Care.* New York: Howell Book House, 1998.

———. *You and Your Pet Bird.* New York: Alfred A. Knopf, 1994.

Birmelin, Immanuel, and Annette Wolter. *The Parakeet Handbook.* Hauppauge, NY: Barron's Educational Series, 2000.

Bittner, Mark. *The Wild Parrots of Telegraph Hill: A Love Story . . . with Wings.* New York: Harmony Books, 2004. *The Wild Parrots of Telegraph Hill* documentary is available on VHS or DVD from Pelican Media (www.pelicanmedia.org/store.htm).

Doane, Bonnie Munro, and Thomas Qualkinbush. *My Parrot, My Friend: An Owner's Guide to Parrot Behavior.* New York: Howell Book House, 1994.

Forshaw, Joseph. *Parrots of the World.* Neptune, NJ: TFH Publications, 1977.

Freud, Arthur. *The Parrot: An Owner's Guide to a Happy, Healthy Pet.* New York: Howell Book House, 1996.

Hanna, Jack, and Hester Mundis. *Jack Hanna's Ultimate Guide to Pets.* New York: G. P. Putnam's Sons, 1996.

Koepff, Christa, and April Romagnano. *The Finch Handbook.* Hauppauge, NY: Barron's Educational Series, 2001.

Lantermann, Werner. *The New Parrot Handbook.* Hauppauge, NY: Barron's Educational Series, 1986.

Lantermann, Werner, and Susanne Lanterman. *Cockatoos: A Complete Pet Owner's Manual.* Hauppauge, NY: Barron's Educational Series, 2000.

Masson, Jeffrey M., and Susan McCarthy. *When Elephants Weep: The Emotional Lives of Animals.* New York: Delacorte Press, 1995.

McCluggage, David, DVM, and Pamela L. Higdon. *Holistic Care for Birds: A Manual of Wellness and Healing.* New York: Howell Book House, 1999.

McClung, Robert M. *Lost Wild America: The Story of Our Extinct and Vanishing Wildlife.* Hamden, CT: Linnett Books, 1993.

Morton, Eugene S., and Jake Page. *Animal Talk: Science and the Voices of Nature.* New York: Random House, 1992.

Moustaki, Nikki. *Parrots For Dummies.* Hoboken, NJ: Wiley Publishing, 2005.

O'Neil, Jacqueline. *The Complete Idiot's Guide to Bird Care and Training.* Indianapolis, IN: Alpha Books, 1998.

Paradise, Paul. *Canaries.* Neptune, NJ: TFH Publications, 1988.

Reed, Nancy A. *Cockatiels! Pet—Breeding—Showing.* Neptune, NJ: TFH Publications, 1991.

Robar, Tani, and Diane Grindol. *Parrot Tricks: Teaching Parrots with Positive Reinforcement.* New York: Howell Book House, 2006.

Rogers, Cyril H. *Zebra Finches: The Bird Keeper's Library.* Edinburgh: K & R Books, 1979.

Short, Lester L. *The Lives of Birds: Birds of the World and Their Behavior.* New York: Henry Holt and Co., 1993.

Spadafori, Gina. *Birds For Dummies.* Hoboken, NJ: Wiley Publishing, 1999.

von Frisch, Otto. *Mynahs: A Complete Pet Owner's Manual.* Hauppauge, NY: Barron's Educational Series, Inc., 1986. New York: Henry Holt and Co., 1993.

————. *Canaries: Everything About Purchase, Care, Diseases, Nutrition and Song.* Hauppauge, NY: Barron's Educational Series, 1999.

Vriends, Matthew M., Ph.D. *The Cockatiel Handbook.* Hauppauge, NY: Barron's Educational Series, 1999.

————. *The Complete Book of Finches.* New York: Howell Book House, 1987.

————. *Lovebirds: A Complete Pet Owner's Manual.* Hauppauge, NY: Barron's Educational Series, 1986.

Wolter, Annette. *Cockatiels: A Complete Pet Owner's Manual.* Hauppauge, NY: Barron's Educational Series, 1991.

————. *African Gray Parrots: A Complete Pet Owner's Manual.* Hauppauge, NY: Barron's Educational Series, 1987.

About Behaviors That Indicate Illness

Doane, Bonnie Munro. *The Parrot in Health and Illness: An Owner's Guide.* New York: Howell Book House, 1991.

Gallerstein, Gary A., DVM. *The Complete Bird Owner's Handbook.* Minneapolis, MN: Avian Publications, 2003.

Ritchie, Branson W., DVM, Ph.D., Greg J. Harrison, DVM, and Linda R. Harrison. *Avian Medicine: Principles and Application.* Lake Worth, FL: Wingers Publishing, 1994.

About Breeding Behaviors

Gonzalez, Fran. *Breeding Exotic Birds: A Beginner's Guide.* Cypress, CA: Neon Pet Publications, 1993.

Schubot, Richard, Susan Clubb, DVM, and Kevin Clubb. *Psittacine Aviculture.* Loxahatchee, FL: Avicultural Breeding and Research Center, 1992.

About Training

Athan, Mattie Sue. *Guide to a Well-Behaved Parrot.* Hauppauge, NY: Barron's Educational Series, 1999.

Hubbard, Jennifer. *The New Parrot Training Handbook.* Fremont, CA: Parrot Press, 1997.

Murphy, Kevin. *Training Your Parrot.* Neptune, NJ: TFH Publications, 1983.

Magazines/Newsletters

Bird Talk, P.O. Box 57347, Boulder, CO 80322-7347

Bird Times, 7-L Dundas Circle, Greensboro, NC 27407

Birds USA, look for it in your local bookstore or pet store.

Online Resources

Bird-specific sites have been cropping up regularly on the Internet. These sites offer pet bird owners the opportunity to share stories about their pets, along with trading helpful hints about bird care.

If you belong to an online service, look for the pet site (it is often included in more general topics, such as "Hobbies and Interests," or more specifically "Pets"). If you have Internet access, ask your Web browser software to search for "bird behavior" or "parrot behavior."

Organizations

The American Federation of Aviculture
P.O. Box 7312
N. Kansas City, MO 64116
Publishes bimonthly magazine, *The Watchbird,* devoted to bird breeding (all species, not only those kept as pets).

Avicultural Society of America
P.O. Box 5516
Riverside, CA 92517-5517
Publishes monthly bulletin detailing society's activities.

The Association of Avian Veterinarians
P.O. Box 811720
Boca Raton, FL 33481

Bird Clubs of America
P.O. Box 2005
Yorktown, VA 23692

International Aviculturists Society
P.O. Box 341852
Memphis, TN 38184

National Parrot Association
8 N. Hoffman Lane
Hauppage, NY 11788

Society of Parrot Breeders and Exhibitors
P.O. Box 546
Hollis, NH 03049

Parrot Conservation Organizations
United States World Parrot Trust
P.O. Box 341141
Memphis, TN 38184

Other Organizations
National Animal Poison Control Center Hotline
(888) 426-4435

Parrot Rehabilitation Society
P.O. Box 6202213
San Diego, CA 92612-0213
The Parrot Rehabilitation Society rescues and rehabilitates abused and neglected parrots.

Videos

The Positive Approach to Parrots as Pets: Understanding Bird Behavior (tape 1) and *Training Through Positive Reinforcement* (tape 2). Natural Encounters Inc., P.O. Box 68666, Indianapolis, IN 46268.

INDEX